The Naylor Report

THE NAYLOR REPORT
ON UNDERGRADUATE RESEARCH IN WRITING STUDIES

Edited by Dominic DelliCarpini,
Jenn Fishman, and Jane Greer

Parlor Press
Anderson, South Carolina
www.parlorpress.com

Parlor Press LLC, Anderson, South Carolina, USA

© 2020 by Parlor Press
All rights reserved.

Printed in the United States of America
S A N: 2 5 4 - 8 8 7 9

Library of Congress Cataloging-in-Publication Data on File

978-1-64317-155-5 (paperback)
978-1-64317-156-2 (hardcover)
978-1-64317-157-9 (PDF)
978-1-64317-158-6 (ePub)

1 2 3 4 5

Cover design by Ophelia Chambliss

Printed on acid-free paper.

Parlor Press, LLC is an independent publisher of scholarly and trade titles in print and multimedia formats. This book is available in paper, cloth and eBook formats from Parlor Press on the World Wide Web at http://www.parlorpress.com or through online and brick-and-mortar bookstores. For submission information or to find out about Parlor Press publications, write to Parlor Press, 3015 Brackenberry Drive, Anderson, South Carolina, 29621, or email editor@parlorpress.com.

Contents

Acknowledgments   *ix*

Foreword   *xi*

The Transformative Power of Undergraduate Research in Writing Studies   *xi*
    Jenny Olin Shanahan

Introduction

Building Capacity, Cultivating Consequences: Charting the Course of Undergraduate Research in Writing Studies   3
    Dominic DelliCarpini, Jenn Fishman, and Jane Greer

Many Generous Hands: A Narrative Reflection on the Naylor Symposium on Undergraduate Research in Writing Studies   14
    Cynthia Crimmins

Participants in the Naylor Symposium   25

Part One   27

Defining Characteristics of Undergraduate Research in Writing Studies: What We've Learned   27

1 Mentoring: Partnering with All Undergraduate Researchers in Writing   29
    Jessie L. Moore, with Sophia Abbot, Hannah Bellwoar, and Field Watts

Reflection on Chapter 1

The Importance of Reciprocity in Mentoring: Benefits and Challenges   45
    Sophia Abbot, Hannah Bellwoar, and Eric E. Hall

2 Research Methods: Designing Methods Instruction and Experiences That Invite Undergraduates into the Field   49
    Emily Murphy Cope, Kim Fahle Peck, Kristine Johnson, and Shurli Makmillen

Reflection on Chapter 2

Research Methods as Declarative Knowledge
in Writing Studies   65
    Doug Downs

The Place of Research Methodologies in
Undergraduate Research Development   68
    Emily Murphy Cope and Gabriel Cutrufello

3 Contributing to Knowledge: A Defining
Characteristic of Undergraduate Research   71
    Jane Greer, Laurie Grobman, and Heather Falconer

Reflection on Chapter 3

Contributing to Whose Knowledge?   88
    Heather Falconer

Faculty and Undergraduate Co-Authoring and
Contributions to Knowledge   91
    Laurie Grobman

4 Circulation: Undergraduate Research as
Consequential Publicness   94
    Doug Downs, Laurie McMillan, Megan Schoettler, and
    Patricia Roberts-Miller

Reflection on Chapter 4

From "Dissemination" to "Circulation" with Consequential
Contributions: A Note on Process   106
    Doug Downs

The Temptation to Privilege Traditional Academic
Modes of Circulation   108
    Laurie McMillan

Part Two   111

Blazing Future Paths Together: Accessible and
Equitable Ways Forward   111

5 Access to Undergraduate Research in Writing Studies   113
    Alexandria Lockett, D. Alexis Hart, and Rebecca Babcock

Reflection on Chapter 5

Impact and Access: Opportunities for Repurposing,
Listening, Learning: *132*
    Heather Brook Adams

Undergraduate Research and Labor Practices
in Writing Studies   *135*
    Elizabeth Kleinfeld

6 Curriculum; or If You Build It, They Will Do It   *138*
    William FitzGerald

Reflection on Chapter 6

Serendipity and Bureaucratization: Loosening
the Gordian Knot   *154*
    Dominic DelliCarpini

7 Beyond "Cosmetic Surgery": An Action Plan
for Institutional Support   *158*
    *Dominic DelliCarpini, Michael Mattison, Andrea Rosso
    Efthymiou, Gabriel Cutrufello, and Michelle Grue*

Reflection on Chapter 7

Institutional Support for Emerging Scholars in
Undergraduate Research in Writing Studies   *181*
    Michelle Grue

The Impact of the Raab Writing Fellows Program at UCSB   *184*
    Ljiljana Coklin

Institutional Support for Investigating the Impact of
Undergraduate Research in Writing   *187*
    Jenn Fishman

Afterword   *191*

Being Bold: Undergraduate Research in Writing Studies   *191*
    Joyce Kinkead

Appendix A: A Guide for Assessing Institutional
Support for Undergraduate Research   *201*

Appendix B: Available Resources for Undergraduate Research in Writing Studies   *212*

Appendix C: Conference on College Composition and Communication Position Statement on Undergraduate Research in Writing: Principles and Best Practices and Bibliography   *215*

Works Cited   *225*

Contributors   *251*

Index   *261*

Acknowledgments

As with the practices it describes, this book is the work of many generous hands. Most centrally, it is a product that could not exist without the many hours of labor and thoughtful reflection done by undergraduate researchers and their mentors. The authors and editors of this volume hope that it reflects that labor and reflection faithfully and gratefully, helping to bring recognition to that work and to generate the further support it needs to flourish.

This book also represents the labor of the group of generous scholars whose thoughts and expertise informs the words on these pages. Forty-three national experts agreed to spend three intensive days of their already busy life to participate energetically in the Naylor Symposium on Undergraduate Research in Writing Studies, and to spend the following year writing together to create a book that they hope will add value to the future of this high-impact practice and to our discipline more generally. It also reflects the efforts of countless other mentors and undergraduate researchers whose ground-breaking efforts, and day to day labor, inform a set of practices that is clearly influencing the future of our discipline—as well as the future of the students with whom we are so fortunate to work. Part of our message is that more resources are clearly needed to make these practices sustainable; but we also acknowledge gratefully the support of institutions that are indeed providing support for the exemplary practices noted throughout in this book.

Likewise, we are grateful to those who have created and who sustain the various publication and presentation venues for undergraduate researchers, to those organizations such as CCCC that have opened spaces for this work through its poster sessions and committee leadership and the other organizations noted in Appendix B. (We also thank CCCCs for granting us an earlier research grant that helped us to learn more about these practices through focus groups with undergraduate researchers and their mentors.) The Council of Undergraduate Research has also embraced the entry of Writing Studies into their sphere; and more personally, the attendance of Jenny Shanahan at our Symposium and her Foreword to this volume has helped us to see our place within these practices throughout higher education.

Finally, we must acknowledge that none of this could have happened without the generous support of Mr. Irvin S. Naylor. The endowment he established to support the Naylor Professorship in Writing Studies, and his willingness to earmark its proceeds for the benefit of undergraduate research and social justice initiatives within our field, funds our annual workshop for undergraduate researchers. That endowment pays for the travel, lodging, and meals of hundreds of students and mentors who have attended and will continue to attend this event. Proceeds from that endowment also funded the Naylor Symposium, allowing us to gather this rich assortment of scholars together to do this work. It is the kind of philanthropy that we value, and should continue to seek—philanthropy that comes with a vision for the good it can do in support of our students' lives and education. We are proud that this report carries Mr. Naylor's name as a tribute to his consistent support.

Irv, thank you. Your generosity is doing the good things you envisioned through your gift.

Foreword

The Transformative Power of Undergraduate Research in Writing Studies

Jenny Olin Shanahan

The global undergraduate research movement is simultaneously far-reaching in its spread to countless institutions and academic disciplines around the world and close-knit in its members' radical, shared commitment to the primacy of student inquiry. In those various institutions and fields of study, proponents of undergraduate research (UR) have dismantled the barriers between learners and educators to foster collaboration in the creation and discovery of knowledge. That embrace of undergraduates as fellow scholars has transformed higher education. More importantly, it has transformed our students' lives. We have substantial and diverse forms of evidence attesting to the power of authentic scholarly experiences to ignite students' excitement about their field of study, to teach them a vast array of valuable skills, to inspire their academic and post-graduation achievement, and to contribute to their persistence and timely graduation. Represented in all of that data are countless stories of students whose life trajectories were fundamentally changed by the opportunity to engage in meaningful inquiry with the guidance of a mentor. Student transformations through UR occur across programs and majors, student demographic groups, types of institutions, and levels of experience, from students' first to final semesters of study.

The profound benefits of participating in UR are most pronounced for students who have been underserved in higher education: students of color; indigenous students; English Language Learners; and low-income, working-class, and first-generation students. The high level of support they receive from faculty mentors, the mutual encouragement they enjoy with their peers, and the unparalleled opportunities they receive as a result of their research (e.g., to travel to and network at conferences) are advantageous for all students but provide particularly valuable forms of social and cultural capital for students from underserved groups. The preponderance of that evidence points to a moral imperative to ensure equitable access to UR.

Writing Studies faculty and administrators have been particularly responsive to the call for equity in UR, likely because it resonates strongly with fundamental values of the discipline. Distinctive aspects of Writing Studies teaching and learning praxes—especially the centering of student inquiry and student voices—align with inclusive practices of UR that resituate power as shared between students and professors. That congruence of student-centered values with student-centered practice in the teaching, learning, and scholarship of Writing Studies serves as a model for fair access to UR across the disciplines. Even with extensive data about the transformative power of UR for underserved and at-risk students, and despite federal funding in the sciences to support diversity in STEM, the demand to democratize UR remains largely unfulfilled. The opportunities to participate in UR continue to be channeled toward students of privilege. In most fields of study at most institutions, access to UR disproportionately favors economically advantaged students with high GPAs and family legacies of higher education (Finley & McNair 2013; Kuh & O'Donnell 2013; McNair, Albertine, Cooper, McDonald & Major 2016). The challenge of broadening access to UR across the disciplines remains as relevant today as it was two decades ago, when the Boyer Commission Report (1998) called for making inquiry-based learning the norm, with opportunities for all students to conduct meaningful research.

As this book makes evident, Writing Studies is particularly well situated, philosophically and practically, to advance UR more equitably—and to do so in new, interdisciplinary forms and a diverse array of methods. Undergraduate research opportunities are advancing knowledge and deepening student engagement in this multifaceted field—sometimes in innovative ways made possible by technology and emerging fields of study, such as the digital humanities and writing about writing, but just as often through the core teaching and learning practices that characterize Writing Studies. Undergraduate research is what teacher-scholars in Writing Studies have been doing for decades: guiding students in processes of inquiry and creativity and providing opportunities and support for their voices to be heard. Undergraduate research in Writing Studies takes a myriad of approaches, shaped by the topic and rhetorical situation of the particular study or project, the level of experience and skills of the student, the faculty mentor's role on the spectrum of heavy scholarship to heavy teaching, and the institution's priorities and forms of support.

Each of the chapters of this book highlights UR in Writing Studies as capacious, inclusive, and disruptive, in the best sense of the term. It comprises all the characteristics of UR promulgated by the Council on Undergraduate Research (CUR)—an inquiry or investigation that is mentored, makes an original contribution, uses disciplinary methods, and is disseminated (Osborn & Karukstis 2009)—yet significantly expands UR beyond those boundaries.

The primary attribute that distinguishes UR from traditional research-project assignments is mentorship (Osborn & Karukstis 2009). Undergraduate research is guided by faculty—and, in doctoral-granting institutions, by graduate students and postdoctoral fellows—to ensure intellectual rigor, disciplinary significance and integrity, and meaningful participation in scholarly discourse about the topic. Mentoring UR includes working closely with students at each stage of the project, such as through holding regular individual or small-group meetings, setting interim deadlines, providing frequent feedback, and focusing on each student's learning process—in other words, offering the forms of guidance that writing instructors provide as a matter of course. Chapter 1 of this text expands predominant ideas about the role of mentors in UR by detailing a diversity of mentoring methods, including the many forms "mutual mentoring" can take—from co-mentoring by more than one faculty member to peer-to-peer mentoring and the students-as-partners model. In doing so, the authors transform our understanding about who mentors are and about how different mentoring relationships enrich the processes and outcomes of research.

The diversity of research mentoring roles and configurations in Writing Studies not only subverts the traditional notion of a single, expert "mentor," but also the forms and processes the mentored research takes. This book's discussion of the scholarly practices of Writing Studies, particularly in chapter 2, expands the notion of research methods into a rich array of ways of thinking and learning. Undergraduate researchers in Writing Studies are not trained in firmly agreed-upon methodologies but, instead, learn versatile research "moves" they can adapt to different situations. In those various situations, they cultivate habits of mind, such as curiosity and perspective-taking, that they can bring to all sorts of ill-structured problems.

Disciplinary, prescribed methods have traditionally been taught to undergraduate researchers to ensure the quality of their work—to guide them systematically through established inquiry processes to their original discoveries. The expectation that undergraduate researchers make "original contributions to the discipline" (CUR 2019), however, has been a controversial notion for at least the fifteen years I have been involved in CUR. Many research mentors have likened "original contribution" to what doctoral students and professors are expected to produce: unprecedented, publishable results. My recollection of the discussions at CUR business meetings in which we debated the intent of that "original contribution" benchmark, however, is that most CUR Councilors intended it to mean that undergraduate researchers engaged in authentic, inquiry-based scholarship, using their skills of research, analysis, and critical thinking to arrive at their own (i.e., original), as opposed to prescribed, conclusions. "Original contribution" signifies going beyond reporting on others' research and beyond "practicing" research techniques and arriving at planned results, such as what students might do in an introductory science course with a "cookbook" lab assignment. The idea was to encourage authentic inquiry and discovery processes. The debate has continued, though, even a decade after two leaders of CUR suggested a continuum between "original to the discipline" and "original to the student" (Beckman & Hensel 2009, 40).

I am therefore especially grateful for the attentive and beneficial discussion of the complex idea of "original contribution" in chapter 3 of this book. The authors' reframing of "original contribution" as *contribution to knowledge* provides an insightful clarification of the appropriate expectations of undergraduate researchers' contributions. The consideration of diverse forms of contributions by novices in Writing Studies (just as ranges of contributions exist for faculty, as the authors point out) is freeing. By moving well beyond the academy (where "original contribution to the discipline" lives) to many other kinds of communities to which undergraduate researchers contribute, the discussion invites readers to consider innovative and comprehensive understandings of scholarship.

"Contribution to the discipline" varies greatly not only among students of different levels of experience and among academic and community-based audiences, but also, of course, across disciplinary norms. I was first invited in 2004 to participate in CUR discussions and workshops about UR in the social sciences, humanities, and arts for the very reason that scholars employ varying processes, forms, and products in different fields and contexts. It has been the philosophy in CUR that, like graduate and faculty scholarship, UR should be rooted in appropriate, recognized, disciplinary methods; it should, in other words, mirror the work that more advanced scholars do, even though adapted for students' levels of expertise, the time constraints of a semester, and other variables.

The many forms of research in Writing Studies logically lead to multiple ways of disseminating it. I have told countless students over the years who were nervous about presenting their research at a campus symposium or reluctant to submit a piece of writing for possible publication, that the real power of UR is realized through dissemination. Sharing what was learned with an audience for whom it matters is essential to scholarship. The point of research is to discover, create, or learn something that furthers human thought; research that does not go beyond the researcher (and the professor who grades it) loses much of its purpose. I have witnessed, as anyone who has helped students disseminate UR likely has, that when students know their work will be seen by classmates and other members of the campus community because they are presenting at the institution's student symposium, or that it will be found by online searchers because it is part of a digital humanities project, they quickly get out of the mode of "writing to the professor" and become much more invested in the work. Rather than focusing solely on meeting the criteria on a rubric to get a good grade, they think more intentionally about the purpose and quality of the work. The rhetorical situation suddenly matters because a real audience is expecting something from them, such as accurate information, new understanding, or an artistic experience.

This book's reframing of "dissemination" as *circulation* in chapter 4 is another powerful example of how the authors enlarge our understanding of the possibilities of UR, not only in Writing Studies, and not only across academic disciplines, but also beyond colleges and universities. *Circulation*, as opposed to the unidirectional act of dissemination, implies reciprocal exchanges and the sharing of and adding to ideas well beyond the initial site. It is how the spread of knowledge actually occurs in the world.

Although each part of this text advances the cause of equity in UR by revealing inclusive ideas about the breadth of mentorship, methods, and contributions to and circulation of knowledge, chapter 5 makes an especially powerful case for removing barriers and intentionally welcoming all students to engage in this high-impact practice. The authors put forth a bold and compelling vision of all students accessing UR in Writing Studies as a matter of social justice. That degree of access depends on our making opportunities to engage in UR straightforward and open to all. The surest way to do so is through the courses that every student will take in pursuit of their degrees. Chapter 6 of this text, on UR in the Writing Studies curriculum, offers a specific set of recommendations for embedding authentic scholarly experiences in the classroom and various types of coursework so that UR is no longer reserved for students who have the luxury of extra, unpaid time to dedicate to it. Chapter 7 takes those curricular recommendations to the next level, detailing a range of institutional supports within and beyond the classroom that are critical to the success of UR in different types of higher-education institutions.

In all of these ways of expanding the boundaries of UR—from broader models of mentorship, to more diverse methods, inclusive access, research-rich curricula, various forms of contributing to knowledge, means of circulating ideas, and systems of institutional support—this text makes significant contributions not only to UR in Writing Studies, but also to the comprehensive, global practice of UR across disciplines, institutions, and sites of discovery and creation. The expansive ideas in this book reflect some of the myriad ways feminist and indigenous ways of knowing have transformed Writing Studies over the last several decades—namely, in transgressing boundaries that keep people out and finding ways of welcoming and including everyone's voices. As this book demonstrates, UR is integral to Writing Studies, and it is a model of the kind of integrative learning that deepens students' experiences and can be a richly rewarding teaching and scholarly experience for faculty. When faculty are involved in guiding students in iterative scholarly processes; when students are encouraged to make their own contributions to the communities they care about; when they experience as undergraduates what scholars and other practitioners actually do in their chosen fields; and when they have opportunities to circulate their ideas and learn from others, our students' lives and future possibilities are transformed.

The Naylor Report

Introduction

BUILDING CAPACITY, CULTIVATING CONSEQUENCES: CHARTING THE COURSE OF UNDERGRADUATE RESEARCH IN WRITING STUDIES

Dominic DelliCarpini, Jenn Fishman, and Jane Greer

Two auspicious anniversaries occurred in 2018. The Boyer Commission Report, *Reinventing Undergraduate Education*, marked twenty years since its publication in 1998, and George D. Kuh's *High-Impact Educational Practices: What They Are, Who Has Access to Them, and Why They Matter* marked ten years since its publication in 2008. The former directly addressed the need to improve undergraduate education at research universities. The latter, written for a broader audience, has been helping faculty and staff at a wide range of colleges and universities prioritize the most impactful experiences they might offer students for the past decade. Notably, both documents bring undergraduate research (UR) to the fore. While the Boyer Commission called for "research-based learning" to become the standard (15), Kuh's work provided convincing evidence that participation in UR increases engagement and retention for students from many backgrounds (9).

These anniversaries provided the impetus for forty-three scholars, researchers, and teachers in Writing Studies to convene at York College in Pennsylvania for the 2018 Naylor Symposium on Undergraduate Research in Writing Studies. Fittingly, the symposium took place on the fifth anniversary of the Naylor Workshop on Undergraduate Research in Writing Studies. Established in 2014, the annual workshop invited undergraduate researchers from across the country to share projects-in-progress over three days of intensive mentoring with Writing Studies experts. Celebrating UR as an educational movement both within and beyond our discipline, the broad goals of the symposium were to assess the state of UR in Writing Studies and to chart a course for the ongoing development of this critical work. Traveling from across the US, symposium participants included teachers, scholars, writing administrators, and graduate students, as well as adjunct, contract, and tenured/tenure-track faculty. They represented flagship state universities, historically black colleges and universities (HBCUs), private and religiously affiliated institutions, small liberal arts colleges, regional comprehensive universities located in rural communities, and urban research universities.

Symposium participants worked from the definition of UR put forward by the Council on Undergraduate Research (CUR): "An inquiry or investigation conducted by an undergraduate student that makes an original intellectual or creative contribution to the discipline" (Council on Undergraduate Research 2019). Toufic Hakim, a past president of CUR, further stipulates four key characteristics of the UR experience:

- Undergraduate researchers are mentored by faculty members or more experienced researchers.
- Undergraduate researchers use research methods and methodologies that are widely accepted in their fields of study.
- Undergraduate researchers make a contribution, however modest, to knowledge in their disciplines.
- Undergraduate researchers circulate the results of their work to audiences beyond the classroom. (1998, 190)

These characteristics served as the basis for symposium working groups on mentoring, methods, contribution to knowledge, and circulation, and participants in each group were charged with articulating how these aspects of UR are (or should be) manifested in UR opportunities in Writing Studies. Four additional working groups were formed to address the challenges faced by UR practitioners in Writing Studies in relation to two specific goals: making this high-impact educational practice a defining characteristic of our field and making it more widely available to students from all backgrounds and across diverse post-secondary institutions. These working groups focused on access, curriculum, impact, and institutional support.

This report represents participants' energetic dialogue, productive disagreements, and hard thinking over three days at York College and throughout subsequent months of writing and revising the chapters that make up this volume. Not a traditional edited collection, the *Nay-*

lor Report on Undergraduate Research in Writing Studies reflects ongoing interactions among the symposium participants, and it invites readers to join the conversation. To that end, each chapter centers on research-based recommendations for best practices as well as specific steps readers can take to involve their own students in UR in Writing Studies. Rich examples of practice from classrooms, writing centers, writing programs, and other spaces stand as resources to help readers imagine how they too might engage in this work. By offering brief but richly detailed examples of practice along with concrete recommendations, the Naylor Report aims to be both actionable and aspirational.

Each chapter, most of them collaboratively authored, is followed by one or more reflections written by symposium participants. These reflections recreate the dialogic dynamic of the symposium; they also highlight some of the ideas that became critical in working group discussions, whether as points of agreement or divergence. Additionally, since identifying and documenting the impact of UR is so crucial, commentary on impact appears in reflections throughout this volume, highlighting the critical connections symposium participants made across working groups. Throughout our work on this collection, we have kept in mind that UR, like all educational practices, depends on relationships between specific people positioned within particular institutional contexts. Campus cultures, financial and infrastructure resources, labor conditions, curricular structures, institutional missions, and countless other local exigencies affect how UR in Writing Studies is (and can be) carried out. The editors and contributors to this volume recognize that teachers, researchers, and academic leaders will need to think with, through, and beyond the best practices and recommendations put forward here if they are to realize the potential of UR in Writing Studies for their students, themselves, their institutions, and our field. To this end, this introduction articulates how the long-standing traditions, values, and norms of Writing Studies align with the principles and practices of UR; it also identifies the unique affordances that Writing Studies brings to UR. Additionally, the introduction highlights two main themes that thread throughout the volume: the importance of building capacity for UR in Writing Studies and the desire to ensure that UR in Writing Studies can be consequential for all stakeholders, including students, teachers, researchers, institutions, community partners, and professional organizations.

Writing Studies and Undergraduate Research: An Alignment of Principles & Practices

Students and their rhetorical education have always been at the center of the boundary-stretching field of Writing Studies, from Plato's dialogues with Phaedrus (370 BC) to Hallie Quinn Brown's reciter, *Bits and Odds* (1880); from Hugh Blair's *Lectures on Rhetoric and Belle Lettres* (1783) to Mina Shaughnessy's *Errors and Expectations* (1977); and from Jovita Idar's articles in *La Crónica* (1911) to Asao Inoue's calls for critical race writing pedagogies and assessments (2015). The "students" with whom Writing Studies researchers and teachers engage span from people of all ages pursuing post-secondary education at colleges and universities to immigrants working to master the English language in classes offered at local community centers, from military veterans learning to compose their stories in online workshops to low-wage workers developing new literacy skills at coding boot camps. In trying to define or map the field of Writing Studies, numerous scholars and researchers have wrestled with epistemological and ontological foundations of the field as well as the diversity of its pedagogical commitments and research traditions (e.g., Berlin [1984]; North [1987]; Phelps [1991]; Fulkerson [2005]; Horner [2016]; Ruiz [2016]; Mueller [2017]); Malenczyk, Miller-Cochran, Wardle, and Yancey [2018]). But there can be little doubt that students and their literacy repertoires occupy a privileged place within Writing Studies. As Joseph Harris might say, Writing Studies is indeed a "teaching subject" (2012).

The centrality of student learning to Writing Studies combined with the ubiquity of writing and the prominence of college-level writing requirements positions Writing Studies uniquely within the larger landscape of UR. In the twenty-first century, people matriculating at post-secondary institutions are almost universally required to complete one or more entry-level writing courses. According to the National Census of Writing, 96% of four-year institutions and 75% of two-year institutions have an explicit or embedded first-year writing requirement. While nearly all students thus study writing, it is researchers and teachers in Writing Studies who ensure that writing courses, as well as other sites of writing instruction, enable students to develop critical skills with language in all its forms. It is also Writing Studies educators who are likely to remain engaged with students from across the academy through upper-level, writing-intensive classes, writing centers, and other resources and programming.

Few other fields of study have similar opportunities to welcome students with a vast range of interests, abilities, and aspirations into the academy or to play such a crucial role in their post-secondary experiences. Faculty in Biology, Sociology, or Art History, for example, might teach an introductory course to initiate first-year students into their discipline or offer a general education course for a wide-range of beginning students. However, they work primarily with students who choose to major in their subject areas. Of course, the growing number of writing minors and majors on campuses across the country allows Writing Studies faculty to devote increasing attention to students who choose to make writing a primary area of study (see Giberson, Nugent, and Ostergaard, 2015). As a result, Writing Studies faculty and administrators bring distinctive breadth and depth to UR. Because of their institutional positions and the range of their work, they can engage a diversity of students in UR, and they can bring their acute understanding of writing and varying students' talents and desires as writers to general conversations about UR.

Writing Studies faculty also benefit greatly. As many UR mentors attest, the work of introducing students to inquiry in our field creates rich opportunities to intertwine research, teaching, and leadership locally on individual campuses and nationally through professional organizations. In the chapters and reflections to come, readers will find examples of undergraduate researchers and faculty collaborating on consequential projects: studies that gauge the impact a writing center has on its campus community; archival inquiries that enable faculty mentors to complete monograph projects; community-engaged, course-embedded research that leads to local activism and deepens campus-community relations. Rather than "one more thing" that writing teachers and scholars are called upon to do, UR offers a means of meaningful synthesis that can mitigate the sense of fragmentation and the loneliness that many Writing Studies educators experience in their jobs. UR in Writing Studies brings together research, teaching, and service and can be a "high-impact" practice that enriches the work lives of mentors as well as the educational experiences of their students.

Ultimately, the primary beneficiaries of both UR and Writing Studies are undergraduate researchers themselves. For UR is a fundamentally student-centered activity, which places priority on student learning as well as the contributions students make as researchers to disciplinary bodies of knowledge. This orientation is reflected in widely-used assessments of UR, such as EvaluateUR and SURE (Survey of Undergraduate Research Experience), which focus on learning outcomes, including students' acquisition of disciplinary knowledge and their development of competencies connected to communication, creativity, autonomy, persistence, self-confidence, and ethical conduct (EvaluateUR; SURE). The priority UR places on mentorship also affirms the importance of student learning. The first defining characteristic of UR is a mentoring relationship, which involves a more experienced researcher acting "as a guide, role model, teacher, and sponsor" for a less experienced researcher. Such a mentor offers "knowledge, advice, counsel, challenge, and support" with the goal of building the capacities of the novice researcher to pursue their own goals and future work (Johnson 2002, 88). Mentored undergraduate researchers learn research methods, they contribute to knowledge, and they circulate their research findings through various means.

In Writing Studies, the suite of activities that defines UR distinguishes it from more traditional and less empowering approaches to teaching. Compare the examples of UR included throughout this volume with the way "research" is often taught, including the infamous "research paper" critiqued by Alexandria Lockett in *Bad Ideas about Writing* and by Laurie Grobman and Joyce Kinkead in their introduction to *Undergraduate Research in English Studies* (2010). As contributors to this volume attest, UR does more than align with the student-centered core values of Writing Studies. UR also offers a means by which we can build upon our values and improve writing instruction along with students' access to it and institutional support for it. Indeed, we might say UR is a teaching activity that befits a teaching discipline such as Writing Studies.

BUILDING CAPACITY FOR UNDERGRADUATE RESEARCH IN WRITING STUDIES

Across the entire volume, readers will note that the authors identify both strategies and tactics for building capacity for UR in Writing Studies. As a discipline, Writing Studies sponsors not only curricular opportunities for UR but also opportunities for students to conduct UR in co-curricular spaces both online and off. As a result, undergraduate researchers in Writing Studies can pursue projects that connect them to different communities on their own campuses or adjacent to them, in their home neighborhoods and workplaces, and in digital spaces. Along the way, undergraduate researchers in our field may learn a host of research methods, including qualitative case studies and ethnographies, analytics and big data, historiographic and archival inquiries, rhetorical and discourse analyses, to name but a few. Likewise, the work produced by undergraduate researchers in Writing Studies takes many forms and takes into account many different audiences and goals. In fact, UR in our field may well open new areas of impactful research for us all.

To activate the full potential of UR in Writing Studies, contributors to this volume accept no limits on who can participate: a first-year student enrolled in a developmental writing class at a community college, a senior completing a professional writing degree at a mid-size regional university, an English major at a small liberal arts college who hopes to attend graduate school and join the professoriate, a computer science major at an elite research university who studies coding as a digital literacy practice. Likewise, UR practitioners include a writing program administrator (WPA) at a research university's satellite campus eager to integrate primary research into first-year writing, a graduate student developing course-embedded UR experiences along with her own career profile as she prepares for the academic job market, a digital scholar seeking ways to create co-curricular opportunities for students on her campus to participate in digital research. It should go without saying that a variety of institutional locations and institution types can—and should—be sites where students and their mentors take up UR in Writing Studies. Required first-year composition classes at two- and four-year brick-and-mortar and online campuses are simply the start. To build capacity for UR in Writing, we can also look to the sequenced curricula of many writing studies or professional writing majors as well as writing in the disciplines courses, writing center tutor training programs, courses that include community-engaged components, and senior theses or independent studies.

Collectively, the editors and authors of this report also acknowledge the responsibility that comes with such a broad call for inclusion. Too often in higher education diversity initiatives do not progress past inaugural events, and programming created to counter the exclusion of faculty and students from historically un- and under-represented groups fails to effect actual change. Throughout this volume, each chapter invites readers to consider actionable issues of access, recognizing that mentorship, research methods, and opportunities to share work contribute to who may—and who may not—see themselves as welcome to participate. We also dedicate a chapter to examining systemic issues of access in Writing Studies, and we attend to the ways in which the distribution of available resources, including curricula and institutional support, directly affects our ability to envision UR as an activity without compass and to work individually and together toward achieving this ideal.

UNDERGRADUATE RESEARCH IN WRITING STUDIES AS CONSEQUENTIAL WORK

When Kuh established UR as a highly consequential educational experience for students, he affirmed the Boyer Commission recommendation that research-based learning become the norm. In turn, the *Naylor Report on Undergraduate Research in Writing Studies* establishes that UR is also particularly consequential for our students and for our field. Further, contributors to this volume also assert that UR in writing has a central role to play in the advancement and expansion of this high-impact practice. Through UR, the students we have traditionally written about and for become our collaborators, writing with us and even about us. A powerful shift, this transformation positions undergraduate researchers to also become our partners in (re)shaping the future of Writing Studies, both in local contexts and on a broader stage.

The field of Writing Studies can take pride in the number of venues where undergraduate researchers can circulate their work. Our nationally-circulating, peer-reviewed journals include *Xchanges*, *Young Scholars in Writing*, and the *JUMP+*. Writing Studies also provides undergraduate researchers with regular opportunities to present their work at regional and national conferences. Perhaps most notably, the flagship national professional organization for college writing educators, the Conference on College Composition and Communication (CCCC), has been hosting a juried and mentored event, the Undergraduate Researcher Poster Session, annually since 2012. More than mere vanity outlets, these venues are selective and rigorous opportunities for emerging research and scholarship. Citation studies are one indication of how seriously UR in Writing Studies is taken, demonstrating that work produced by undergraduate researchers is regularly taken up by other scholars. That is to say, it is cited and re-circulated alongside scholarship by professional academics. We also see undergraduate researchers' work referenced and reproduced in textbooks and listed among course readings on syllabi. We will continue to learn more about the impact undergraduate researchers are having on our field as we develop increasingly sophisticated tools that can ascertain and compile how often electronic publications are clicked, how frequently students' work is cited on social media, how often it appears on learning management system sites, and whether it is deposited in open access institutional repositories, as well as in other spaces and places.

But the impact of UR in Writing Studies goes much further than scholarly contributions. Yes, the methods that undergraduate researchers learn to use are increasingly rigorous, valid, and reliable. They also reflect our collective efforts to be increasingly historically, culturally, and theoretically informed. But it may be even more important that UR in Writing Studies reflects our field's constant striving to contribute to the public good. Thus, *The Naylor Report* includes examples of undergraduate researchers whose work has made a difference—by helping to establish a new approach to tutoring in a campus writing center, by contributing to curriculum revisions undertaken by a first-year composition program, by strengthening a campus partnership with underserved members of a local community. Even as they expand their own research and writing repertoires, undergraduate researchers are authoring new scripts for writing instruction. As they do so, they and their mentors are model citizens of our field, demonstrating how all of us might best seek and share both knowledge and expertise to address pressing issues in ways that can make a true difference to others on our campuses and communities.

Using this Book: A Note on Our Rhetorical Situation

The Naylor Report on Undergraduate Research in Writing Studies begins with a brief narrative composed by Cynthia Crimmins, Director of the Center for Academic Innovation at York College of Pennsylvania. She provides readers with a glimpse into the Naylor Symposium, where work on this volume began. The body of *The Naylor Report* is then comprised of two interlocking parts.

Each of the four chapters in Part One take up one of the defining characteristics of UR: mentoring, research methods, contribution to knowledge, and circulation. Individually and together, these chapters serve two purposes. First, they illuminate how these characteristics are currently manifested in UR in Writing Studies. Second, they offer recommendations for building upon successes (and avoiding pitfalls) in practice on contributors' own campuses, in their communities, and within our field. Readers who are new to UR may find these first four chapters particularly helpful.

Part Two of this volume focuses on critical questions that Writing Studies might consider as UR continues to expand. Who has access to UR—and what challenges exist in opening these practices to under-represented groups and within a wide variety of institutional types? What curricular structures and sequences enable and support UR—and how might course-based opportunities widen the scale and scope of participation as well as the sustainability of this high-effort enterprise? And what institutional resources are necessary if a culture of UR in Writing Studies is to thrive on our campuses and throughout our discipline? By addressing each of these questions in turn, this section of the report offers recommendations for extending the reach and effect of UR in years to come.

The structure of the report is pragmatic. While we wished to engage with and illuminate the body of scholarship that examines UR and related issues in our discipline, we also strived to produce a practical resource for readers who plan, maintain, and deliver UR to our students, as well as to those who wish to do so. The genre, format, and style of this volume were designed to make *The Naylor Report* as usable as possible for those audiences as well as administrators and faculty from other disciplines who may play a role in sponsoring UR in Writing Studies. More specifically, we include the following features:

- A Foreword by Jenny Olin Shanahan, which explicitly relates UR in our field to the larger landscape of UR nationally, while also calling out the unique opportunities Writing Studies offers undergraduate researchers;
- Recommendations in each chapter, which can help you develop, maintain, and/or revise UR programs at your institution;
- Examples of successful UR practices, which appear in each chapter to help you envision steps you can take on your own campus;

- One or more reflections on each chapter, which are meant as an invitation to readers of this book to continue the dialogue of the symposium and this report;
- A self-study instrument, included as Appendix A, which can be used as a guide by readers who wish to assess current UR activities on their campus or collect information in preparation for new efforts;
- A list of existing resources for mentors and undergraduate researchers included as Appendix B;
- The CCCC Position Statement on Undergraduate Research, included as Appendix C.

Like the Boyer Commission, participants in the Naylor Symposium were eager for both dialogue and action, and *The Naylor Report*, like the Boyer Report before it, is designed as a toolkit to help guide the ongoing reinvention of undergraduate education through undergraduate research.

Final Words

There is no shortage of vital projects in Writing Studies that need the attention of talented researchers. In the twenty-first century, we grapple with growing income inequality, climate change, white nationalism, ableism, racism, heteronormativity, sexism, and the long-enduring structural inequities in modern society that have privileged the few and oppressed the many. If we are to write a different and better future for ourselves and for generations to come, many hands and minds will be needed to take up critical inquiries about how people use language to shape their worlds. Undergraduate researchers can and should be fully invested partners who join with their fellow students, teachers, scholars, and campus leaders in Writing Studies to deploy their considerable intellectual and rhetorical talents in the pursuit of a safer and more just future for all.

Many Generous Hands: A Narrative Reflection on the Naylor Symposium on Undergraduate Research in Writing Studies

Cynthia Crimmins

> *We believe passionately in the transformative power of meaningful, authentic research for our students.*
>
> Joyce Kinkead and Jessie L. Moore (2017)

Kinkead and Moore easily could have been speaking for every one of us who gathered during the Naylor Symposium to reconsider the past, present, and future of undergraduate research (UR) in Writing Studies. I was asked to chronicle the event and provide readers with some context for the development of this book. I hope this narrative can help you participate after the fact in the dialogues that occurred there. For, while this Symposium reflects the considered thoughts of some of the most crucial voices in undergraduate research in our field, there are scores of other mentors and undergraduate researchers nationally who do this work every day—often without sufficient resources. As Joyce Kinkead notes in the Afterword to this volume, the symposium was "yet another bold move to solidify what has come before and to take an activist and forward-looking view." We owe a debt of gratitude to all these generous scholars (including undergraduate scholars), whose mutual mentoring and energy is reflected throughout each chapter, especially in the various illustrative snapshots you will find there.

History and Context of "The Naylor"

The annual Naylor Workshop for Undergraduate Research in Writing Studies debuted in 2014. During "The Naylor," as it's fondly called by participants and alumni, students from around the country gather to

Figure 1. Participants in the 2016 Naylor Workshop on Undergraduate Research in Writing Studies.

learn from national experts about the research practices of our discipline as they develop their own projects. Unlike many undergraduate conferences and research celebrations, this workshop is meant for students who are in the throes of the questions and the struggles that all researchers face. Acknowledging the key role of mutual mentoring (see chapter 1), the workshop provides structured learning about methods in conjunction with less structured time for experts and novices to interact as co-learners. To date, over 130 students from thirty-nine states and three countries have attended the Naylor Workshop, held at York College of Pennsylvania, to work with mentors from forty-five different institutions from across the United States (indeed, some have attended multiple times). This unique workshop is funded through an endowment established by Mr. Irvin S. Naylor, a successful entrepreneur who has supported access to high-quality education for all students at all levels.

Figure 2. A 2017 Naylor participant shares his perspective with the group.

First developed by Dominic DelliCarpini, the Inaugural Naylor Endowed Professor of Writing Studies, with input from his student Megan Schoettler, the Naylor Workshop helps students to learn about a wide range of methods in Writing Studies, and to discern which method(s) best serve their goals. Students spend three intensive days in workshops and consultations with faculty mentors to refine their research questions, review relevant scholarly literature, determine appropriate research methods, and develop a research plan. Students leave The Naylor with new knowledge, sound advice, and the impetus to see their research through to its conclusion.

TIME TO TAKE STOCK

For the fifth anniversary of the Naylor Workshop and the twentieth anniversary of the Boyer Commission Report, *Reinventing Undergraduate Education*, the leaders of the Naylor Workshop felt it was time to take stock, both of the Workshop's achievements and the state of UR in the field. Rather than hold the usual workshop, Jenn Fishman, Jane Greer, and Dominic DelliCarpini designed a symposium for UR experts and launched a call for proposals to attend the first ever "Naylor Symposium on Undergraduate Research in Writing Studies." In response to their bold invitation, colleagues from all quarters of Writing Studies (many of whom who had acted as mentors for previous Naylor workshops) came together to assess the state of this high-impact educational practice in Writing Studies and to steer UR into the future. (The Workshop format returned in September 2019, and was attended by thirty-five students and seventeen mentors.)

A FITTING ATMOSPHERE

The Naylor Symposium convened at the York College of Pennsylvania Center for Community Engagement, an 1830s-era home with a rich history as a meeting space for collaborations about the future. Originally built as a residence for a wealthy York family, the building later became an exclusive club for prominent members of the York community who would socialize and discuss local and national issues. Women and people of color were restricted from joining until the 1990s. The building's mission changed fully in 2016, when York College was gifted the building by local philanthropist, Louis Appell. Dominic DelliCarpini, who serves as the Center for Community Engagement's first Dean, was charged to use the space for the good of the York community. It gave one Naylor Symposium participant a chuckle to learn that the venue for our work was once a club for elite white males but is now a space for work that disrupts notions of privilege—including the idea that faculty are the only "researchers" who matter.

Figure 3. The ribbon-cutting for the re-purposed Lafayette Club as it became York College's Center for Community Engagement, where the Naylor Symposium took place.

Our symposium break-out sessions took place in parlors adorned with murals and artwork about a more inclusive version of York's history. Local artist Ophelia Chambliss visited one evening to share stories of past African-American leaders in York who inspired her paintings. Her exhibition in the Center, "Casting Shadows," is a visual representation of Black American history and community designed to change the stories we tell about Black history and the Black community. Her images are products of scholarly research and conversations with York's current residents. (Ophelia also designed the cover for *The Naylor Report*.) Holding the Naylor Symposium in this restored historical landmark offered a fitting atmosphere. It was full of inspiration for the work of linking past with future, and it truly gave the Symposium a sense of place.

Figure 4. Diversifying the York College Center for Community Engagement on First Friday Latino.

Figure 5. Artist Ophelia Chambliss poses in the York Center for Community Engagement with her artwork, which offers visual narratives on York's black leaders and its racial history.

We also visited the Goodridge Freedom Center, site of one of the nation's first underground railroad sites, which had been established by a formerly enslaved individual, and we had lunch at the Marketview Arts art gallery, another historical site transformed by York College's Center for Community Engagement into a hub of creative expression for community members and students alike. In these ways, the setting of the Naylor Symposium within a challenged third-tier, post-industrial city reminded us of the social justice message of our field and how UR can stretch into the community.

Figure 6. The Goodridge Freedom Center, site of an Underground Railroad House in York, Pennsylvania.

A Design-Thinking Approach: Day One

In addition to helping symposium participants better understand our host city, these tours also helped members of the group get better acquainted with each other as we worked through our rigorous three-day agenda designed to promote collaboration and innovation based on the framework of Human-Centered Design or "Design Thinking." Prior to the first meeting, participants joined one of eight working groups, which match the themes addressed in this report. Each group was organized by a senior or "lead" scholar with relevant expertise. On the first morning, lead scholars presented framing pitches about each working group theme, identifying key premises, points for discussion, and lines of inquiry to be pursued during the remainder of the symposium. Each working group went on to develop "framing statements" for their theme, stating what they believed to be possible in the future and why. These statements operated as anchors throughout the symposium and beyond.

During our afternoon Town Hall Meeting, working groups re-convened and delivered these framing of "possibility" statements as posters, slides, and graffiti boards. We responded with statements that began "I like . . ." and "What if . . .," a feedback strategy based in Design Thinking. This process elicited both new and reinvigorated ideas, and the session itself became a threshold moment for the future of UR in Writing Studies. Lead scholars took notes, and everyone listened for overarching principles, re-imagined priorities for UR, and key operating assumptions.

Day Two: From Possibilities to Recommendations

On the second full day, each working group concentrated on transforming the previous days' conversations into recommendations that could drive forward and guide growth of UR in Writing Studies. Perhaps the hardest part of this assignment: recommendations were meant to identify concrete action items that both acknowledged and accommodated differences across sites of UR and among UR practitioners. To promote collaboration during the drafting sessions, Jenny Shanahan and I moved from group to group, identifying when groups should merge temporarily to discuss overlapping themes or test out their ideas on others.

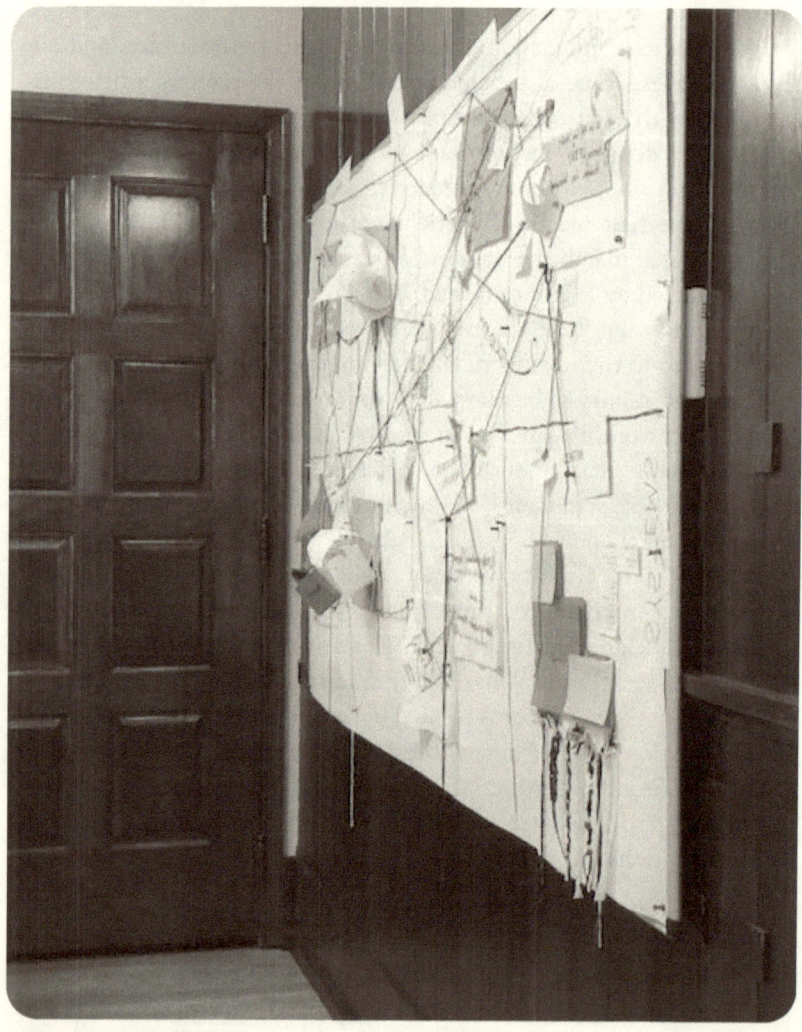

Figure 7. Mapping key motifs in undergraduate research on day one of the Naylor Symposium.

Next, the Naylor Symposium featured a Gallery Walk, which gave participants a chance to examine artifacts developed during the symposium, including diagrams, drawings, and lists that represented groups' recommendations and the thinking behind them. We carried sticky notes and pens as we circulated, adding input at each display. Following the Gallery Walk over lunch, free-form discussions helped everyone consider the feedback their group received and synthesize ideas. We also held a more formal debriefing session, where groups were able to raise questions, propose new ideas, and test revised versions of their recommendations. Some of the most widely discussed (and at times fervently debated) questions at this time and over the course of the symposium included:

- What is the definition of research? What does it mean to contribute new knowledge to a discipline? Do we need an expanded notion of research?
- What counts as dissemination of research? Does research need to be original to be publishable? Who is validating the research?
- What are sites of entry in the curriculum for students to be exposed to undergraduate research? What's realistic for an undergraduate researcher to accomplish?
- How can access to undergraduate research opportunities be equitable? What does it mean to invite everyone into this space? Do we have different expectations for different students?
- Do we have an obligation to teach research to all undergraduates? What role does reflection and student learning play in undergraduate research?
- What does it mean for research to have impact? How can assessment be useful? Should research be attached to grades?
- What resources are needed to develop a UR program that is based in equitable labor practices?

Day Three and Beyond: Our Bold Future

On the third day, the symposium may have ended but the work did not. For the next several months, lead scholars continued to elicit input from participants to craft this report, which, like the Boyer Commission Report, captures what we know (or think we know) about the impact of UR upon our discipline. *The Naylor Report* also contextualizes and differentiates the practices and products of UR in Writing Studies within the larger field of UR across the disciplines and envisions a way forward for this work.

In the end, it was the deep generosity of symposium participants that characterized this landmark event. Everyone gave freely of their time, sharing their experiences, their expertise, and their hopes and dreams for UR in Writing Studies. They embody a spirit of generosity that also characterizes UR in our discipline. This book is the result of that ongoing work, the work of many generous hands.

Participants in the Naylor Symposium

September 27–30, 2019

Sophia Abbot, Elon University
Heather Brook Adams, University of North Carolina, Greensboro
Rebecca Babcock, University of Texas, Permian Basin
Hannah Bellwoar, Juanita College
Ljiljana Coklin, University of California, Santa Barbara
Emily Cope, York College of Pennsylvania
Gabriel Cutrufello, York College of Pennsylvania
Cynthia Crimmins, York College of Pennsylvania
Dominic DelliCarpini, York College of Pennsylvania
Doug Downs, Montana State University
Andrea Efthymiou, Hofstra University
Kim Fahle Peck, York College of PA
Heather Falconer, Curry College
Jenn Fishman, Marquette University
William FitzGerald, Rutgers University, Camden
Angela Glotfelter, Miami University of Ohio
Jane Greer, University of Missouri, Kansas City
Laurie Grobman, Pennsylvania State University, Berks
Michelle Grue, University of California, Santa Barbara
Alexis Hart, Allegheny College
Justin Hodgson, Indiana University
Kristine Johnson, Calvin College
Elizabeth Kleinfeld, Metropolitan State University of Denver
Ethna Lay, Hofstra University
Alexandria Lockett, Spelman College
Shurli Makmillen, Claflin University
Mike Mattison, Wittenberg University
Laurie McMillan, Millersville University
Jessie Moore, Elon University
Enrique Paz, Miami University of Ohio
Michael Rifenburg, University of North Georgia

Trish Roberts-Miller, University of Texas, Austin
Megan Schoettler, Miami University of Ohio
Khirsten Scott, University of Pittsburgh
Jenny Shanahan, Bridgewater State University
Yvonne Teems, Hofstra University
Lee Torda, Bridgewater State University
Field Watts, University of Michigan
Jennifer Wells, New College of Florida
Mike Zerbe, York College of Pennsylvania

Part One

Defining Characteristics of Undergraduate Research in Writing Studies: What We've Learned

Part One of this report addresses some of the defining characteristics of successful undergraduate research (UR): creative and scalable models of mentoring, opportunities for students to learn a plurality of research methods, a wealth of options for undergraduate researchers to contribute to shared knowledge of writing, and multiple modes of circulating UR in ways that matter to diverse audiences, including researchers themselves.

Each chapter reviews key insights that theorists and practitioners of UR in Writing Studies have learned in the twenty years since the Boyer Commission was published. Each chapter also offers *recommendations* for activating the lessons that can be gleaned from our collective knowledge to advance UR at both local and national levels. As such, Part One serves as a storehouse of ideas about how these four key characteristics—mentoring, methods, contribution to knowledge, and circulation—can form a backbone for successful UR in Writing Studies.

1 Mentoring: Partnering with All Undergraduate Researchers in Writing

Jessie L. Moore, with Sophia Abbot,
Hannah Bellwoar, and Field Watts

> *Universities are communities of learners, whether those learners are astrophysicists examining matter in the far reaches of space or freshmen new to an expanded universe of learning... At many universities, [though,] research faculty and undergraduate students do not expect to interact with each other.*
>
> —Boyer Commission

> *Ideally, the campus environment is enriched by interaction among faculty members in disparate fields, with graduate students enlivened by their exploration of faculty roles, and with undergraduates, whose questions and fresh approaches may open new paths of inquiry.*
>
> —Boyer Commission

We open this chapter of *The Naylor Report* by deliberately echoing the Boyer Commission report, *Reinventing Undergraduate Education* (1998), which boldly called for "a mentor for every student" (1998, 17). Since the Boyer Report's publication, a growing body of evidence has affirmed that having a mentor in college matters. The 2014 Gallup-Purdue Index, for example, demonstrates that long-term benefits of mentored experiences include greater engagement at work and increased well-being. Arguably, mentoring also makes undergraduate research (UR) in Writing Studies a high-impact educational practice. George Kuh and Ken O'Donnell identify eight key elements of high-impact practices:

> Performance expectations set at appropriately high levels; significant investment of time and effort by students over an ex-

> tended period of time; interaction with faculty and peers about substantive matters; experiences with diversity, wherein students are exposed to and must contend with people and circumstances that differ from those with which students are familiar; frequent, timely, and constructive feedback; periodic, structured opportunities to reflect and integrate learning; opportunities to discover relevance of learning through real-world applications; [and] public demonstration of competence. (2013, 10)

Many of these elements have the *potential* to occur as part of mentored UR due to the mentoring relationship with a faculty or staff member, a near-peer, a graduate student, or another more experienced researcher in the field. For example, a mentored UR experience adds interaction with the mentor to the student's significant investment of time and effort and increases the likelihood of frequent feedback.

Within their examination of six themes of transformative undergraduate experiences, Felten, Gardner, Schroeder, Lambert, and Barefoot suggest, "High-impact practices are powerful in part because they are relationship rich" (2016, 48). High-impact UR mentoring relationships can foster belonging, scaffold learning challenges, and promote peer and professional networks (Felten et al. 2016). High-quality, mentored UR allows students to engage in real-world, complex problems and strengthen their self-awareness (Brew 2013; Kuh 2008; Johnson, Behling, Miller, and Vandermaas-Peeler 2015). These learning gains are most likely to occur when students work closely with faculty mentors throughout the research process, from developing a research question to sharing their findings (Kuh and O'Donnell 2013; Lopatto 2003).

Given the demonstrated gains of mentoring relationships, this chapter proceeds from the foundational belief that *Writing Studies faculty should engage in mutual-mentoring with undergraduate researchers in all our writing programs and majors*. Mutual-mentoring recognizes that mentoring may involve a network of participants who each contribute strengths to collective goals. With potential sites of writing UR including first-year writing and professional writing programs, writing majors, writing across the curriculum programs, and writing centers, Writing Studies is poised to have a transformational impact on the undergraduate experience by scaling up access to high-quality UR via mutual-mentoring. Our discussion of this foundational belief and key characteristics of mentoring is followed by four recommendations regarding the mentorship of undergraduate researchers in Writing Studies.

Research-Informed Mutual-Mentoring

What, then, does a mutual-mentoring relationship entail? W. Brad Johnson defines *mentoring* as, "a personal and reciprocal relationship in which a more experienced (usually older) faculty member acts as a guide, role model, teacher, and sponsor of a less experienced (usually younger) student or faculty member. A mentor provides the mentee with knowledge, advice, counsel, challenge, and support in the mentee's pursuit of becoming a full member of a particular profession" (2016, 23). Mentoring is not synonymous with teaching or advising, though some teachers and advisors may extend their relationships with students to include mentoring. Whereas teaching and advising roles often have parameters established by curricular structures (e.g., learning outcomes) or institutional priorities (e.g., a student's four-year course planning) and often assume a hierarchical relationship, mentoring relationships are reciprocal and broadly encompassing of the whole person, including emotional and social support. As Johnson illustrates in his Mentoring Relationship Continuum, teaching and advising roles often move towards mentoring when they shift from transactional to transformational structures and when they embody strong working alliances with high social support (2016, 29). Of course, a mentor is not always a faculty or staff member; near-peers, graduate students, postdoctoral fellows, and industry professionals also contribute to mentoring networks.

Mutual-mentoring "encourages the development of non-hierarchical, collaborative networks; . . . each 'node' or person in the network provides specific areas of knowledge and experience, such as research, teaching, tenure, or work-life balance; and the network relationships are formed to benefit" all members (University of Massachusetts Amherst Institute for Teaching Excellence and Faculty Development n.d.; see also Sorcinelli and Yun 2007). Mutual-mentoring may include co-mentoring, peer mentoring, and near-peer mentoring.

Ketcham et al.define co-mentoring as "the collaborative, simultaneous mentoring of a student by two or more faculty members" (2018, 155). Ketcham and colleagues examine the impact of co-mentoring not only on undergraduate researchers but also on faculty mentors. Because co-mentoring, one form of mutual-mentoring, entails "intentional, collaborative, multi-mentor structures . . . in which mentors build a relationship and work together to mentor a trainee . . . [and] mentors are mentored simultaneously . . . [T]his structure includes reciprocal teaching and learning, the move to level power structures, and an open dialogue on the needs and contributions of all mentors" (Ketcham et al. 2018, 157). While some dissertation committees might approximate this type of mentoring structure, depending on the working relationship of the committee members, co-mentoring remains largely absent from UR in Writing Studies. Yet, co-mentoring could serve as a pivotal strategy for implementing sustainable research teams, particularly in writing majors and minors, writing centers, and writing fellows programs, while fostering a community of practice among writing studies mentors. Co-mentoring distributes responsibility so that mentors can work with more than one mentee, and when co-mentoring results in research teams, mentees also can mentor each other—broadening access to these meaningful relationships beyond the traditional one-to-one mentoring that is more common in the humanities.

SALIENT PRACTICES OF MENTORING

Mutual-mentoring practices should be informed by salient practices of mentoring (Shanahan, et al. 2015, 362–70). Based on an extensive review of literature on UR mentoring, Jenny Olin Shanahan et al. identify ten salient practices of mentoring that offer undergraduate researchers intellectual, personal/emotional, and professional socialization support. Presented approximately in the order that they might occur during a mentored UR relationship, ten evidence-based practices are:

1. Engage in strategic pre-planning.
2. Set clear, and well-scaffolded expectations.
3. Teach technical skills, methods, and techniques.
4. Balance rigorous expectations with emotional support and appropriate personal interest in students.
5. Build a community among members of the team.
6. Dedicate time to one-on-one, hands-on mentoring.
7. Increase student ownership over time.
8. Support students' professional development through networking and explaining norms of the discipline.
9. Create intentional opportunities for peers and near-peers to learn mentoring skills.
10. Encourage and guide students through the dissemination of their findings. (Shanahan, et al. 2015, 362–70)

As the researchers note, these salient practices could form a mentoring pedagogy and the basis for faculty development for mentors. Although some salient practices mirror aspects of writing pedagogies, few writing programs devote professional development resources to preparing UR mentors, a professional identity that shares traits with, but is distinct from, identifying as a writing teacher. As a result, if writing programs and majors embrace the challenge of engaging in mutual-mentoring for UR, research-informed mentoring pedagogies like salient practices offer a helpful entry point for new professional development offerings.

STUDENTS-AS-PARTNERS FRAMEWORK

Mutual-mentoring also should be informed by students-as-partners (SaP) frameworks (Cook-Sather, Bovill, and Felten 2014; Healey, Flint, and Harrington 2014) when the mentoring context allows. A SaP pedagogical approach forefronts students and faculty working in collaboration to enhance teaching and learning. SaP projects and related practices for engaging student voices in the scholarship of teaching and learning (see, for example, Center for Engaged Learning 2018, and Werder and Otis 2010) offer strategies for implementing research teams that are attentive to co-inquiry across higher education's traditionally hierarchical roles. Though mentored UR and SaP initiatives have evolved with different lexicons in different bodies of scholarship, they share similar goals as potential high-impact educational practices (Moore 2016). The Council of Undergraduate Research defines UR as, "An inquiry or investigation conducted by an undergraduate student that makes an original intellectual or creative contribution to the discipline" (Council on Undergraduate Research 2019). UR is mentored by faculty, but the primary focus is on student learning—not the faculty mentor's research (Osborn and Karukstis 2009), so UR projects might explore slices of faculty mentors' larger research projects or students' own inquiry questions. SaP makes explicit this need for shared goal setting and co-inquiry, beginning with the shared development of research questions. Even when students are belatedly joining projects, the ethos of students as partners pushes for shared ownership of the process and reciprocity in the work. Mentored UR that attends to SaP frameworks may become even more high impact: fostering opportunities for students and faculty to contend with diverse perspectives within their team, and encouraging not only feedback for the student partner, but reciprocal feedback for the faculty partner.

Building on our foundational belief that Writing Studies faculty should engage in mutual-mentoring with undergraduate researchers in all our writing programs and majors and our brief introduction to key characteristics of mutual mentoring, we now turn to four recommendations for making the practice high-impact.

Recommendation #1: Because mentoring is a critical component to making UR a *high-impact* educational experience, writing studies should embrace multiple models of mentoring in order to scale up access to *mentored* UR.

The one-to-one mentoring models that many faculty associate with their masters and doctoral studies are not sustainable models for ensuring all students have access to mentored UR. When writing centers employ dozens of consultants and writing majors matriculate hundreds of students, for example, one-to-one mentoring enables only a fraction of students to participate in high-quality UR. To offer high-impact, mentored UR experiences to more students, including historically underrepresented minority students, writing studies should employ mutual-mentoring, including co-mentoring and near-peer mentoring, across UR models.

Although much published scholarship focuses on faculty/staff mentors (e.g., the 2018 Strada-Gallup Alumni Survey), research teams and near-peers also contribute significant mentoring. In a multi-institutional study of mentored UR at four universities in the US and Canada, Palmer et al. note that, "11 percent [of student participants] indicated that the initiator [for their involvement in an undergraduate research project] was a graduate student, 16.2 percent indicated a more senior student, and nearly 12 percent indicated a peer" (2018, 24). Palmer et al. also learned that students identified peers, near-peers, graduate students, and mentoring constellations as significant sources of support for their identity development during their UR experiences.

Near-peer mentoring is embedded in some of writing studies' *practices* (e.g., writing center peer consultants), but near-peer mentoring and research teams are less common in the discipline's undergraduate *research*. Indeed, for teacher-scholars who identify with the humanities aspects of the discipline's roots, research may continue to exist as a solitary activity. Yet, embracing the affordances of near-peer mentoring and research teams could facilitate increased access to UR experiences for students, while extending the potential of research projects.

One-to-One UR Mentoring

While one-to-one mentoring presents challenges for scaling access to mentored UR, this model is familiar to faculty and can serve as a starting point for trying out mutual mentoring informed by SaP and the salient practices of mentoring. Laurie Grobman (2007) affirms the value of the one-to-one, or independent, research model, including examples from *Young Scholars in Writing* to illustrate humanities students' capacity to contribute knowledge to their disciplines and to engage in sophisticated research processes. When faculty adopt the mindset that students bring their own knowledge and experiences to UR, mutual-mentoring via one-to-one mentoring has the potential to increase access to UR by providing more individualized support and development for students who may not traditionally be considered, or consider themselves, researchers—opening access beyond the "star student" model. For example, at a mid-sized liberal arts college, a faculty member mentored several undergraduate researchers whose life experiences (e.g., service trips, semesters abroad) led them to ask research questions related to the faculty members' research area—second language writing. The students had not taken courses with the faculty member and were not in any of the university's research-focused honors programs; fortunately, other faculty recognized their shared interests and made introductions. In other cases, though, a mutual-mentoring mindset may help faculty be attentive not only to which students demonstrate a capacity for research but also to which students are asking interesting inquiry questions that could be cultivated as UR through mentoring.

Team-Based UR Mentoring

Mutual-mentoring via research teams has the potential to increase access to UR by providing a collaborative atmosphere made up of individuals with varying levels of research experience who can mentor and learn from each other. In a Writing Studies research team, students initially might explore slices of a faculty member's research while multiple members of the team provide mentoring on the research topic, research methods, data analysis, and professional identity development. As students' experience and confidence increases, they might move along the continuum to shared development of new or follow-up research questions and then potentially to student-led inquiry, which also might be supported by other members of the team. At the same time, students become near-peers for newer members of the research team.

> ### One-to-One Mutual-Mentoring at a Small Liberal Arts Women's College
>
> **Context:** Students as Learners and Teachers Seminar of 15 students from various disciplines and academic levels
>
> **Snapshot:** Students in a small seminar observe other classes on campus, meet weekly with the faculty teaching those courses to share their student perspectives on inclusive teaching efforts in the observed classes, and meet weekly as a seminar group to discuss strategies for supporting their faculty partners (Cook-Sather and Des-Ogugua 2018). A student in the pedagogical partnership seminar describes the processes she uses as a student partner as "translation." Her professor affirms this metaphor, asks her to expand on it, and references it throughout the semester as a useful frame for the seminar participants. Near the end of the semester, the professor asks the student if she would like to write together on the topic. In **one-to-one mentoring**, they look through interviews and previously published writing on the process, seeking examples of this metaphor in practice. The student and professor describe themselves as research partners, and they navigate their varying expertise: the professor's on literature in this field, and the student's three years of practice in this area. They adapt the student's theoretical framework and write together on their findings. The student grows as a researcher and scholar, and she begins to identify herself as a legitimate creator of knowledge in this field. The professor grows as a scholar too, adopting a new understanding of her field and gaining energy and vitality through this collaborative process. The student helps the professor write more accessibly—clarifying passages that are initially written in a formal and jargon-filled way to be more straightforward and open to readers. They feel mutually empowered by this process as they both contribute to their field, but also use this new frame in teaching and interactions on their campus. It generates agency to develop and share this new framework and to mutually create knowledge. It legitimizes the student, who then uses this language when working with peers. In recognizing the value of new perspectives, both continue to affirm the contributions of other students they work with – extending this listening, care, and mentorship to others.
>
> **Reflection on Mutual-Mentoring:** How does this differ from a traditional one-to-one mentorship process? The two grow together and affirm their different but equally valuable expertise. They continue to talk beyond this project about shared interests. They co-author and think of each other as colleagues.

What, then, might be the roles of various members of (and mentors in) a research team? In a research team examining the writing lives of students, for example, new undergraduate researchers might practice analyzing survey or interview data in collaboration with more experienced near-peers, who also can offer mentoring on balancing research team responsibilities with other aspects of their undergraduate experience. Undergraduate researchers also might partner on discourse analysis of participant literacy narratives, offering an opportunity to establish interrater reliability and to refine a shared code book. More experienced undergraduate researchers might propose, draft IRB applications for, and ultimately implement follow-up data collection strategies related to research questions emerging from their own previous data analysis for the team. Team members then co-present at conferences, where faculty mentors connect students to broader professional networks and both faculty mentors and near-peers help newer team members navigate the conference experience.

Course-Based UR Mentoring

In some institutional contexts, scaling access to UR might be best achieved through course-based UR experiences (CURE). Mutual-mentoring via CURE has the potential to increase access to mentored undergraduate research by introducing all students enrolled in a course (or a sequence of courses) to mentored research practices. To approximate the mentoring relationships that make UR a high-impact experience, CURE should be carefully designed to foster cohort-based research teams and to reflect the salient practices of mentoring. An early course in a writing major, for instance, might "teach technical skills, methods, and techniques" (Shanahan et al. 2015, 362) while students conduct research for a local, community partner. A junior-level course might "increase student ownership over time" both by continuing the research partnership initiated during the earlier course and by requiring students to propose their own research project, to complete during a capstone course that "encourage[s] and guide[s] students through the dissemination of their findings" (Shanahan et al. 2015, 362). Even when students are unable to complete courses in a sequence that allows them to continue working with the same community partner, program-wide showcases of capstone projects and other CURE research allow all students to celebrate progress on these community-partner research projects, and a well-scaffolded

Undergraduate Research in a Research Team at a Large University

Context: A writing center with undergraduate and graduate consultants who are compensated for research as part of their working in the writing center

Research team description: The writing center at this institution provides a space for research teams to be formed, to discuss ideas, and to develop and work on research projects through employing a model of *inquiry groups*. These groups are made up of consultants exploring and discussing topics of interest as they relate to the work of the writing center. Inquiry group topics at this WC include (but are not limited to) feminism in the WC, STEM writing, supporting graduate students, supporting LGBT+ students, working with and/or being a multilingual writer, and working with and/or being a creative writer. These inquiry groups provide a space for research questions to be asked and for research teams to be formed.

Snapshot: Near the beginning of the semester, the LGBT+ inquiry group leader (a graduate student) reached out to the entire WC staff via email and the weekly consultant meeting to advertise the group. Undergraduates working hourly in the WC were encouraged to attend this (and other) inquiry group meetings in the place of one of their regularly scheduled consulting hours. Both graduate and undergraduates attended the LGBT+ inquiry group meetings (in the space of the writing center) in which they discussed articles related to supporting LGBT+ students and explored different possibilities for connecting these ideas to their realities in the center. The inquiry group leader was mentored by the WC director in terms of receiving support with managing group dynamics and direction **(one-to-one mentoring)**.

Through the mentorship of the inquiry group leader **(peer/near-peer mutual-mentoring)**, the group conversations began to focus on the more specific topic of inquiry that grew into a research project focused on exploring the use of gender-neutral language in the WC. Once the research project became more defined and specific, the research team developed out of a subset of the inquiry group—those involved who were committed and interested in doing the research. This team consisted of the graduate student inquiry group leader and two undergraduates, all mentored by the WC director. Despite the apparent power dynamic created by the different levels of research experience each team member brought to the project, the WC director was explicit about encouraging each group member by reminding them of their capability to contribute in a meaningful way.

> This allowed for a collaborative atmosphere in which all participants could voice their ideas.
>
> The team itself was able to meet to develop and work on the project, in meetings both with and without the WC director depending on the need for guidance, support, and advice. As the research team was also situated within the larger inquiry group—which was further situated within the even larger writing center—ideas could be shared with different people with different levels of involvement in the project (i.e., with inquiry group members outside of the research team as well as with writing center consultants outside of the inquiry group). This provided numerous opportunities to gather multiple perspectives allowing for the fruitful growth and development of the research. This had further benefit when it came time to disseminate the research at both a regional and an international writing center conference, as the other consultants in the WC provided a low-pressure audience for practicing the conference presentations.
>
> **Reflection on Mutual-Mentoring:** In all of the mentoring relationships within the research team, co-mentoring was apparent in that all involved were able to learn and develop as researchers (and mentors) by working with each other in this collaborative and open space—with the WC director empowering all voices, the research team sharing ideas with each other, and the research team seeking feedback from peers within the WC.

curriculum gives students experience with the discipline's research methodologies and methods.

Mutual-mentoring across these contexts has the potential to help students identify as *researchers* moving towards conducting (undergraduate) research. Mutual-mentoring may include research members from multiple disciplines and multiple institutions; because mutual-mentoring informed by the salient practices and SaP is attentive to explicit goal setting and negotiation of priorities, mutual-mentors have opportunities to negotiate outcomes that match their professional/personal goals.

Course-Based Undergraduate Research Experiences at a Small Liberal Arts College

Context: Professional writing degree program with twenty majors

Program Description: The professional writing major provides students with the opportunity to hone writing and communication skills while developing the ability to create and edit a piece of writing from start to finish. Students learn the fundamentals of copy editing and comprehensive editing, become immersed in multimedia writing and visual rhetoric, and create websites, screenplays, and blogs. All of this activity, in addition to courses from the Communication, Art, and IT departments, makes for a well-rounded major experience indicative of a liberal arts education.

Snapshot: A key part of mentoring is relationships. This snapshot shows how mentors and students might build mentoring relationships in class-based research projects throughout a major to eventually support one-to-one mentoring for students' senior research projects.

- In Introduction to Professional Writing, an introduction to qualitative research methods, students use interviews to learn about what people write and how they learn to write at work. Embedded mentoring includes one-to-one conferences and discussions of research in the field of professional writing in class.

- In Public Health Writing, students complete a Community Engaged Learning project, creating public health posters for the health center on campus. Students research the organization they're writing for and the audience, conducting focus groups with members of the audience. Students create posters and produce write ups that contribute knowledge to the field of health writing. Experienced students serve as TAs and both these near-peers and the faculty member guide students through the research process and provide feedback on their writing.

- In Writing Across Media/Writing for Video Production, students create blogs, podcasts, and videos about their chosen areas of inquiry. Students research their audience and their topic. They read about and engage with multiple ways to disseminate their research to their audience. Embedded mentoring includes small group workshops with peers and the professor to workshop their multimodal writing projects; the professor models how to provide feedback to their peers.

- In Peer Tutor Training, as students are learning to work as writing peer tutors for a class or in a writing center, they study writing pedagogy and peer mentorship. Students create a final project where they research topics related to their work as peer tutors and create posters. Embedded mutual mentoring includes student consultation sessions with each other about their writing and opportunities to shadow experienced peer tutors.

- Ultimately, in students' Internship/Thesis research, they have an extended one-to-one UR mentoring experience on the students' area of inquiry.

Reflection on Mutual-Mentoring: As students move through the curriculum, they encounter multiple forms of embedded mutual-mentoring (e.g., peer-mentoring, near-peer mentoring, one-to-one mentoring) and gain experience with different parts of the research process, including research methods and circulation of findings. To help students transfer their research strategies and experiences among courses, beginning-of-term writing or discussion prompts could ask students to identify their previous course-based and co-curricular UR experiences that might be applicable to the semesters' projects; similarly, end-of-term prompts could ask students to reflect on the applicability of the semester's research experiences to their future coursework and goals.

Recommendation #2: Mutual-mentoring should extend from question-formation to shared writing, presenting, and publication, with an explicit assumption that all members are capable of contributing meaningfully.

As noted above, learning gains associated with UR are most likely to occur when students work closely with faculty mentors throughout the research process, and the Salient Practices offer a mentoring pedagogy for working with undergraduate researchers from pre-planning through circulation. Some students approach potential mentors or research teams because they have a research question that aligns with the mentor's or team's scholarship. When programs embrace multiple models of mentoring, though, undergraduate researchers often contribute to question-formation in other ways. In a CURE model, for instance, a student might brainstorm several research questions in a methods course, receive feedback from faculty and peers, and then advance one of the questions in a capstone project. In a team-based model, advanced undergraduate researchers might propose follow-up questions based on their understanding of the team's existing research. Regardless of the mentoring models

Course-Based Undergraduate Research Experiences at a Mid-Sized University

Context: 200-level Writing as Inquiry course that counts as an elective in two majors and in multiple minors

Course description: This course is designed to introduce students to research methods employed by practicing writers and to emphasize that writing as a rhetorical practice always involves active inquiry. In addition to surveying writers' research methods, students will gain hands-on experience with a variety of methods. In the context of specific assignments and projects, students will learn how to choose, sequence, and adapt forms of inquiry to specific rhetorical situations, enhancing their artfulness as writers and professional rhetors.

Snapshot: Students have been working with a local non-profit throughout the semester. Early in the semester, the course used public transportation to travel to the non-profit's office; they met the director, learned more about the non-profit's mission, and heard firsthand about the non-profit's hope to attract a larger audience for fundraising events like an annual ice cream social and an annual art gala. Having negotiated the scope of the collaboration earlier with the instructor, the director asked the class to research community interest in the non-profit's mission and events, as well as ways that local community members feel compelled to contribute—via donations, ticketed events, or purchase of items—to area non-profits.

The class split into two sub-teams, one focusing on surveys of current and potential supporters of the non-profit and one conducting focus groups with the non-profit's Board members and longstanding supporters. The two teams started each class session with within-team scrum sessions in which each team member shared their responses to the following questions:

- What did you do since our last class session?
- What will you do before our next class session?
- How can the team help you work towards your next goal?

Once a week the teams reported their progress to the whole class with similar prompts. The instructor also met with them each time briefly during working class sessions to help troubleshoot challenges. Twice during the project, an advanced student currently interning with the non-profit visited the class to hear update reports from the teams and to offer feedback, creating space for near-peer mentoring focused on both content and practice. At the end of the project, the class synthesized their research and presented research-informed recommendations to the non-profit director.

Reflection on Mutual-Mentoring: Within this CURE context, mentoring took peer, near-peer, and faculty-to-group structures, with discussion prompts and conversations routinely acknowledging and inviting the varied expertise different group members brought to the shared research. In addition, students had the opportunity to present their research to an authentic audience. All aspects of the project also benefited from the safety net of a class structure with intentional mentoring opportunities.

in play, adopting a SaP framework for mutual mentoring acknowledges the valuable perspectives undergraduate researchers bring to posing inquiry questions and developing corresponding research plans.

As a consequence of mutual mentoring that extends throughout the research process, we should expect to see more undergraduate researchers as co-authors in all the journals and edited collections in our field, not only those designed to showcase UR. Grobman's reflection on chapter 3 in this volume addresses faculty/student co-authorship as a form of knowledge production, and chapter 4 offers additional public outcomes for UR in Writing Studies.

Recommendation #3: Institutions should explicitly demonstrate that they value mutual-mentoring.

High-quality mutual-mentoring requires institutional support. Promotion/tenure criteria should reward mentoring that reflects the salient practices of mentoring, including mentoring that occurs with members outside the institution. Institutions also should showcase mentoring via undergraduate research events and ongoing public displays of mutual-mentoring partnerships (e.g., posters featuring mutual-mentors in highly visible buildings). As Baker, et al. (2018) advocate, colleges should celebrate mentoring success, initiate conversations about the role of mentoring in promotion and tenure criteria, and acknowledge the significance of mentoring in developing the next generation of scholars. That scaffolded development requires significant time and merits institutional recognition of the teaching and mentoring that occurs in research settings, sometimes at the expense of research productivity (Buddie and Collins 2011). If colleges and universities want students to experience high-impact educational practices like mentored undergraduate research, they must visibly value and reward their alignment with the central mission and goal of higher education—student learning.

Recommendation #4: Institutions should provide professional development opportunities for mutual-mentoring, for faculty, staff, graduate students, peers, and near-peers.

With the possible exception of consultant development programs from writing center consultants, coursework and professional development programs rarely, if ever, focus on mentoring strategies and theories. Given that teaching and advising are not inherently mentoring relationships, even students, faculty, and staff who have pursued professional development related to these roles would benefit from opportunities to learn about and reflect on their use of mentoring pedagogies. The Salient Practices of Undergraduate Research Mentors, introduced above, offer a powerful heuristic for this professional development.

Conclusion

Regardless of our institution types, program contexts, and faculty/staff research interests, if Writing Studies as a discipline values UR, we must adopt curricular and co-curricular practices that reflect the notable value of *mentored* UR. The relationships students experience as part of mutual-mentoring across mentored UR models (i.e., one-to-one mentoring, research teams, and CURE) ultimately differentiate *high-impact* UR from UR.

Reflection on Chapter 1

The Importance of Reciprocity in Mentoring: Benefits and Challenges

Sophia Abbot, Hannah Bellwoar, and Eric E. Hall

We are wholeheartedly committed to the foundational belief that undergirds the first chapter of *The Naylor Report*: "Writing Studies faculty should engage in mutual-mentoring with undergraduate researchers in all our writing programs and majors." Thus, our response provides more details on the reciprocity involved in mutual-mentoring, and the challenges and opportunities which arise from that reciprocity.

The Process of Mutual-Mentoring: Emphasizing Reciprocity

Moore et al. define mutual-mentoring as encouraging "the development of non-hierarchical, collaborative networks"; we would add that that mutual mentoring centers on reciprocity as a goal. We want to emphasize a truth not often acknowledged: mentoring is not a unidirectional process. At the Naylor Symposium in 2018, many Writing Studies faculty shared stories about feeling positively transformed by the students they have mentored. These experiences were meaningful for the students, but they also breathed life into these instructors' work, inspiring and energizing them to explore new directions in research, or simply learn and grow from this human connection. We hope this reciprocity is appropriately reflected in the phrase "mutual-mentoring."

Chapter 1 connects this reciprocity to the Students as Partners (SaP) movement, and we suggest that the value of a SaP framework for mentoring is the intentionality it imparts. SaP pushes mentors to begin a mentor relationship with reciprocity and mutuality as an *intention*, rather than an accident. This intentionality can become an attitude or habit of mind that faculty continue to develop around mentoring. Mutual-mentoring offers us a way of entirely rethinking what mentoring looks like so that it becomes more open and democratic. As faculty continue to develop their mentoring habits through the intentionality of a SaP framework, they may also develop a deepened capacity for co-mentoring and mentorship teams.

Mutual-mentoring for many Writing Studies faculty might initially and primarily take the form of Moore et al.'s first side bar: one-to-one mutual mentoring. But co-mentoring is another form of mutual-mentoring that offers a way of rethinking mentoring and emphasizing reciprocity in which two or more scholars collaborate to mentor one or more students. Ketcham et al. write that the co-mentoring "structure values a culture of learning and development where researchers / mentors at all levels have something to gain and to give in a connected relationship, in some cases disrupting a typical power structure" (2018, 157). Aside from dissertation committees, faculty in writing studies may have limited experience with co-mentoring. As a result, it may be difficult for faculty to imagine what co-mentoring might look like at their institutions or in their relationships with their undergraduate students. However, as Moore et al. acknowledge, countless networks of people serve as mentors and mentees (e.g., peers and near peers, graduate students), and we wish to add to this list: librarians, instructional technologists, community members, alumni, student affairs staff, and work-study supervisors, in addition to contingent and tenured faculty. As faculty mentors work with these networks, they experience reciprocity through faculty development.

Faculty experience a distinctly reciprocal relationship in co-mentoring, as Ketcham et al. describe: (1) enhancing and broadening their pedagogical skills as they learn from each other's successful models, (2) sharing the work of mentoring and gaining "psychosocial" support, and (3) growing and developing new research skills in collaborations with folks from different disciplines and/or methodological background (2018, 163). Through co-mentoring, faculty and other mentors find personal benefits that help to make mentoring sustainable and sustaining. This sustainability can also help mentors scale up access to mentoring.

Internal Resistance and Challenges

In scaling mentoring, it is important to understand the challenges experienced by undergraduate research (UR) mentors and the ways reciprocity in mutual mentoring can reduce or resolve these challenges. Hall et al. (2018) interviewed twenty-four award-winning UR mentors with challenges and motivations in mind. These mentors' common challenges include: colleagues not valuing UR mentorship because it was not seen as fitting within the typical roles of faculty; amount of time needed to work with undergraduates; university structures (e.g., workload and criteria for tenure and promotion) that do not recognize or value UR mentoring; and lack of funds to support research and related activities.

Despite these challenges, these same mentors often spoke about the importance of undergraduate mentoring as part of their academic identity (e.g., mentoring aligned with career goals, specifically in terms of development of students). Indeed, these instructors held a growth mindset about mentoring and its potential. Additionally, many of them viewed mentoring as providing a synergy between their teaching and research. Mentoring is commonly assumed to decrease research productivity, but these award-winning mentors mentioned specific examples of how it actually helped them increase their research productivity by co-authoring papers with students and by expanding their research interests and the way that they thought about their work. Another interesting finding was that many of these mentors mentioned the importance of relationships with other colleagues as helping them become better mentors. As we saw in the stories at the Naylor Symposium, these faculty were experiencing the reciprocity of mutual mentoring.

Navigating External Challenges

Moore et al. highlight the importance of institutional support in creating successful, high-quality mutual-mentoring networks. Hall et al. (2018) share four different recommendations that may help institutions support these initiatives: (1) Emphasize the importance of UR mentorship and its potential for blending of faculty roles, (2) help faculty see mentoring as a way to enhance research productivity (not hinder); (3) develop reward systems that emphasize the importance of UR mentorship, and (4) create opportunities for faculty to share excellent practice in UR mentorship. Enacting these recommendations would help reinforce the value and reciprocity involved in UR mentoring and create a more positive environment that supports UR mentorship in writing studies and across the disciplines.

As Moore et al. point out, a common obstacle for UR mentoring is determining ways to increase the scale of such efforts. Shanahan et al. (2017) asked thirty-three award-winning UR mentors about the future of UR, and all expected to see an increased growth in the number of students involved and there to be more equitable access to UR for students. Their responses included comments related to the democratization of UR: (1) for underrepresented students, (2) for "average" students, (3) in the curriculum, and (4) through the use of technology. This intentionality towards providing access to more students was obviously an important issue discussed by Moore et al., and is one reason why the mutual-mentoring model seems to be an ideal model. Similarly, using the curriculum as a way to scale up access to students in these populations has been suggested by others. Moore et al. and Wuetherick, Willison, and Shanahan (2018) offer good examples. Finally, the use of technology as a way to increase scale is not often discussed, but new technologies around writing and communication can allow for a greater number of mentors, including professional writers, writing studies faculty, graduate students, and peers at other institutions, to provide mentorship to undergraduate students. Constellations of mentors can also derive personal benefit from these long-distance mentorship relationships such as finding allyship and fulfillment from connecting around a specific shared topic for which there may be limited local interest or support. This reciprocal benefit should not be overlooked. New technologies may open up many different, creative opportunities for mutual-mentoring constellations that have been discussed in chapter 1 and here as well.

CONCLUSION

Focusing on the reciprocity of mutual-mentoring can help us overcome the internal challenges and resistances we contend with as mentors of UR in Writing Studies. Mutual-mentoring itself may make mentoring more sustainable and sustaining. The SaP movement offers some lessons here: just as the goals and work of research are mutually decided in a SaP framework, so too are the benefits of partnership mutually experienced. Thus, the growth, support, energy, and joy present in mentoring relationships for mentees can and should also be experienced by mentors.

2 Research Methods: Designing Methods Instruction and Experiences That Invite Undergraduates into the Field

Emily Murphy Cope, Kim Fahle Peck, Kristine Johnson, and Shurli Makmillen

> *In writing studies, undergraduate research reflects the breadth of available methods and methodologies developed and used by professional writing researchers, including textual, archival, and digital scholarship; quantitative and qualitative empirical research; and creative inquiry.*
>
> —Conference on College Composition and Communication, Position Statement on Undergraduate Research in Writing (2017)

As the CCCC Statement on Undergraduate Research emphasizes, research in Writing Studies is defined by our objects of study rather than by a particular set of methods, making Writing Studies unique compared with other disciplines that more narrowly define what constitutes research. The breadth of research methods available to Writing Studies scholars is exciting and beneficial; it provides many paths for investigating questions that animate the field and opens up possibilities of cross-disciplinary collaborations and teaching.

In this chapter, we suggest that undergraduate researchers in Writing Studies need opportunities to learn about and practice a range of research methods. Doing so positions them to select and use the most appropriate research methods as they pursue questions they are curious about and whose answers are consequential for them personally, for their local contexts, and for the field of Writing Studies. But we also acknowledge that the wide range of possible research methods poses challenges for teaching methods and mentoring undergraduate researchers. Laurie Grobman and Joyce Kinkead argue that the multiplicity of research methods in Writing Studies makes research methods feel less "transparent" to would-be undergraduate researchers:

> Our suspicion is that we as faculty have not articulated to our students the methodology of inquiry in our fields [. . . .] Though the scientific method is transparent, this is not always the case in the humanities. We may not always agree on a process of inquiry; some might even call the discipline fragmented. (2010, x)

Even though Writing Studies scholars frequently use empirical research methods that are systematic, the barriers to teaching and learning field-specific research methods remain significant.

While Writing Studies faculty often have experience using several research methods, they are unlikely to be experts in all of the relevant research methodologies or all of the specific data collection and analysis methods that undergraduate researchers might wish to employ. It would be unreasonable to expect individual mentors to develop expertise in all available research methods. Indeed, expertise with a research method is complex, entailing understanding of research methodologies and paradigms, ethical considerations, data collection methods, data analysis methods, and method-specific genres. The size and constitution of departments may favor the teaching of some methods over others in local contexts. A second significant barrier to teaching and learning the field's range of research methods is time. Some types of research do not fit well into the constraints of an academic term, limiting the possibilities for course-based undergraduate research (UR). For example, grounded theory and longitudinal research methods may be less feasible than other research designs.

Given these constraints, it is not surprising that the "CCCC Position Statement on Undergraduate Research" claim that UR in the field "reflects the breadth of available methods and methodologies developed and used by professional writing researchers" may be more aspirational than fully realized. Our analysis of one key site for UR in the field—*Young Scholars in Writing* (*YSW*)—reveals a limited range of research methods represented in the published UR. While *YSW* does not represent the entirety of UR in the field, it is one of the field's long-standing journals dedicated to UR, and its articles serve as models for undergraduate researchers in the field. A search of terms in articles published in *YSW* (as of October 2018) reveals that approximately half of the student authors use rhetorical theory and methods (68 articles used the term *rhetoric* while 16 used "rhetorical analysis"). Other terms we looked for include *method* (2), *methodology* (2), *theory* (16), and *theoretical* (5). This suggests a need to diversify methods that students are exposed to throughout their undergraduate education.

In the rest of this chapter, we offer five recommendations for designing opportunities for undergraduates to learn about and practice using a range of disciplinary research methods. Although we call for more explicit teaching of research methods, we believe that research expertise does not begin with learning about and practicing specific research methods. Rather, becoming a researcher is a developmental process that benefits from scaffolded, developmentally appropriate instruction and repeated opportunities for practice. We avoid mapping these principles onto particular times within the undergraduate curriculum because of the variety of curricular structures at different institutions and different paths students take through curricula. These recommendations outline ways of designing and providing methods instruction to support UR in Writing Studies across, up, and beyond the curriculum. These recommendations aim to bridge the gap between our aspirations—that undergraduate researchers in Writing Studies would learn a wide range of research methods and, thus, be able to choose methods that allow them to best answer their questions—and the real constraints facing undergraduate researchers, faculty, mentors, programs, and institutions.

Recommendation #1: Writing Studies programs, faculty, and mentors should seek to teach the field's methodological diversity and the field of writing studies should support resources for learning about diverse methods.

Undergraduate researchers in Writing Studies will benefit from learning about the field's methodological diversity and understanding how their own research projects fit into that larger landscape. Faculty and mentors do not need to be experts in the entire range of research methods to help undergraduate researchers develop broad perspectives of the field's research activities and understand the relative affordances and limitations of various methods. At most institutions, colleagues in other disciplines have expertise in specific research methods used in Writing Studies and can become partners in teaching those methods. For example, colleagues in the social sciences may be able to help students learn about common quantitative and qualitative methods and even more specialized methods such as A/B testing or web analytics. Institutions can also support UR in Writing Studies by providing funding for faculty and mentors to participate in institutes and workshops that offer instruction in methods (e.g., Dartmouth's summer seminars for composition research) and cross-institutional research collaborations (e.g., Elon University's research seminars).

For faculty and mentors who wish to learn more about the range of research methods used in Writing Studies, we recommend resources such as "Writing Into the 21st Century: An Overview of Research on Writing, 1999 to 2004" (Juzwik et al. 2006) and *Written Communication*'s web-resource "Written Communication in the Classroom: Resources for Teaching Methods" (Bakke and Dreher n.d.). Juzwik et al. outline seven categories of research methods that were present in the Writing Studies research they reviewed. These categories provide a starting point for exploring and introducing undergraduates to the field's range of methods:

- experimental and quasi-experimental (including causal-comparative research, factorial designs, comparison of groups),
- single subject research,
- correlational research (including regression, multiple regression, structural equation modeling, cluster analysis),
- content analysis (including latent semantic analysis and thematic analysis),
- discourse analysis (including corpus linguistic analysis; text, genre or register analysis; literary or rhetorical analysis),
- other interpretive research (including interviews, focus groups, observation, case studies, ethnography), and
- historical research. (Juzwik et al. 2006, 462)

"Written Communication in the Classroom" curates articles on broad research principles as well as example publications that demonstrate the rigorous use of common disciplinary methods.

Resources like these can never capture the full array of disciplinary methods, but they do provide useful frameworks for helping undergraduates understand the diverse landscape of research methods used in Writing Studies and locate exemplars of many methods. Faculty and mentors can draw from such resources to expose undergraduates to a wide range of data collection and analysis methods by assigning texts that showcase multiple methods. For example, even if we don't teach students to use eye-movement-tracking methods, students could read about studies that use this method. Faculty mentors and undergraduate researchers can take advantage of and participate in the development of online resources for teaching and learning specific research methods. For example, corpus linguists have amassed video tutorials, MOOCs, and data repositories for researchers across the world. Such digital resources make particular research methods more accessible.

The growing collection of undergraduate textbooks in Writing Studies that include some research methods content demonstrates the field's interest in introducing undergraduates to methods. While there are many textbooks designed for first-year writing courses or writing in the disciplines courses that include generalized discussions of research methods, some textbooks are more narrowly focused on writing studies as a field of study and introduce research methods in that disciplinary context (Fitzgerald and Ianetta 2015; Kinkead 2015; McNealy 1999; Wardle and Downs 2017). In addition to textbooks, undergraduate researchers in Writing Studies would benefit from comprehensive handbooks for methods-based research. In particular, we see a need for handbooks and other resources that include specific, step-by-step guidance on the full range of textual, historical, qualitative, and quantitative data collection and data analysis methods employed in Writing Studies along with annotated examples of undergraduate research projects.

Recommendation #2: Within the field of Writing Studies, research ethics should be a primary focus of research methods instruction.

Providing rigorous instruction with disciplinary methods includes helping students develop awareness of ethical considerations implicated in all research activities. Explicit instruction in research ethics is necessary not only for qualitative or quantitative research with participants ("human subjects"), but also for archival and textual studies. Writing faculty and mentors can introduce undergraduates to principles for evaluating the ethics of research design and methods. *The Belmont Report* is accessible for undergraduates, especially when discussed in terms of the historical context from which it arose. Conversations about research ethics can occur throughout the curriculum as undergraduates read published scholarship or learn about research methods and as they design and conduct their own research projects.

Institutional Review Boards (IRB) can serve as sponsors of undergraduate researchers' learning about research methods and ethics. Many IRBs have options for course-based approval, so that the review process is not too onerous for students and can be put in place before the course starts. In some institutions, students complete online certificates at the proposal writing stage, before they begin collecting data. Their obligation after that is to get participants' informed consent, signed off on by the instructor as principal investigator. Having a guest speaker from the IRB can supplement students' learning and help them see their research activity from another point of view.

A recurring problem with asking students to do research with human participants in Writing Studies is time constraints—there is simply not enough time in one academic term to complete the research cycle. One potential solution is to take students all the way through to the proposal writing stage and make a proposal with an IRB application the final assignment in a course. In a vertical curriculum, for example, students in a research methods course could prepare a proposal and IRB application for their capstone project. In other contexts, a culminating assignment could be proposals for research studies undertaken in independent studies or in collaboration with campus or local organizations (e.g., writing centers, internship sites, nonprofits).

Institutional review boards vary widely in their requirements for UR. Some boards do not require a formal review unless the project will be presented or published beyond the institution; in such cases, institutions rely on faculty mentors to ensure the ethical treatment of participants. Additionally, some boards do not require studies that could be considered educational assessment or evaluation (categories that often could include writing center research) to go through formal review if the research will not be presented or published beyond the institution. When IRB approval is not required by the institution, faculty and programs may find that creating a process for ethics review and feedback benefits students' learning in this area. For example, peers in a course or a small faculty panel could provide feedback on research design focused on ethical considerations.

Even when IRB approval is not required or relevant, students benefit from discussing ethical considerations. Applying ethical principles in UR, Enoch and VanHaitsma argue that students can be mentored toward what they would call critical archival literacy, following the work of numerous scholars who see archives in terms of "their rhetorical properties" (2015, 216 emphasis in original). Their article is a practical resource for those wanting to mentor students through digital archival methods, and includes ideas for projects and assignments, for example comparing academic and non-academic archival sources on a particular topic for what they "reflect" and "deflect" (using a Burkean framework). Lueck, Law, and Zhang's chapter "Inclusivity in the Archives: Expanding Undergraduate Pedagogies for Diversity and Inclusion" highlights ethical considerations and pedagogical practices for faculty to consider when working with undergraduates in archives that reinforce white privilege through their collection practices.

To think critically about research design, faculty, mentors, and undergraduate researchers need some exposure to critiques of Writing Studies methods, especially those emerging from historically disenfranchised communities. New questions and methodologies have emerged from the study of African-American rhetorics and linguistic traditions (e.g., Alim and Smitherman 2012). In her promotion of Afrocentric pedagogy, Staci Perryman-Clark asks students to "make connections between African-American communicative practices and literacies, and their own literacy experiences as they investigate personal literary practices, online literary practices, and disciplinary literacy practices" (2014, 260). H. Samy Alim also involves students in ethnographies of communication, described as "sociolinguistic and ethnographic analyses of their own speech behavior" (2007, 170). Similar concerns arise from studies of Indigenous rhetorical traditions (e.g., Cushman 2008; Lyons 2000); indeed, Linda Tuhiwai-Smith's (2012) call for "decolonizing methodologies" has challenged and invigorated many disciplinary communities, demanding our attention. In response, Thieme and Makmillen (2017) have argued for a contingent approach to method when researching writing in contexts of Indigeneity, recognizing limits of standard methods and protocols, such as those surrounding confidentiality. Individual Indigenous communities may determine method locally, as part of what Lyons (2000) calls "rhetorical sovereignty," and researchers need to recognize that practicing some research methods in Western academic frameworks is not always appreciated or desired. Students engaging in what Stó:lō scholar Jo Ann Archibald (2008) calls "Storywork," for example, may not want their method subsumed under the framework of narrative inquiry.

Contributing to critical writing studies scholarship is work conducted within the field of feminist writing studies. A gender perspective has recently become particularly salient in the Writing Program Administration (WPA) community, as WPA scholars had reason to pause and reflect on the gender assumptions of the field at the most basic level (e.g., who takes authority to speak when a woman makes a request on a professional list-serv used by many in the field of Writing Studies). Feminist rhetorical and sociolinguistic methods came to the fore as a way to understand and reflect on this disruption, and as a result the WPA community has been urged to build on what one participant described as "the tenacity, the anger, and the ever-bubbling desire to make the WPA landscape into a workable and equitable space" (Lewis 2018). This was a salient example of how methods in Writing Studies can shape the very field we work in and how methods, like genres, arise out of rhetorical situations (Thieme and Makmillen 2017).

Gender imbalances in the field have also been noted in research in technical and business writing studies; White et al. (2016) conducted a corpus-supported content analysis of the field's leading journals to note that research through a gender studies lens makes up less than five percent of the research output, and this percentage has declined significantly from 1989 until 2012. They quote Ronald and Ritchie: "Feminist theories offer alternative stances for working in and against the male dominated cannon of rhetoric . . ., for demonstrating ways of rereading rhetoric, and for expanding received definitions of authority and effective communication" (White et. al. 2016, 39-40). With only slight adjustments to curricula—e.g., through readings that exemplify them—students can be made aware of feminist methodologies and the types of research they can frame.

Recommendation #3: Writing studies programs, faculty, and mentors should seek ways to foster research moves and dispositions.

Alongside learning specific methods, undergraduates must also begin to think like researchers. Thus, we recommend that faculty, mentors, and programs intentionally teach research moves and foster dispositions that support all types of methods-based research. We borrow this language of "moves" from studies that uncovered rhetorical and discursive patterns in academic writing and texts that argue that students benefit from being taught these moves explicitly (Bazerman 1988; Graff, Birkenstein, and Durst 2018; Lancaster 2016; Swales 1990). We extend this term to research as a way of emphasizing the recurring moves in methods-based academic research that students need to understand and practice. These moves are not only discursive or rhetorical, found in written products, but also represent ways of thinking and learning that can be fostered up and across the undergraduate curriculum.

Undergraduates can learn to recognize and practice the following "research moves":

- Recognize an issue or point of curiosity.
- Find out what scholars already know about the issue or question and identify unanswered questions.
- Identify a narrow and feasible research question.
- Evaluate options for answering that question.
- Determine what information will be collected, how to collect it, and how to analyze it in order to answer the research question.
- Put information collected into conversation with what has been said before to offer answers, offer new interpretations, or offer solutions.
- Determine appropriate avenues to share what was discovered through the research.

These moves entail secondary research as well as a range of primary research methods. Although we present these moves linearly, we recognize that in practice these moves are recursive and messy. The goal of teaching these moves is not only developing methodological rigor but also inviting students to imagine themselves as knowledge producers. Regardless of the curricular (or co-curricular) context or a faculty member's expertise, faculty and mentors can create opportunities for undergraduates to notice researchers engaging in these moves and provide opportunities for them to practice these research moves in a variety of contexts and using a variety of methods.

> ## Teaching Foundational Research Moves in a First-Year Writing Course
>
> The University of Tennessee's second-semester composition course focuses on inquiry and asks undergraduates to practice research moves with a variety of methods: (1) secondary research, (2) archival research, and (3) qualitative research. In each unit, students identify open questions or gaps in a body of literature, identify sources of information or research methods that might enable them to address their questions, collect and interpret data or sources, and articulate and present their research-informed arguments in conversation with prior arguments or research. By engaging with these foundational research "moves" repeatedly across three units, students have the opportunity to observe commonalities and differences across research traditions.

Such research moves are enabled and supported when faculty and mentors help undergraduates imagine themselves as knowledge producers by fostering particular dispositions, or habits of mind. *The Framework for Success in Postsecondary Writing* (Council of Writing Program Administrators et al. 2011) highlights habits of mind that students need to succeed in a variety of fields: curiosity, openness, engagement, creativity, persistence, responsibility, flexibility, and metacognition (1). These habits of mind are valuable in the context of UR and can be developed through research experiences. For example, researchers who are creative may envision a wider range of research methods through which to approach a question, while researchers who are persistent and flexible may not be deterred by the productive messiness of the research process.

The Association of Research and College Libraries also names several dispositions that enable students to engage in research as an iterative process:

- Appreciate that a question may appear to be simple but still disruptive and important to research.
- Maintain an open mind and a critical stance.
- Value persistence, adaptability, and flexibility and recognize that ambiguity can benefit the research process.
- Seek multiple perspectives during information gathering and assessment.
- Demonstrate intellectual humility (i.e., recognize their own intellectual or experiential limitations). (American Library Association 2015)

These dispositions enable researchers to conduct methods-based research and can be fostered up and across the curriculum. In many contexts, writing studies faculty and mentors may productively collaborate with librarians to develop instruction related to research skills and information literacy.

While we are positioning these research moves and habits of mind as foundational, they can be intentionally fostered through coursework and research experiences, returned to repeatedly across a student's academic career. Just as foundational research moves may be expressed differently at different points in the curriculum, so will the habits of persistence, adaptability, and intellectual humility develop throughout the undergraduate years. Programs and faculty can intentionally support undergraduates' learning of these foundational research moves and dispositions by articulating course-level and assignment-level learning outcomes related to these moves and habits of mind or researcher dispositions throughout the curriculum.

Recommendation #4: Writing Studies programs, faculty, and mentors should seek ways to teach research methods up and across the curriculum and co-curriculum.

The question of when and where students will gain exposure to various research methods is local and contextual. While some programs offer a research methods course as part of a vertical writing curriculum, not all institutions are able to offer such a course—or an undergraduate major in Writing Studies. However, even for programs with a research methods course situated in a Writing Studies major, we suggest that methods instruction needs to occur at various points within the undergraduate experience. We agree with the Boyer Commission report: "In a setting in which inquiry is prized, every course in an undergraduate curriculum should provide an opportunity to succeed through discovery-based methods" (1998, 17).

> **MAKING RESEARCH DESIGN & METHODS VISIBLE THROUGH A JOURNAL READING CLUB**
>
> Undergraduate students in linguistics and language education courses at Calvin College meet methodological outcomes in part through a "journal club." With small discussion groups, they read published scholarship from one methodological perspective (such as ethnography, survey research, or corpus linguistics) and construct a grid that tracks elements of a research study: the research question, gap addressed, relevant literature, participants and site, data collected, coding scheme, results, implications, etc. By reading and comparing numerous studies, students gain broad knowledge of methods-based research and gain knowledge of what characterizes specific methodological perspectives.

First, faculty and programs can identify methodological learning objectives for each writing course in the curriculum. All writing courses—and courses in related disciplines such as English, linguistics, and language education—explicitly or implicitly ask students to do methodological work, and instructors need to consider which methods students will be expected to engage in their courses. These methods can be explicitly taught and interrogated, particularly through scaffolded reading of published scholarship. When methodological knowledge is articulated as a course outcome, programs can build a curriculum that ensures exposure to and training in various methods throughout the program.

Second, students at all levels deserve to receive explicit instruction in research methods and can be made responsible for the research processes in ways that are developmentally appropriate. Just as Writing Studies scholars rail against those who expect a first-year composition course to teach students everything they need to know about writing in a single course, we cannot expect one course to provide everything students need to learn about research in Writing Studies. Faculty can scaffold undergraduates' learning of research methods by giving them practice with smaller pieces of the research process. A whole class might collect data together, to reduce the workload for each individual. Or, a faculty member might give students a research question and have them work in teams to develop a research plan, thereby focusing student learning on research design rather than knowledge of a particular disciplinary conversation. In programs with a vertical writing curriculum, faculty can identify appropriate methodological work at various levels and sequence activities accordingly. (Chapter 6 in this volume offers further discussion and recommendations about undergraduate research and curricular structures.)

SCAFFOLDING RESEARCH METHODS LEARNING UP A VERTICAL CURRICULUM

At York College of Pennsylvania, the professional writing major includes a second-year, 200-level research methods course in which students learn about and practice archival, qualitative, and quantitative research methods in small, collaborative projects and then individually produce a research proposal. Students execute that research project in a capstone course, a sequence that allows time not only for obtaining IRB approval or traveling to archives but also for further intellectual development.

While instruction in research methods will likely take place primarily within the curriculum, students, faculty, and programs can also envision the co-curriculum—writing centers, writing programs, community organizations, and internship placements—as sites for methodological instruction and encourage research questions prompted by experience in those sites. These co-curricular opportunities not only support the instruction students receive up and across the curriculum, but also decrease the burden of faculty to be experts in all methods, instead sharing the responsibility with other possible knowledgeable mentors.

Writing centers are one potential site outside of the classroom for methods instruction that have a rich history of UR. Writing centers often offer tutors opportunities for practical research, inviting them to consider problems or points of curiosity they experience within this space and to think through practical applications of any research findings that may impact their experience in their positions as tutors. Fitzgerald (2014a) specifically highlighted writing centers as co-curricular sites for research in our field, pointing to the possibilities provided by research in co-curricular spaces that can "allow students the time to pursue the often-circuitous paths that research can take" (96). Students often spend more time in the writing center than a single academic term, allowing them to undertake research projects that use methods not feasible within the limitations of a course-based project.

Internships may provide another key site for methods instruction for undergraduate researchers in writing studies. Scholarship has discussed the role and position of internships in our field (Balzhiser and McLeod 2010; Durack 2013); however, UR and internships are often positioned as distinct experiences for students. We suggest considering internships as sites for research and the professionals supervising students as additional mentors for research and methods instruction. Internships can introduce students to methods used in professional writing contexts including, for example, usability testing and market research through focus groups, or digitally focused methods like server-log analysis or social-media analytics. Internships provide opportunities for undergraduate researchers to draw on knowledgeable mentors outside of the academy and learn how to conduct research with practical outcomes for an organization.

The field of Writing Studies also provides opportunities for undergraduate researchers to learn research methods. The banner event for undergraduate researchers in the field is the Naylor Workshop for Undergraduate Research in Writing Studies. Students arrive at this event with research questions and ideas for research projects, and workshop leaders and faculty mentors help them identify the most appropriate research methods. The workshop provides undergraduates with an overview of qualitative and quantitative methods; an introduction to specific methods such as participant-observation, interviews, surveys, focus groups, and coding; and information about basic research concepts and project management skills. Students who have attended the Naylor Workshop report a greater sense of confidence about their projects and their ability to conduct methods-based research.

There are other events for undergraduate researchers that provide sometimes incidental instruction or support in research methods. When students apply for the UR poster session at the Conference on College Composition and Communication, they have the opportunity to receive feedback at the proposal stage—and this feedback may include methods. The Rhetoric Society of America also hosts an Undergraduate Research Network at its conference; undergraduate researchers workshop their projects with peers and a a faculty mentor.

These field-sponsored events provide opportunities to learn, experiment with, and refine knowledge of research methods; however, students' access to them is dependent on institutional and extra-institutional support and may be constrained by geographical considerations. The field needs more events held throughout the country aimed at supporting undergraduate researchers in Writing Studies to learn about the methods available in our field. Major disciplinary conferences have begun including pre-conference seminars and workshops on research methods, and conference workshops could be developed for undergraduate researchers. Special workshops at regional writing center conferences and regional CCCC summer conferences may be ideal locations to provide more students access to extra-institutional opportunities for methods instruction.

Recommendation #5: Writing Studies programs, faculty, and mentors emphasize the many benefits of learning research methods beyond the field of writing studies and beyond the academy.

To help undergraduates understand the value of learning the field's research methods and to help them draw from that learning in other situations and contexts, faculty can highlight how these and similar methods are used in professional contexts and other disciplines. In many academic institutions, this work is already underway in courses that focus on the genres of research and writing (Giltrow et al. 2014; Devitt, Reiff, and Bawarshi 2004) or on writing about writing (Wardle and Downs 2017). Writing programs can introduce undergraduates to examples of disciplinary research methods being used beyond the field of Writing Studies: for "applied" purposes, in other disciplines, or in professional contexts. Faculty can work toward this by assigning articles from other disciplines, incentivizing attendance at research presentations on campus, or having students interview working professionals about the research methods they use.

In addition to writing courses, the co-curriculum may provide opportunities for helping undergraduates notice and extend their learning about research methods. For example, students from across the disciplines who work in writing centers can engage in research based on their work as tutors and writing fellows, according to well-established methods in the field (Babcock and Thonus 2012), as well as have opportunities to engage in interdisciplinary studies on writing.

Cross-disciplinary collaborations such as co-taught courses or multidisciplinary research projects can also enrich students' learning about and facilitate their transfer of research methods knowledge: this kind of collaboration benefits students from other disciplines who gain exposure to writing studies research methods as well as students in writing studies programs who gain exposure to other disciplines' research methods and traditions.

Students' learning about research methods from Writing Studies is valuable beyond the academy. Students may be surprised to learn how the research methods they've learned are used in forensic linguistics (e.g., Shuy 2001), psycholinguistics (e.g., Pennebaker 2011), or marketing (e.g., Elliot 1996). Writing Studies methodologies are also relevant in the legal profession, in the form of comparative textual studies and content analysis (Hutchinson 2010). This exchange of benefits between workplace and disciplinary methods is mutual: if degree programs involve internships, students will be more prepared to bring an academic perspective to their internship, rather than see it as only "on-the-job training"; and they will also be prepared to bring data from workplace communities of practice forward for academic inquiry.

> ## Teaching Writing Studies Research Methods in an Interdisciplinary Course
>
> At the University of British Columbia, Vancouver, some undergraduates take an interdisciplinary course titled "Knowledge-Making in the Disciplines." This course gives students practice using discourse analysis methods to "explore the styles of expression which characterize knowledge-making activities—the key practices of research and scholarly discourse—in particular fields of discursive practice, or disciplines" (University of British Columbia n.d.). Students take an applied language approach to studying the discourses of their disciplines. They work individually or in groups to create their own corpora of research genres in their discipline, and in some cases use corpus analysis software for their analyses. The papers they write constitute contributions to this growing field, and some students have presented their findings at conferences at UBC and beyond.
>
> Faculty member Katja Thieme describes how this course and other initiatives foster methodological awareness in these students:
>
>> In addition to recognizing how stylistic practices vary across research genres and between research disciplines, students gain practice in the research methods of applied language studies, discourse analysis, and writing studies. In the process, they learn metalanguage about research genres and the language patterns associated with them. Such metalanguage not only links students' in-class research (in a field they hitherto had no training in) to published work in the field of writing studies, but also assists them in orienting themselves in future writing situations. (2019)

Finally, the field of Writing Studies is well-positioned to help students understand the value of research methods in civic and community contexts. Many writing faculty and programs already partner with community organizations and nonprofits to engage students in civic conversations and practice writing for real, local stakeholders. Just as students can engage in community-based writing tasks, they can engage in community-based research, partnering with local organizations and groups to solve problems and answer questions that matter to the community.

Reflection on Chapter 2

Research Methods as Declarative Knowledge in Writing Studies

Doug Downs

I write as a theorist of high-transfer/declarative knowledge (HT/DK) composition pedagogies. These, including "writing-about-writing," (Downs and Wardle 2007; Bird et al. 2019), "teaching for transfer" (Yancey, Robertson, and Taczak 2014), and other "writing-studies" approaches, ground writing instruction in the disciplinary knowledge of Writing Studies. They premise that declarative knowledge about writing, and more effective conceptions of and dispositions toward writing, are highly transferable to later scenes of writing, and are well built through encounters with Writing Studies research itself—both as students engage its scholarship and as they conduct primary research on their own questions related to writing, writers, discourse, literacy, and rhetoric. HT/DK instruction centers on students' mindful participation in our professional conversations about writing—and is thus congruent with undergraduate research (UR). I've been asked, then, to consider convergences between HT/DK pedagogies and this chapter's recommendations. The thinking the chapter offers is so superb that it leaves me with as many questions about HT/DK pedagogies as about its own suggestions. Here I'll consider three: *showcasing* methods through readings, *verticality* and *time* in curricular arrangements, and *transfer* of methodological knowledge.

The chapter's first recommendation is teaching our methodological diversity, in part by "assigning texts that showcase multiple methods." *Showcasing* is one of the clearest convergences between these writers' thinking and HT/DK pedagogies and resources. For example, the 4th edition of Wardle and Downs's textbook *Writing about Writing* (2019) includes a primer on research methods, and its *raison d'etre* has long been anthologizing accessible scholarship featuring a variety of research methods and dispositions. Likewise, Laurie McMillan's textbook, *Focus on Writing: What College Students Want to Know* (2019), dedicates a chapter to contributive research and offers a wonderful set of foci for student inquiry: the roles of discourse and literacy in our world; rhetorical theory; writing practices and process; and writing in "public" genres. It's less clear how the "teaching for transfer" pedagogy developed by Yancey, Robertson, and Taczak (2014) attends to research methods, but we can imagine students using primary inquiry and engagement with scholarship to help reach keywords and reflection that develop the "conceptual framework of writing knowledge" the pedagogy seeks (Robertson and Taczak 2017, 96).

While HT/DK pedagogies well support this recommendation, the chapter also suggests a showcasing not yet so well done: research ethics. Included in recommendation 2 is an argument that we show "critiques of writing studies methods, especially those resulting from contributions from scholars in historically disenfranchised groups." This reminds us just how rich the vein of research ethics has become in Writing Studies. (Far more so than standard IRB pablum.) Along with building a selection of key ethics-oriented scholarship into textbooks, we could imagine a research ethics course (or unit) built on engaging readings and enacting principles from them.

The next convergence I'll emphasize is around *verticality* and *time*. In their recommendations 3 and 4, the writers make a smart and strategic distinction between teaching *moves and dispositions* and teaching *methods* in scaffolding and integrating primary research *vertically* across curricula. HT/DK pedagogies specialize in conceptions and dispositions; in first-year courses, teaching moves and dispositions (recommendation 3) is a good fit with both what's feasible for students and for working on their prior knowledge and new conceptions of research. I've taught MacNealy (1999) in, and looked at Kinkead's (2015) methods handbook for, first-year WAW courses, but the time crunch and need for context are real. The idea of examining more methods in later gen-ed or major courses (recommendation 3) is helpful. Similarly useful is the chapter's push toward fostering team and multi-semester projects. I'm aware of few HT/DK implementations, either gen-ed or major, that vertically integrate a series of coordinated experiences across courses. Developers of HT/DK pedagogies should design multiple course to leverage such experiential sequences, playing for time and interweaving dispositions and methods.

Finally, I'm struck by convergence between "high transfer" declarative knowledge pedagogies and this chapter's concern for *transfer* of methods-related knowledge to non-scholarly scenes of writing and citizenship. To what extent have HT/DK pedagogues thought about methods *as* declarative knowledge? Fields outside the humanities have long taught their research methods as explicitly transferable and required knowledge, while historically English Studies imagined "close reading" as a transferable *skill* but rarely framed it as methodology available for reflection and metacognition.

While the chapter's fifth recommendation advocates applying methodological knowledge outside the scholarly sphere, how we should do so is less clear. Yet this is a *must*, not a "could." Two aspects emerge here. First, *dispositions* matter: adopting a scholarly disposition toward knowledge-making is huge for life-after-school. To understand research as narrative, to recognize the value of systematic inquiry, to know the roles of subjectivity and owning bias in research? Such methodological awareness is huge for citizenship and democracy. Second, it's not just *writing-about-writing*; we need *writing-about-numbers*—building a quant/stats element into our methods teaching, so that we're also focusing on numeracy.

Clearly, high-transfer/declarative knowledge pedagogies create a helpful framework for the kinds of methods instruction these writers advocate. And HT/DK instructors would do well to incorporate much of this chapter's thinking into our designs.

Reflection on Chapter 2

THE PLACE OF RESEARCH METHODOLOGIES IN UNDERGRADUATE RESEARCH DEVELOPMENT

Emily Murphy Cope and Gabriel Cutrufello

As we reflect on chapter 2, we wonder about the place of research methodologies in undergraduate Writing Studies methods instruction. While methods are the specific "analytical tools and procedures" researchers use to address research problems, methodologies are "the epistemological assumptions and worldviews that surround and shape specific methods" (Haas & Bakke 2013, 233). In our experiences, undergraduates experience learning about methods as more immediately useful and concrete than research methodologies. Chapter 2 encourages faculty and mentors to understand research as a developmental activity and makes practical recommendations for designing methods instruction that is developmentally appropriate. But what does it mean to think about research methodologies developmentally? What do undergraduates need to know about the field's research methodologies? When?

We both teach in York College of Pennsylvania's Professional Writing major, which has a vertical research curriculum: a second-year Research Methods in Writing Studies course, in which students explore a range of disciplinary research methods and develop a proposal and IRB-materials for their own undergraduate research (UR) project, and a fourth-year Senior Seminar, in which students undertake the research project and "go public" with their findings. Our program also offers several third-year courses in which students study a specific aspect of Writing Studies and conduct research using specific methods to approach topic-related research questions. We've chosen to prioritize hands-on learning, letting students learn by playing with methods in small, collaborative projects and then by conducting their own research studies (Earley 2014). We emphasize the importance of starting with research questions and then selecting research methods that can address those questions. While these priorities support student engagement and situate learning, we worry that learning about research methodologies might be getting short shrift.

Despite the relative challenges of learning about methodologies, we believe that knowledge of methodologies is important for undergraduate researchers for several reasons and can be supported "up and across the curriculum." We understand knowledge of methodologies as an aspect of discourse community knowledge. As a way of thinking about the place of knowledge about methodologies in developing research expertise, we turn to Beaufort's (2007) model of the knowledge domains that expert writers draw from; while this model describes a particular type of expertise-disciplinary writing expertise—it is nevertheless useful in teasing apart the multiple, overlapping domains of knowledge that might be present in disciplinary research expertise. In Beaufort's model, writing expertise is developed as multiple kinds of knowledge—rhetorical awareness, genre awareness, knowledge of processes, and subject-specific knowledge—work together and are connected to knowledge of a discourse community. We suggest that the ability to identify research problems and questions requires subject-matter knowledge and that the ability to make use of disciplinary research methods is a type of process knowledge. While methods operate at the level of process knowledge———what to do and how to do it—methodologies seem to operate as part of discourse community knowledge. Understanding research methodologies, including the ontologies and epistemologies that underlie various methods, helps us understand why communities of practice use particular methods.

Our students typically need repeated opportunities to learn about research methodologies. In our second-year research methods course, we introduce them to three major "families" of Writing Studies research: quantitative, qualitative, and historical. Students read about the differences between quantitative and qualitative research paradigms in an undergraduate-level research methods textbook (Flick 2015), and we explore these differences through in-class lessons and inductive reading of published scholarship. Emily's first enthusiastic attempts to introduce second-year students to the ontological and epistemological assumptions underlying quantitative and qualitative paradigms, as well as conceptions of research quality and the role of researcher values in both paradigms resulted in students' eyes glazing over. In other words, the level of detail and the timing may not have been developmentally appropriate.

We've seen better engagement with research methodologies later on, when students are already interested in a specific research problem and are grappling with research design and ethics in very specific ways. Students planning to conduct human-subjects research are required to develop an IRB application in the end of the 200-level methods course, but often end up working with us to revise their methods and IRB applications before commencing the research. This seems to be one of several moments when students "need to know" about research methodologies. As they work to explain their choices to the IRB, methodologies supply the language they need to describe the appropriateness of their approaches. Other kairotic moments occur when students are grappling with their data. Students can be frustrated, for example, that there was no clear "consensus" view on a particular topic they interviewed participants about; this is a wonderful opportunity to reinforce student learning about social constructionism. In the context of the 200-level research methods course, students may not have been ready to think about the possibility that "realities exist in the form of multiple mental constructions, socially and experientially based, local and specific, dependent for their form and content on the persons who hold them" but in the face of the data they collected, they might (Guba 1990, 27).

Repeated exposure to engagement with real audiences and situations where students need to articulate choices is key for approaching the teaching of methodologies. There is no one perfect moment that is developmentally appropriate, and there is no one perfect way to help students explore methodological questions. In fact, teaching methodology is the *sine qua non* of mentoring undergraduate students in Writing Studies because doing so requires an investment of time, expertise, and attention on the part of the faculty member to know when to move in that direction and how depending on our students' research and academic and professional audiences. Research methodologies and the surrounding pedagogical questions help to sharpen our own understanding of how to mentor undergraduate researchers precisely because they are so keyed to the individual learner, which is what UR mentoring is purported to support.

3 Contributing to Knowledge: A Defining Characteristic of Undergraduate Research

Jane Greer, Laurie Grobman, and Heather Falconer

Definitions of undergraduate research (UR) are remarkably consistent in their insistence that this "high-impact" educational practice (Kuh 2008) features undergraduates making an original contribution to a discipline. The Council on Undergraduate Research (CUR) defines UR as "An inquiry or investigation conducted by an undergraduate student that makes an original intellectual or creative contribution to the discipline" ("Who We Are—Mission" 2019). Physics professor and former CUR President Toufic Hakim emphasizes that "[u]ndergraduate research leads to a meaningful contribution by the student to the subject of inquiry." As he elaborates: "The research problem must revolve around a new question, a new hypothesis, or a new twist on an old question. It must give the students the chance to leave their marks behind, no matter how small or insignificant it may seem from the faculty mentor's perspective" (1998, 190). Writing more specifically about UR in English Studies, Joyce Kinkead and Laurie Grobman argue: "Ideally, undergraduate research is based on the same principles that drive faculty scholarship: it is meant to fill a gap in our knowledge base and be shared with the scholarly community" (2011, 219). And the Conference on College Composition and Communication (CCCC) Position Statement on Undergraduate Research in Writing Studies (2017) specifies that well-defined UR projects "[m]ake a genuine contribution, however modest, to public knowledge of writing, whether academic (e.g., disciplinary knowledge), professional, or community-based."

Despite these seemingly clear guidelines, however, challenges of defining and measuring "contribution to knowledge" in Writing Studies persist and are not confined to UR. As Horner and Lu have argued, the work of Rhetoric and Composition/Writing Studies as a discipline is concerned with "a wide array of practices, bodies of knowledge, and institutional sites" (2010, 471). As a field, we sometimes struggle to distinguish the work we do from other disciplines (e.g., communication, literature, education), and the multiplicity of methodological approaches, theoretical frameworks, and research populations means that there are, likewise, a multiplicity of outcomes in the pursuit of knowledge. Incorporating undergraduates into these disparate research practices complicates the "contribution" question further. For example: What is considered a reasonable contribution to a research project from a novice? Where does the boundary lay between a student learning about research and actively engaging in research? Thus, in conceptualizing what constitutes contribution to knowledge in Writing Studies for undergraduate researchers, we must recognize that the end result is deeply entwined with the work we ourselves do as scholars, as well as the other considerations discussed in this report, for example, mentoring, methods, circulation, access, curriculum, and institutional support.

Because contributing to knowledge is a defining characteristic of UR and because Writing Studies is a diverse, interdisciplinary field that places student voices at the center of intellectual inquiry, we recommend that writing teachers, researchers, institutional leaders, and other constituencies (1) adopt a capacious notion of what constitutes a contribution to knowledge by undergraduate researchers in Writing Studies, (2) recognize and work against the potential for hyper-professionalization that may occur if all undergraduate students are expected or required to make contributions to knowledge in our field, and (3) make informed decisions that are responsive to local exigencies when identifying students' work as UR that makes a contribution to knowledge in Writing Studies.

What Counts as a Contribution?

When faculty in any discipline evaluate tenure and promotion dossiers or determine merit raises for their colleagues, they must wrestle with questions about how to define meaningful contributions and how to determine the impact of a specific project on broader scholarly conversations. The field of Writing Studies faces particular challenges in defining and measuring contributions to knowledge due to the diversity of knowledge production in our field—a challenge that prompted the adoption of the CCCC Position Statement on Scholarship in Rhetoric, Writing, and Composition: Guidelines for Faculty, Deans, and Chairs (2018). "Contributions" include traditional monographs, edited collections, and articles in peer-reviewed journals; webtexts and other digital genres; textbooks and pedagogical materials used in classrooms and in writing centers; administrative documents, including model syllabuses, professional development materials for new teachers and/or tutors, and assessment reports; and a wide-range of texts that arise from community-engaged writing. In addition to the myriad textual artifacts produced as a result of their work, researchers, scholars, administrators, and teachers in Writing Studies are also often positioned as public advocates. As the Position Statement notes, "We are often called on to respond to language-related issues (e.g., the English-only movement, gendered and racialized expression, the teaching of grammar, the use of inclusive language) by way of editorials, radio and news interviews, and panels."

Just as faculty in Writing Studies produce a wide range of materials that are recognized as contributions to knowledge in our field, so too do undergraduate researchers contribute via an expansive range of modes. They apply and extend classroom learning. They combine extensive secondary and primary research and ground their inquiry in defined theoretical frameworks. They engage with local communities and help develop solutions to long-standing issues. They conduct confirmation studies, demonstrating that insights generated by other researchers are valid in new contexts. They develop and deploy new methodologies and technologies to address persistent questions in the field.

Such contributions to knowledge can be generated through an array of collaborative relations. As Todd McDorman (2004) observes, undergraduate researchers may become partners on faculty-driven research projects; they may work in tandem with more experienced mentors, pursuing independent but related projects while sharing insights, ideas, and feedback; or they may pursue an independent project that reflects their own interests under the guidance of a mentor. (See chapter 1 for further discussion of such mentoring relationships.) While traditional forms of scholarship, such as peer-reviewed articles or presentations, are an important aspect of circulating the work students do as undergraduate researchers, as with faculty in writing studies, other forms of knowledge may result from UR.

Recommendation #1: Writing Studies should recognize that contribution to knowledge has multiple meanings; faculty and other academic leaders—both nationally and in local contexts—should adopt a capacious notion of what constitutes a contribution to knowledge.

Traditional Contributions of Knowledge

Tracking how undergraduate researchers contribute to knowledge in Writing Studies is perhaps easiest when such work appears in the most traditional academic forms: a peer-reviewed publication or presentation. The field of Writing Studies is fortunate to have a number of such outlets where students can publish their work. Long-standing national and international journals in Writing Studies that publish the work of undergraduate researchers include *Xchanges*, founded in 2001; *Young Scholars in Writing*, founded in 2003; and *JUMP*, now *JUMP+*, founded in 2010.

Citations to work published in such peer-reviewed journals can stand as a measurement of how undergraduate researchers are contributing to knowledge in our field. For example, Jennifer Corroy's essay (2003) on the Writing Fellows Program at the University of Wisconsin, which appeared in Volume 1 of *Young Scholars in Writing*, has been cited eleven times by scholars who published in *The WAC Journal*, *Writing Center Journal*, and *New Directions in Higher Education*. Corroy's work was also re-printed in a 2005 volume of essays on course-based tutors, *On Location: Theory and Practice in Classroom-Based Writing Tutoring*, edited by Candace Spigelman and Laurie Grobman. Miriam Gofine's "How Are We Doing? A Review of Assessments in Writing Centers," which appeared in *The Writing Center Journal*'s 2012 special issue devoted to work by undergraduate researchers, has similarly been taken up by other scholars—it has been cited fifteen times. As Amy E. Robillard notes, "To be cited is to know that one is being read, but, perhaps more important, such citations function as a form of exchange value in the academic marketplace. When my work is cited, I can materially represent my 'impact on the field,' and my value in the academic marketplace increases" (2006, 260). Tracking citations to UR published in peer-reviewed journals is one way to document how undergraduate researchers have contributed to knowledge to our field.

Knowledge for/to/of Communities

New knowledge in Writing Studies is also created when scholars, including undergraduate researchers, engage with communities beyond the academy. The CCCC Position Statement on Community-Engaged Projects in Rhetoric and Composition (2016) provides some guidance in measuring the impact of academic work that circulates through non-academic networks. The position statement takes up issues of evaluating community-based scholarship, suggesting criteria that include reciprocity,

CONTRIBUTING TO KNOWLEDGE—
TRADITIONAL SCHOLARSHIP

Context: An upper-level, undergraduate course in English and Women's & Gender Studies at an urban research university in the Midwest.

Along with thirty other students enrolled in a course on Girls and Print Culture, a returning adult student, Leah, is required to complete an archival research project that recovers the voice of a girl or girls. The syllabus for the course is scaffolded to support students in what for many of them is the first archival research they have ever tackled. As a class, they use databases to identify possible primary materials, including diaries, scrapbooks, school yearbooks and newspapers, autograph albums, and other documents. The students visit campus-based archives and learn from archivists and librarians about using finding aids and working with manuscript materials. Class assignments include composing a project proposal; writing short analyses of primary documents; and compiling an annotated bibliography. The students also submit a "best effort" draft for instructor feedback and engage in numerous peer response activities throughout the semester.

Leah identified a diary kept by a teen-aged girl in the 1850s and wrote an outstanding class paper on how the diarist used her literacy skills to document her economic contributions to the household headed by her older brother upon their father's death. Once the course ended, Leah continued working on the project. Through her institution's Office of Undergraduate Research and Creative Scholarship, she applied for a small grant so she could travel to New England to examine other nineteenth-century diaries. She revised her original class paper, presenting her more developed project at a campus-wide UR symposium and sharing her research with state legislators via a poster symposium in the Capitol. Leah went on to publish her work in an international journal of UR in Writing Studies, and she also volunteered at the archive to transcribe the entire diary so that future researchers could more easily access it.

Leah's research experience demonstrates how undergraduate researchers engaged in traditional scholarly activities that contribute to knowledge in the field of Writing Studies. She recovered an intriguing text that had yet to be studied by other scholars and framed an innovative argument about the use of diaries as economic records for nineteenth-century girls. Leah drafted and revised her work over an extended period of time, sharing it with multiple audiences and honing the presentation of her findings based on the feedback she received. She ultimately published her work in a peer-reviewed journal and worked to ensure that future researchers would have greater access to the primary text she studied.

the potential for all stakeholders to engage in criticism and self-critique, and sustainability.

Germaine for consideration here is the criterion that includes the development of new knowledge: "New knowledge can take any number of forms, including published artifacts, performance events, media for community organizations, new teaching curricula, or new opportunities for community-university dialogue" (CCCC Position Statement on Community-Engaged Projects 2016). Students may contribute to a community's historical record or public and collective memory, often by contesting dominant narratives and uncovering previously silenced or marginalized voices. Students may conduct, transcribe, and archive oral histories. They may write research and recommendation reports for city governments, offering solutions to problems, such as littering or the need for accessible mass transit, and they may contribute policy briefs to city councils, addressing the need for more diversity in committees and advisory boards. Students may also produce videos, develop social media campaigns, and revise website content for nonprofits.

Faculty research often demonstrates the value and impact of UR that is situated in community contexts. For example, in Georgina Guzmán's community-engaged writing project, students read and discussed Chicana/o-Latina/o literature with farmworker families living near the campus in low-income farmworker housing tracts in Oxnard and Camarillo, California. Guzmán's analysis of these reading circles emphasizes the power that she and her Latina students had to provide models of what Latinas could achieve. The Latina women and families in the project came to see the "university itself as a democratizing place where they were welcome—a space that now figured into their and their children's present and future reality" (2018–19, 9). In another example, Claudia Monpere McIsaac's course on Creative Writing and Social Justice at Santa Clara University (SCU) in 2015 involved first-year students who read and wrote poetry with community members in a transitional housing project, a residential treatment program, and a youth community center. McIsaac's course illustrates that community members feel empowered "through their poetic voices" (2015, 189). In a University of Maryland-based community literacy program called Writing for Change, college students and ninth-grade students from a predominantly low-income local public high school collaboratively create a multimodal advocacy project. Research by the faculty, Heather Lindemann and Justin Lohr, "demonstrates myriad benefits of the partnership" for the high school students, "extending from personal growth to a heightened sense of social responsibility" (2018, 8).

Additionally, undergraduate students in Laurie Grobman's class made a substantial impact when they researched, documented, and shared local African-American history in collaboration with a museum in their community. Despite numerous challenges and complexities, "community members saw this project as crucial to their ongoing agenda of calling attention to the long-neglected history of African Americans in the region and to continued efforts to empower their people, especially the children" (2009b,136–137). Deborah Mutnick's analysis of a university-school oral history project in an elementary school in Brooklyn, New York, concludes: "The rendering of the stories concretizes them and signifies the importance of everyday life, thereby entering them, however modestly, into the historical record" (2007, 639). Despite significant language and cultural divides between the immigrant Mexican, Spanish-speaking population and the working and middle-class, English-speaking US population, participants were able to see themselves as connected and part of the same school community.

As these rich examples make clear, undergraduate researchers who undertake community-engaged projects contribute to knowledge in diverse ways that are best measured as a "matter of lived consequences" (CCCC Position Statement on Community-Engaged Projects, 2016).

Applied Knowledge

In *Scholarship Reconsidered* (1990), Ernest L. Boyer makes a powerful argument for including "the scholarship of application" in understandings of what constitutes substantive intellectual work. Harkening back to the traditions of land-grant universities founded in the late nineteenth and early twentieth centuries as well as to original missions of institutions like the University of Chicago and Rensselaer Polytechnic Institute, Boyer asks "How can knowledge be responsibly applied to consequential problems? How can it be helpful to individuals as well as institutions?" (21).

Writing program administrators (WPAs), writing center directors, sponsors of WAC/WID programs, designers and managers of digital labs, and other campus leaders in Writing Studies spend much of their intellectual energy producing knowledge and applying their insights to solve significant local issues. For example, a writing center director might be called upon to produce a report for a provost that justifies the center's currently assigned space on campus, separate from tutoring and other academic support initiatives offered through the university's academic advising office. Or, to inform curriculum design, a WPA who is responsible for first-year composition (FYC) courses may initiate a robust biennial assessment program that involves student focus groups, a review of randomly selected electronic writing portfolios produced in FYC, and a large-scale survey of graduating seniors about their post-FYC academic writing experiences. As the Council of Writing Program Administrators (CWPA) statement on "Evaluating the Intellectual Work of Writing Administration" (1998) makes clear, such applied intellectual work must be "grounded in disciplinary knowledge, demanding expertise, and producing knowledge or other valued ends" (1998, 5).

Such work can afford rich opportunities to undergraduate researchers as they partner with mentors who serve in a variety of administrative and teaching roles. Undergraduate researchers may engage in data collection as they help design and distribute surveys, comb institutional archives, facilitate focus groups, map usage patterns, or undertake ethnographic observations. They can participate in the analysis and interpretation of data as they code interview or focus group transcripts or deploy statistical analysis software. And they can co-present such applied research to a wide range of campus constituencies from faculty to deans, provosts, and alumni. By engaging in these kinds of activities, undergraduates have opportunities to learn research methods widely used in Writing Studies, gain exposure to existing scholarly literature in the field, enhance their critical thinking and metacognitive capacities, expand their rhetorical repertoires while communicating with various stakeholders, and build their own networks of professional relationships across campus. Through such applied work, undergraduate researchers are making important contributions to the field of Writing Studies.

To differentiate such applied research from routine bureaucratic practices, the CWPA argues that two broad criteria must be met: "First, it needs to advance knowledge—its production, clarification, connection, reinterpretation, or application. Second, it results in products or activities that can be evaluated by others" (1998, 10). In the case of the undergraduate researcher who collaborates with a writing center director to determine usage patterns, data is produced about who visits the writing center, how often, and for what purposes. This information is applied to make an argument about preserving the autonomy of the writing center and its physical space separate from other tutoring and support services. The provost and other administrators evaluate the research and its credibility as part of their decision-making processes about how to best support students and deploy scarce financial resources. Contributing knowledge to projects within one's own institution may indeed be as consequential as delivering a conference presentation, publishing in a peer-reviewed journal, or partnering with a community organization.

> ## Contributing to Knowledge—
> ## Applied Scholarship
>
> **Context:** A private liberal arts college in the Mid-Atlantic region
>
> A transfer student from a community college, Stacey wanted to work in the writing center when she matriculated at a four-year institution. She, thus, enrolled in a course on theories of writing and tutoring that was required for all writing center staff, and she found a powerful mentor in the professor teaching it. Based on Stacey's high level of engagement, the professor arranged for her to work as a summer intern in the campus writing program, which was about to embark on a revision of its curriculum. The internship involved helping to code qualitative surveys completed by over two hundred students in the college's current first-year writing classes. Initially, Stacey's mentor suggested particular coding categories based on widely recognized terms in the field of writing studies (e.g., mechanics, process). After working through a few dozen surveys, however, Stacey discovered that students' ways of describing their writing experiences were at odds with the coding categories suggested by her mentor. Stacey went on to develop new coding categories, which her mentor approved, and she was able to finish coding the surveys over the summer. She then helped to present the survey results to the entire writing faculty, who used that information to re-shape how writing was taught at the college.
>
> Stacey's UR project stands as a powerful example of applied research. Through her coding work and insights, she contributed to new knowledge about how students experience writing instruction at her institution. Stacey circulated her work to campus stakeholders who were able to evaluate it and determine how is should be used to inform their ongoing curriculum development efforts.

Knowledge for/of Methodologies

Undergraduate research can and should follow the field's direction in expanding the repertoire of methodologies, theoretical frameworks, and technological tools used in conducting research. New technologies are providing Writing Studies scholars with opportunities to explore rhetorical practices and community discourses in ways previously unforeseen.

The use of digital historiography in documenting the community experience of the Boston Marathon bombings in 2013, for example, allowed students to assist in the examination of traditional archival documents (e.g., newspapers) alongside oral history and digital writing (About Our Marathon 2019). Advancements in the digital humanities are allowing for the use of computer coding (e.g., XML and TEI) to examine not only what people write about but also how. Kevin G. Smith (2017), for example, uses XML coding in his undergraduate writing courses to help foster awareness of genre and composing practices. However, rather than provide the coding schema, his students design it as part of their work:

> Students begin with a (basically) bare schema and—iteratively and deliberately over the course of an entire semester—design and revise the schema for a range of writing tasks using document analysis and modeling, qualitative writing research methods, and their own experiences of authorship. The result is a shift from annotation to production, from product to process.

Through this process, students are not only constructing knowledge about the fluidity of genres, but about composing processes more broadly and ways to use technology in the examination of those processes.

While the contribution to the field's knowledge base may be the result of the application of new methodological approaches, it may also be the methodological approach itself. All scholars come to research with unique positioning and backgrounds, and students are no exception. Their prior knowledge and experience affect the questions they pose, as well as the methodological approaches they take to answer research questions. "Students are never just 'students,'" Asao Inoue argues, "They are classed, gendered, and raced (among other dimensions), so our research methods must account for these dimensions" (2012, 128). Thus, there is great potential for students to contribute to the field's knowledge of methodologies when they are involved in research design. This might involve a reconsideration of hypotheses posed, observation strategies, or approaches to data collection from a given population. Or, it might involve choosing a unique combination of data streams to shed new light on existing lines of inquiry. The immediate contribution to knowledge from students in these contexts may stem from their in-depth knowledge of particular communities or cultures or it may be a product of their positionality as students in relation to the subjects of their research.

Recommendation #2: While contributing to disciplinary knowledge is a defining characteristic of UR, faculty and other academic leaders in Writing Studies should recognize and work to forestall the dangers of hyper-professionalization for undergraduate students.

As a high-impact practice that introduces students to the epistemological and ontological orientations of a discipline and positions them to make contributions to the field, UR can be seen as a rung on the ladder toward an academic career in Writing Studies. UR experiences undoubtedly make students competitive for graduate programs in Writing Studies and help to ensure students are prepared for the rigors of advanced intellectual work. However, it is important to recognize that the skills and abilities students develop as undergraduate researchers are transferable to a wide range of contexts outside of academia. Researchers, scholars, teachers, and other leaders in Writing Studies are thus encouraged to recognize and work to forestall the dangers of hyper-professionalization for undergraduate students.

It is also the case that opportunities to engage in UR are not equally distributed due to a range of social and material factors. As chapter 5 on access discusses at length, the economic considerations of engaging in UR must be taken into account. When research takes place outside the construct of traditional, for-credit coursework or a paid position on campus, many students are unable to devote time to such activities. Travel to research sites, time away from family and work obligations, and access to materials may create an undue hardship on students that makes UR implausible or impossible. Additionally, many post-secondary institutions themselves struggle with serious financial constraints in an age of ongoing austerity for higher education. Reduced budgets may mean institutions are unable to support undergraduate student grants or travel to conferences, and faculty may not be appropriately compensated for the additional labor of mentoring undergraduate researchers beyond the classroom. Because of these and other constraints, UR that makes a contribution to knowledge in Writing Studies should not be a criterion for scholarship opportunities, acceptance into honors programs, internship placements, or admission to graduate school.

Moreover, it is critical for all stakeholders to realize that making a contribution to knowledge through UR in Writing Studies can benefit all students, regardless of their professional goals. Contributors to *Young Scholars in Writing*, for example, have come from disciplines ranging from English, Communication Studies, Creative Writing, and Rhetoric to Anthropology, Biology, Behavioral Science, Computer Science, History, International Studies, Marketing, Mathematics, Political Science, and Women's Studies among others. And undergraduate researchers' career paths are equally wide-ranging. English major Lindsey Harkness, whose research was published in volume one of *Young Scholars in Writing*, found her "career niche in higher education development and fundraising." Harkness writes that her work as an undergraduate researcher was relevant to her career: "[M]any of those skills I used in preparing to publish are relevant to my current career, in which I must have an appreciation for the editing process, an awareness of audience and the ways in which my words affect those I am addressing, and a strong attention to detail" (Bastian and Harkness 2008, 5). Other undergraduate researchers in Writing Studies have earned their bachelor's degrees and pursued careers in secondary education, technical writing, editing and publishing, the legal profession, library science, public history, public relations, journalism, and marketing to name but a few. By engaging in UR and contributing knowledge to the field of Writing Studies, students are not simply preparing for graduate work in English Studies and related fields; they are developing "the abilities to identify, analyze, and resolve problems [that] will prove invaluable in professional life and in citizenship" (Boyer 1998, 17). In engaging students in the research practices of Writing Studies, researchers, scholars, and teachers should embrace the civic role of Writing Studies in society by viewing the outcome of research not only as a contribution to the knowledge of the field, but also as a contribution to undergraduate researchers' worldviews, which will inform their critical thinking and decision making in all aspects of their lives.

Recommendation #3: As UR expands into new curricular and co-curricular spaces, teachers, researchers, institutional leaders, and other constituencies need to make informed decisions that are responsive to local exigencies when identifying students' work as a contribution to knowledge in Writing Studies.

Along with the other high-impact experiences identified by George D. Kuh, UR has a disproportionately positive effect on retention and graduation rates for first-generation students and members of underrepresented groups. Educational institutions are, thus, working to make these

CONTRIBUTING TO KNOWLEDGE—MORE THAN JUST AN AVENUE TO GRADUATE SCHOOL IN WRITING STUDIES

Context: A faith-based doctoral-granting university in the Midwest

As a first-year honors student, Kaylee was daunted by the requirement that all honors students at her institution engage in UR before graduating. Though she knew she wanted to be an English major, she was unsure about what "research" might look like in English Studies. At orientation, Kaylee connected with an English professor who was studying how women learn in sororities. The faculty member invited Kaylee to join her project, and Kaylee learned qualitative research methodologies and interview techniques while working with her faculty mentor. Together, they made a presentation about their findings at a regional conference for English teachers. They also submitted an article on the project to a national publication.

Kaylee went on to develop her own research project on the International Baccalaureate program (IB). She interviewed thirteen IB graduates, developed fourteen learning narratives (a technique her faculty mentor had used), and then coded the learning narratives using the CWPA Framework for Success in Post-Secondary Writing. Kaylee presented her research at the CCCC Undergraduate Researcher Poster Session.

Pursuing research increased Kaylee's confidence, and she described contributing to wider conversations about education as the "coolest feeling." But Kaylee's long-term career goal was to work in public relations, and she recognized how the skills she developed as an undergraduate researcher would help her advance along the professional path she was most interested in pursuing. She was able to land an internship with a local non-profit because she could interview people and "pull quotes." She was also able to develop her public relations skills by serving as a campus ambassador for the UR program at her university.

While Kaylee certainly contributed to knowledge in the field of Writing Studies through her research, presentations, and publications, she will carry the capacities she developed not to graduate school but into her career and community.

educational experiences more widely available to students, particularly in the early years of their college experiences. UR is emerging in first-year writing courses, first-year seminars, and in general education courses. According to Koch, Griffin, and Barefoot, twenty-three percent of community colleges, which deliver primarily 100- and 200-level courses to students, are providing "opportunities for students and faculty to work on research topics and/or generate scholarship (2014, 28). Institutions that have embraced online learning opportunities for students are seeking to "re-mediate" UR so that a student who may never visit the physical campus can still participate. And the College Board has developed AP (Advanced Placement) Research as the second course in its capstone experience for high school students.

These new spaces and places present exciting possibilities and raise complex questions. For example, can a student completing their first-year writing class in a sixteen-week semester or a 10-week quarter truly contribute to knowledge in Writing Studies (a question also addressed chapter 2)? How does mentoring undergraduate researchers so that they can contribute to knowledge in our field impact the workload of contingent faculty, who may teaching one hundred or more students across multiple general education courses and multiple campuses? Or what professional development opportunities might a secondary teacher delivering dual enrollment courses need if they are to offer a UR experience to high school students that allows them to engage in the kind of inquiries that might make a genuine impact on Writing Studies?

While such questions can seem intractable, a number of intriguing models are emerging. Institutions and programs that offer a writing major may opt to institute vertical curricula that scaffold students' learning about Writing Studies across their academic careers. For example, students in Oakland University's Department of Writing and Rhetoric are required to take three core courses: a gateway class on issues in writing and rhetoric; a course on the history of rhetoric; and a course on literacy, technology, and civic engagement. Students then complete courses in one of three tracks (writing for the professions; writing for new media; and writing as a discipline) before taking a final capstone requirement (Ostergaard, Giberson, and Nugent 2015). From a gateway class through a capstone, students have time to develop and hone both their expertise about writing and the research skills that will allow them to contribute knowledge to Writing Studies.

However, at many colleges and universities a vertically aligned curriculum is impractical, thus requiring other approaches and pedagogical creativity. For example, in first-year writing courses, an instructor might provide students with a limited data set to analyze or ask them to undertake a confirmation or replication study to check the results of previously published research. Other writing teachers have reported designing beginning-level classes that involve students in working with archival materials and other primary documents that have yet to be studied. In a 2018 NCTE blog post, Sarah E. Carter argues for such work in first-year writing, citing successful examples at Arizona State University, University of Tennessee-Knoxville, and Georgia State University. Similarly, Christopher Ervin (2016b) has documented how UR conducted by peer tutors in writing centers can take a number of forms. For example, Ervin describes a single tutor working closely with the writing center director to complete an honors thesis on tutors' relationships with English-language learners. He also describes a group of tutors working informally with a graduate student mentor and their writing center's director to research and address a stubborn issue—student conceptions of plagiarism and Turnitin.com—that they encountered in many tutoring sessions

Even as students' opportunities to contribute to UR in Writing Studies expand in exciting and dynamic ways, teachers and academic leaders need to proceed intentionally, and they need to think carefully as well as strategically about where and when to label particular educational experiences as UR, recognizing the pedagogical and material consequences of that label within the local context. For example, at some institutions characterizing literacy narratives written by students completing FYC as UR and having the students share their narratives at an annual showcase of student work might allow a faculty member or WPA to garner additional resources to support writing teachers and their students from the office of UR on campus. At a different institution, such a move might result in additional labor for over-worked and underpaid contingent faculty, with no additional resources forthcoming. And with no additional resources to support the composition and circulation of literacy narratives as a substantive form of research, students of overtaxed teachers might be in danger of developing an attenuated and dismissive notion of what constitutes research that contributes to knowledge in Writing Studies.

Angela Brew (2013) has developed a circular or "wheel" model for faculty and other academic leaders to navigate such situations as they develop UR experiences and programs. The wheel model acknowledges the centrality of contextual questions about institutional resources, curricula, and disciplinary expectations. The model also moves outward, positioning questions about when undergraduate researchers should be contributing knowledge to a discipline in relation to questions about students' relationships to their teachers, their relative autonomy and agency, the nature of the audience(s) for their research, and the forms of institutionally-mandated assessment that might structure their learning experiences. In working through such questions, writing faculty and other academic leaders do well to remember the eight key elements of UR that Kuh and O'Donnell pinpoint, including "performance expectations at appropriately high levels; significant investment of time and effort by students over an extended period of time; [and] interaction with faculty and peers about substantive matters" (2013, 10). We have little doubt that students who are well mentored and well supported, and thus able to invest significant time in their research and related research communities, will be well-positioned to make contributions that shape the future of Writing Studies.

Conclusion

In privileging students' voices and honoring their abilities to contribute to scholarly conversations, UR aligns with the core values of Writing Studies as a field. As early as 1984, Muriel Harris welcomed undergraduates working in writing centers into the pages of the *Writing Lab Newsletter* via the "Tutor's Column." In founding *Young Scholars in Writing* in 2003, Laurie Grobman and Candace Spigelman articulated the journal's mission as a "commitment to and celebration of undergraduates engaged in scholarship in writing, rhetoric, and related disciplines." They further explained, "Just as students' voices are crucial to the work of composition and rhetoric, student research may significantly contribute to the scholarship, learning, and on-going formation of this disciplinary community" (5). The development of venues such as the CCCC Undergraduate Researcher Poster Session, initiated in 2012, helps to ensure that students' consequential work is circulating through ever-evolving scholarly networks. Likewise, special issues of journals like *Kairos* (2011) and *Writing Center Journal* (2012) devoted to the work of undergraduate researchers also serve as powerful evidence that our field recognizes the vital role that students play in shaping our disciplinary community.

Our collective commitment to involving students in sustaining and enlarging the field of Writing Studies is enabled by our belief that students themselves reap significant rewards from these activities. There is ample evidence that undergraduate researchers value opportunities to find their place in scholarly communities beyond their own classrooms and campuses by contributing to research and scholarship. In reflecting on an essay she published in *Young Scholars in Writing* in 2003, Kate Stuart noted: "The real draw of the project for me was the opportunity to add to the larger discussion of club records, girls' studies, and feminism. I knew that having published an essay would look great on my curriculum vitae, but what I really wanted from the experience was to be a part of that larger academic community and to have an audience" (2013, 7-8).

As the field of Writing Studies continues to expand what "counts" as a contribution to knowledge, we encourage faculty working with students to think more broadly about what students as students bring to research, what a significant contribution looks like in practice, and the kinds of outcomes that will become possible as a result of collaborations that include them. While undergraduate researchers in Writing Studies will go on to work in a variety of professions and communities, they all should benefit from their UR experiences in ways that enhance their lifelong capacity to compose the world in which they want to live.

Reflection on Chapter 3

Contributing to Whose Knowledge?

Heather Falconer

At my current institution (a small liberal arts college in New England), undergraduate research (UR) is slowly gaining a foothold as one way to engage students in the scholarly aspects of our respective fields. At present, however, these opportunities are extremely limited and embraced largely by my colleagues in STEM. Though there is ample evidence to support UR as transformative (Lopatto 2010a, 2010b), faculty in the other disciplines have been hesitant to get involved. The resistance I have observed echoes concerns raised in Brew and Mantai (2017) regarding institutional policies, time, and money. Also prominent have been the questions of academic skill and whether students "at this level" are capable of contributing knowledge. How, for example, can a student make "an original intellectual or creative contribution to the discipline" (Beckman & Hensel 2009, 40) when they are only just learning foundational concepts?

Reflecting on chapter 3, I find myself thinking about the intertwined and generative relationship between contribution to knowledge and other aspects of UR. What have become most salient for me are the implicit questions that *The Naylor Report* authors raise about scalability, assessment, and reproducibility. I wonder, for example, about the multiple ways in which "originality" can be construed and how practical (or possible) it is for large numbers of undergraduates on a given campus to "leave their marks behind," as Hakim suggests they should. How fair, or manageable, is it to incorporate UR into first-year writing courses when a large number of those classes are taught by contingent faculty, who are likely to be teaching multiple courses on multiple campuses in any given semester? And, if UR in Writing Studies is implemented as a means of increasing retention and persistence, how do we handle that assessment? How do we scale it up without diluting its impact?

The recommendations in chapter 3 go a long way toward helping us formulate ways of addressing these questions. Capaciousness, for example, is not only important in conceptualizing contribution, but also in defining what constitutes UR. This quality is critical to access and scalability. Not every student will be capable of conducting research at a level that warrants publication, but many will be able to engage in research that directly benefits their immediate communities or affinity groups. I see this in my own first-year writing courses, where students pursue self-generated lines of inquiry. The nursing student who uses her own experience in mock-clinicals to examine the ways in which medical jargon is conveyed to patients, for example, is not ready to contribute to WAC/WID scholarship. However, when that research involves surveying nursing students in different years about language used in classes, and interviewing nursing faculty about how they teach medical terminology, she is discovering important information about her field's disciplinary discourse and nursing education more broadly. She also discovers agency and autonomy in the process of research. This constitutes a contribution to knowledge.

Similarly, not every student will want or need to engage in individual projects, but many can engage in group-based inquiries. An undergraduate course on teaching writing in K–12 settings can, collectively, contribute to knowledge in community—and school-based literacy if it involves a service-learning and/or research component. Though such courses have historically been seen as distinct from UR opportunities, reconsidering may create a new context for UR and a new way to increase its scale. Just as we can adopt a capacious notion of what constitutes a contribution to knowledge, we can adopt a capacious notion of how such contributions can be accomplished.

Angela Brew's "wheel" framework (2013) was noted at the end of chapter 3 as one way of thinking about expanding UR. This framework is particularly useful in considerations of scaling and assessing contribution to knowledge. Because instructors and administrators work outward, beginning with the student(s) and considering context and realistic learning outcomes, the wheel framework encourages those designing curriculum to be deliberate about what they are asking (and expecting) students to accomplish. By its very nature, research can be nebulous and, as UR continues to evolve and expand, it requires careful, constructive thinking about how we define, assess, and conceive contribution to knowledge for undergraduates. It would be unfair and impractical to establish a single, fixed endgame for UR (i.e., publication). Doing so would undermine UR as a high-impact educational practice. Brew's wheel helps practitioners avoid such problems by privileging UR processes over their products.

As a discipline, Writing Studies has a history of both inward and outward facing research and we have long privileged students: their voices, their work, their growth. As we strive more actively toward building UR opportunities in Writing Studies, it behooves us to remember this history and consistently ask ourselves: "To whose knowledge are we contributing?"

Reflection on Chapter 3

FACULTY AND UNDERGRADUATE CO-AUTHORING AND CONTRIBUTIONS TO KNOWLEDGE

Laurie Grobman

Though still relatively rare, faculty coauthoring research projects with undergraduate students offer powerful opportunities for knowledge-making in Writing Studies. At the same time, when faculty and undergraduates coauthor publications, the complicated questions that arise about how undergraduates contribute to knowledge are magnified by power differentials. Who is an author? How do we assign credit for authorial labor? As Ben Wetherbee suggests, coauthoring with undergraduates "deserves more attention from rhetoric-and-composition scholars, given our investment in understanding the perspectives of our students" (2012, 743). In particular, Wetherbee argues that in most cases, published collaborations "subordinate . . . the student's voice" to the voices of faculty scholars (744), thus limiting undergraduate researchers' knowledge-making potential. In response, Wetherbee proposes collaborations that enable students to "speak back" to academic authors, including their faculty coauthors (745). His suggestion opens the door to powerful new ways for undergraduate researchers to both help dismantle student-faculty authorial hierarchies in Writing Studies and generate new possibilities for disciplinary knowledge production.

In the past five years, I have co-authored three published articles with undergraduates, and I draw on my experience to demystify the process of collaborating with undergraduate researchers for others who might want to consider this form of knowledge-production. To be sure, such collaborations are complex, and they can be fraught in myriad ways. Yet, complexities and challenges open spaces and possibilities for exciting and meaningful journeys. Together, students and I have pushed ourselves to construct disciplinary knowledge together, to enrich our own knowledge, and in some cases to contribute to the public good and social justice.

Elizabeth Kemmerer, Meghan Zebertavage, and I published "Counternarratives: Community Writing and Anti-Racist Rhetoric" in *Reflections: A Journal of Public Rhetoric, Civic Writing, and Service-Learning* in 2017. Kemmerer and Zebertavage were students in my upper-level Writing Studies course in spring 2015. That semester, they worked collaboratively with their classmates and a local African-American history museum to document the Civil Rights Movement in Reading, Pennsylvania. Their work included interviewing twenty-two African Americans ranging in age from seventy-two to ninety. When Kemmerer, Zebertavage, and I analyzed this community writing project, we ended up with a far more complex argument than we initially had in mind, in large part due to the twists and turns our work took throughout our collaborative knowledge-making process.

In this excerpt from an UR stipend application I submitted in August 2015 to fund the work that Kemmerer and Zebertavage wanted to accomplish, the planned partitioning of our efforts is clear:

> Specifically, I will offer important insights about the pedagogy of undergraduate community-engaged oral history partnerships; Elizabeth will focus on some of the most salient issues in oral history, such as verification, authorship, collaboration, power relationships between narrator and writer, and fidelity to the narrator's voice; and Meghan will focus on the significance of Reading to the growing body of research on the CRM [Civil Rights Movement] in the North and in Pennsylvania.

Indeed, we each began our writing and research on separate sections. Kemmerer and Zebertavage expanded on their final essays they wrote for the course, and I focused on reciprocity with community partners and the course pedagogy.

However, as we wrote and revised, particularly after receiving reviewer and editor comments, the "pedagogy" subsection I initially wrote alone became the newly titled "Pedagogy: Competing Narratives in/of Civil Rights History, Oral History, and 'Standard' Evidence," and it included a complex and layered conversation among the three of us. While I described the curriculum, Kemmerer and Zebertavage described their responses to the readings as well as their classmates, community partners, and me. In doing so, they moved from students to writers and full collaborators in the project.

As I look back at the letter accompanying the revised manuscript we submitted to Cristina Kirklighter, *Reflections* editor at that time, I'm struck by this sentence: "We want to stress how much we all learned about anti-racist writing instruction from this revision, Laurie from the perspective of an anti-racist educator and Meghan and Elizabeth from the perspective of students reflecting on coursework from a year ago on the continued racial tensions and injustices in the US today." Even then, and more so now, I see the profound impact coauthoring had on all three of us. In ways that may be invisible to readers, the published article's argument demonstrates how significantly our contribution to knowledge had changed through the nearly two years of writing, revision, peer review, and more revision:

> [W]e argue that constructing and studying civil rights history is a form of anti-racist writing pedagogy. We suggest that the rhetorical, historical project under study illuminates the rhetorical and powerful nature of current narratives of race and racism because, as Victor Villanueva so aptly puts it, "Behind [language] there is a material reality—the reality of racism, still present, and not all that new after all" (n.p.). As we and all our collaborators documented Civil Rights era history together, we began to circulate layers of counter-narratives that both expose and challenge these "not all that new" racial realities in productive ways.

Wetherbee might view the changes that took place as a shift from multivocal to polyphonic knowledge making, which repositioned the students as coauthors "dialogically speak[ing] back to the voices of academic researchers," including their faculty co-author (2012, 746–47). No doubt, the article we published contributes deeper, more profound knowledge to oral history, the Civil Rights Movement in northern states, anti-racist scholarship, and authorship than the article I had initially envisioned. Thus, I encourage faculty, peer-reviewers, and journal editors to welcome articles that represent faculty and undergraduate co-authorship and, perhaps most importantly, to encourage co-authorships that take advantage of "different varieties of authority essential to the integrity of the polyphonic whole" (748).

4 Circulation: Undergraduate Research as Consequential Publicness

Doug Downs, Laurie McMillan, Megan Schoettler, and Patricia Roberts-Miller

In the time since the Boyer Report on "Reinventing Undergraduate Education," significant changes have further opened possibilities for undergraduate research (UR). Perhaps because of the Boyer Report's focus on R1 institutions, its outcomes concentrated on the kind of research whose main value is the extent to which it mirrors academic research done by faculty or graduate students at a research-oriented university. The Council on Undergraduate Research (CUR) has argued for significantly broadening the range of students who should have important research opportunities, and technologies of publication have increased access and reduced cost. Even with this expanded notion of student researchers and the continued value of traditional modes of academic publication, we are concerned that UR is too often narrowly focused on scholarship exactly like the kind that leads to faculty promotion and tenure. As Lindy Johnson et al. (2018) suggest, the purposes guiding student work should not be tied to *sharing* the work as an end goal, but rather with the end goal focused on the *effects* the research might have—effects which tend to be realized *through* sharing research. Such goals are concordant with the research concerns Ellen Cushman urged us to consider in "The Rhetorician as an Agent of Social Change" (1996): ethical human research bears an obligation not just to *learn about* its participants but to *help them*. Such good ends are realized, in part, through the circulation of the research.

What we thus want to emphasize in this chapter is the notion of publics for whom UR has consequence, with a more capacious view of what publics and what consequences might matter. For instance, while several of us have experience working with students whose research was published in peer-reviewed scholarly outlets, presented at scholarly conferences, or displayed in poster sessions at national conferences, we also have seen students share their research findings in both formal and informal ways, with interested publics including university stakeholders, online communities, and local groups or individuals with a shared interest in the topic.

This more capacious understanding of UR in Writing Studies requires reframing traditional expectations for dissemination of research findings within, and as an advancement of the knowledge of, a discipline. By understanding the available "ends" of UR more broadly, as *circulation of consequential discovered stories and stories of discovering to a variety of relevant publics both academic and non-academic*, those fostering UR in Writing Studies can increase the range of what is recognized as UR, decrease the time it takes to bring projects into circulation, and dramatically expand access to and participation in UR projects. In so doing, we can also significantly increase the number of public stakeholders touched by Writing Studies research as well as the production of research, and support for it, in the field.

Therefore, we recommend that professional organizations, universities, teachers, mentors, and others work together to support the circulation of UR in the following ways:

Recommendation #1: Diversify expectations for what kinds of stories might be circulated, recognizing and circulating both discovered stories (that is, research findings) and stories of discovery (that is, narratives of research projects).

At times, such discovered stories and stories of discovery will be told together, but they also have value as stand-alone projects, depending on the audience and the purpose. Those creating, using, and mentoring research should attend to uses of and needs for stories of discovery that create opportunities for their telling and circulation. Such stories not only add to our understanding of knowledge-making but may encourage and guide researchers to come.

"Research findings" may include the application of "old knowledge" rather than the creation of "new knowledge." Researchers and research mentors should resist the traditional notion that value lies only in novelty and instead both emphasize the need for and reward replication and application studies that extend existing knowledge to additional sites.

**Recommendation #2: Support expanded notions of *purposes, forms, and venues* considered appropriate for circulation of research by providing models, opportunities, and possibilities for circulation to have an impact on developing knowledge, growth, or solutions for invested publics and for the researcher, with quantitative and qualitative measures used to measure impact.

Faculty mentors and other academic leaders need to develop and publicize both traditionally academic forms of circulation (presentations, posters, journal articles) as well as nontraditional venues for circulation (speeches and club presentations, community events, local museums and archives, non-scholarly publications, social media). Moreover, institutions must recognize and reward mentorship of consequential research regardless of the networks through which it circulates.

Recommendation #3: Consider ways students can be *enabled and encouraged to* engage such expansive forms of circulation by actively accommodating a variety of research ecologies in the discipline, with specific attention to time constraints, affordances for students at various points in their academic careers, possibilities for material and/or performative modes, and content focused on research findings and/or stories of discovery or impact.

Undergraduate researchers need opportunities for circulating work as an endpoint in a research process as well as a generative and transactional mid-project event. This will require faculty mentors and other institutional leaders to conceive not only long-timeline (multi-year) professional projects but also a wider range of possible timelines and workflows (immediate, semester-length, and year-length) for research leading to circulation.

The following sections offer a fuller rationale and suggestions for implementing our recommendations, with composite and actual current examples of diverse circulation practices highlighted in sidebars.

RATIONALE

Broadening access and participation—increasing the number of new (and frequently youthful) voices in the field—requires first a return to two root questions. What *is* an academic discipline? What is *circulation* of knowledge within a discipline?

While the field of Writing Studies has taken a long time to coalesce around a particular focus and set of problems, we have generally, as Kathleen Blake Yancey (2018) argues, arrived at agreement: our discipline is comprised of people who study questions and problems related to writing and adjacent subjects (e.g., discourse, rhetoric, literacy) and who organize and teach the resulting knowledge. The functions of any discipline include organization of labor and focus (leadership, agenda-setting, convening the field), development and curation of specialized knowledge (primary research, filtering/moderation/quality control, information management and databasing), advocacy (communication with non-specialist stakeholders and development of funding), teaching (circulation of specialist knowledge to fellow specialists and to non-specialists, learners, and new members), and service-driven engagement (including community outreach and support). "The discipline" is, thus, those interested in the study and teaching of its subjects of inquiry, no matter their level of academic preparation or recency of arrival. Understanding Writing Studies as a discipline that produces knowledge may not be a given, as explained in chapter 7 on institutional support. Circulation of student research in Writing Studies, then, may be challenging since it is often not readily recognized. Simultaneously, UR in Writing Studies can be a key strategy for shifting perceptions of the disciplinarity of Writing Studies.

> ### CIRCULATION TO NON-ACADEMIC STAKEHOLDERS AND COMMUNITY INTERESTS
>
> A student studying rhetoric at the University of Texas, Austin, undertook a spatial analysis of his campus focusing on the presence of statues of Jefferson Davis and Woodrow Wilson. Drawing on theories and methodologies from Henri Lefebrve and Kathleen Lamp, he authored a traditional academic paper that analyzed how students had raised concerns about the statues since the 1930s as well as how digital rhetorical platforms in the twenty-first century, such as Twitter, created new rhetorical possibilities for challenging commemorative practices on campus. The student was then able to draw upon this critically important research when he offered testimony at a public hearing to determine the fate of the statues.

The basis for our recommendations regarding circulation of UR within the field is in *re-membering* these root-level functions of discipline and circulation. Disciplines are networks of people who, independent of their academic status or "age," focus their intellect and vocational time primarily on the subjects of those disciplines. And circulation is that set of functions related to the sharing of the discipline's specialized knowledge among and beyond its participants: moderation, adoption, curation, propagation, teaching, (re)application. These essences of circulation extend well beyond the ossified academic-humanities traditions of one-way "dissemination" (seed-scattering) of "finalized," gate-kept knowledge via conference papers, peer-reviewed articles, and scholarly books. To such necessary work, we should add the fostering and curation of massively multi-participant conversations on short time scales and in various stages of knowledge emergence, formation, and narration. If we wished to foster greater openness and the participation of newcomers in Writing Studies, how else, beyond our traditions, could circulation in and beyond the discipline look, particularly given contemporary communication, networking, and curation technologies?

For faculty and graduate students, "research" is usually assumed to be inquiry-based and oriented toward scholarly publication. While inquiry itself is recognized as beneficial for the intellectual and cognitive growth of the researcher, scholarly publication has traditionally been framed as valuable only insofar as it creates original knowledge *for a scholarly discipline*. We argue for a more capacious understanding of research, one in which rather than limiting the possible publics for research to scholarly disciplines, we imagine public-ness as the goal. But we aren't advocating a purely expressive notion of publicness; the goal of research should be the circulation of work that has meaningful consequences for a public. That is, we advocate seeing the goal of research as consequential publicness.

> **CIRCULATION AMONG STUDENTS FOR LEARNING AND GROWTH**
>
> In a first-year composition course, a student researched rhetorics of eating disorders and shared personal consequences of her research with class members. The student analyzed the online sites of a pro-anorexia discourse community, exploring the tensions between these sites as positive therapeutic spaces and as spaces that normalized and encouraged unhealthy behaviors. This research was circulated only within the boundaries of the class, where a few students seemed interested but much of the consequence of the research was to the student herself—she said the project made her realize that it was easy for her to internalize unhealthy messages. This example of UR does not fit traditional definitions of "circulation," but it's important that researchers themselves be considered a "public" who can benefit from UR in writing.

Even then, we aren't arguing that a UR experience is valuable only to the extent that it results in consequential publicness—we see improving UR ability as a good in and of itself. On the subject of circulation, though, we focus on research that seeks to engage an audience beyond the researcher. We imagine a multi-phase, iterative knowledge-making process with circulation in every phase: research questions are excited by intersections of researcher curiosity and existing conversation, inquiry is undertaken, and results are circulated in an interested community.

Even just within scholarly disciplines, what constitutes "consequential public-ness of research" requires new examination. Circulation of specialized knowledge is inherent to being a field; without circulatory mechanisms and operations, a field simply would not *be*. Prior to and during the emergence of academic disciplines as we now know them, circulation was primarily epistolary and face-to-face, carried on through letter- writing, gatherings of small societies in coffeehouses, and convenings of learned academies that were then essentially private clubs of gentlemen "natural philosophers." (See Steven Johnson's *The Invention of Air*, chap. 1.) With exponential growth in both participation and publication, conventions for large-scale quality control and circulation of research emerged and ossified: peer-review, scholarly journals, meetings and conventions to discuss papers resulting in peer- reviewed proceedings, publications of letters, and posters. Efforts at data-basing this circulating knowledge were vastly simplified by digitization and international standards for persistent document identification such as DOI (Digital Object Identifier). The growth of electronic networking has fostered additional explosion of participation and diversity of voices and, in some ways, a return to the epistolary era through informal, pre- or non-peer-reviewed publication via blog, podcast, and wiki, as well as post-moderation, pre-print sites such as ArXiv, and less formal meeting structures such as "unconferences." We can also think about circulation not simply in terms of venues but also in terms of *applications*, even within traditional academic settings. In a university site, for example, undergraduate research can be used to support writing across campus.

> ### CIRCULATION AT HOME INSTITUTIONS
>
> In their 2010 *CUR Quarterly* article, Doug Downs and ZuZu Feder detail how Feder's UR project on metaphors students use for writing demonstrated conceptions of writing that students held and that writing faculty needed greater awareness of. Downs circulated Feder's data to faculty in the writing program he directed. Her demonstration of student conceptions led faculty to revise FYC curricula to better address those conceptions.
>
> A sophomore/junior-level composition theory class explored research questions whose findings could support student writing on- or off-campus. One research group developed a student survey to assess what motivates students to use the campus's Writing Center or keeps them from doing so. They circulated their findings both via poster session at the campus's celebration of student research and in a presentation to the Writing Center Advisory Board. While the poster session focused on graphical presentation of methods and findings, the board presentation focused heavily on recommendations and feasibility for implementation. As a result of their work, the Writing Center improved signage, added the ability to sign up for appointments in person, and prioritized advocating for a professional ELL tutor.

In addition to expanding our sense of what counts as circulation, we argue for seeing publication as not just the moment when a researcher tells the discovered story, but also taking opportunities for telling the story of discovery—such as the research narratives accompanying pieces published in *The JUMP+*. In other words, we should value not only the circulation of research findings, but also the narratives of discovery themselves. In such ways, we imagine circulation not just as an end product, but as a transactional and generative event. Such "social circulation" (Royster and Kirsch) encourages students to engage in the messy work of solving ill-structured problems (King, Brown, and Kitchener 1994; Wardle 2012); in other words, thinking about the consequences of their research and how to best circulate their findings for meaningful change does not encourage one clear answer.

Writing Studies in many respects already recognizes and supports a capacious understanding of consequential UR. Traditional academic modes of circulation are supported by dedicated UR journals such as *Young Scholars in Writing*, *The JUMP+*, and *Xchanges*, and by occasional special issues of professional journals (such as *Kairos* and *The Writing*

Center Journal) dedicated to UR. The field is ramping up its sponsorship of undergraduate poster sessions at conferences like CCCC. Possibilities for sharing process narratives are modeled by *The JUMP+*. UR in and for communities is flourishing. This is not just in traditional, single-semester, upper-division courses, but in multi-semester projects and in first-year writing courses as well. Our argument for circulation as consequential publicness responds to such work by recognizing its value, articulating why and how it matters, and calling for its proliferation.

> ## Untraditional Approaches to Traditional Academic Circulation
>
> **Poster presentations** at academic conferences have been rare in the humanities. In Writing Studies, it was actually supporters of UR who brought the poster format to the annual Conference on College Composition and Communication, as Jessie Moore spearheaded the first session in 2012 ("About CCC UR Poster Session" 2019). CCCC has since expanded the format to be available to all conference applicants.
>
> **Community-based undergraduate research** has appeared in *CCC* and in *Young Scholars and Writing*. Laurie Grobman's 2017 article "Disturbing Public Memory in Community Writing Partnerships" is based on a community-archival research project conducted by one of her Penn State-Berks undergraduate classes into how a community museum memorialized events feature blackface. Rachel Hoffman (2019), as an undergraduate at the University of Missouri, Kansas City, conducted archival research on the fundraising publications of a late-1800s Kansas City charity hospital written by a female M.D., Katherine Barry.
>
> **Research process narratives and responses** are a key feature of articles in the UR journal *The JUMP+*, a site for born-digital multimedia projects which conduct Writing Studies research. Alex Borowitz's 2019 short film "Le Processus d'Ecriture," a four-minute memorialization of a writer's material and conceptual efforts at invention and drafting, is published alongside two student responses (from other universities), his own writing reflection / process narrative, his instructor's reflection, and the original assignment sheet and project timeline. These materials dramatically enrich the conversation around and depth of the work "itself," and it becomes productively unclear which of these pieces are "commentary" and which are "research."

Implementation Strategies for Expanding Circulation of Undergraduate Research

Our overarching call is to expand possibilities for the circulation of consequential research to invested publics. As noted at the start, such work involves commitment not only from individual teachers and mentors but also from the professional field and from colleges and universities. The following strategies focus on these institutional supports to better enable circulation of UR as outlined in our three recommendations. Briefly, the hope is to provide a variety of circulation models and opportunities that accommodate different research ecologies in the discipline, with content focused on research findings and/or stories of discovery or impact.

As chapter 7 makes clear, an Undergraduate Research Network in Writing Studies is needed, and it would help facilitate circulation already occurring and allow more opportunities for circulating and reflecting on UR in Writing Studies. To imagine how this could be so, consider the following scenario of what the UR Network could make possible:

One goal of the UR Network is to maintain a wiki-space dedicated to the discussion of published research in the field; this site could contain channels for podcasting, and student members have their own blogs. The site's purpose is to propagate past scholarship among the next generation of Writing Studies researchers, recognizing that this propagation is affected by conversation that therefore is itself consequential publicness. Teachers can make assignments to do so on the site, or independent undergraduate researchers can earn college credit or be supported by research funding to curate discussions among student researchers on specific works. Special events would include student discussions with authors of the works.

Such a site would address Richard Haswell's critique (2005) that the field too easily forgets to read its own work—that few publications in our field are ever cited extensively, making us ignorant of our own research history. It also addresses Downs's contention (2015) that one of the most difficult aspects of UR in Writing Studies is finding the field's conversation itself. Ultimately, this site would support crowd-moderated informal discussion—blogs, podcasts, wikis—*as* a consequential contribution to the field.

This site could also contain an additional channel that functions as a question-and-methods hive: Students pose research questions that emerge from their own classes, reading, and research, developing a collection that would spur undergraduate, graduate, and professional inquiry projects. Another thread of conversation could consider methods: on a given research question, what methodological suggestions could the hive develop? Such collaborative development of research questions, agendas, and methods by undergraduate researchers and moderators would constitute very consequential contribution.

Undergraduate research journals more broadly should adopt the model used by *The JUMP+* of including "making-of" narratives with published research, and create sidebands (such as blogs) for discussion of them, making the narratives circulated subjects of inquiry. Narratives could be video-based or multimodal so researcher(s) could visually demonstrate their research process. Journals could also incorporate wiki-style "talk" pages with each article published, so that a sideband discussion around a piece would be easily and prominently fostered. Journal websites would also include channels for pre-print discussion of research in progress and emerging findings. Rather than specializing only in "final" accounts of studies, journals could (based on project proposals submitted early in the research process and moderated by the editorial staff) host ongoing reports of and discussions of research in formation.

Such approaches would let journals circulate in-process, emerging, speculative research, allowing students to circulate work on their projects in much shorter timeframes and increasing reflective learning during the process. The researcher's expertise would grow through conversation, instead of prior to it as current notions of publication demand, likely resulting in higher-quality finished projects as well.

The field has for several years hosted undergraduate fora for the presentation and development of research, such as the CCCC Undergraduate Researcher Poster Session and the Naylor Workshop in Undergraduate Research in Writing Studies. We imagine the addition of a UR un-conference in writing studies—much like the current National Conference on Peer Tutoring in Writing, but less about *presentations* and more about *conversation*—in which a forum convenes to discuss crowdsourced, multi-institutional research (emerging, for example, from conversation on the UR Network web-hub envisioned earlier) on a shared question, perhaps reminiscent of the undergraduate research described by Eodice, Geller, and Lerner's *The Meaningful Writing Project* (2017). Such a forum would be video-recorded and ported to the project's collaborative website or the UR Network web-hub. Local celebrations of student research (Wierszewski 2012) could similarly link to the web-hub, allowing the local to be viewed and discussed around the world.

Such UR puts the A (*aggregable*) in Haswell's "RAD" research—replicable, aggregable, data-driven. Uptake of Haswell's work has so far largely focused on "data-driven," but his vision beyond simply *multi-institutional* collaborative research was for multiple *independent* studies sharing the same design, replicated over miles and years to aggregate thousands of data-points. Crowd-sourced data-aggregation projects are ripe for the energy of undergraduate researchers who bring numbers and speed to existing expertise. Through aggregation, we can find meaning and value in the less "finished" and smaller-scale contributions that are often accessible to undergraduate researchers—rendering consequentiality more accessible too.

In a data repository established and supported by UR Network—akin to the Digital Archive of Literacy Narratives (DALN) but devoted instead to the written- and spoken-word process accounts of thousands of professional and student writers—UR teams could curate special collections of data that is linked to the research narratives journals in the field now keep, as well as to relevant discussion threads on the UR Network web-hub. Because the field has grown to understand the value of circulating *informal, pre-moderated* discussion as consequential contribution, the vastly greater amount of data in these conversations requires tracking, curation, and accessible data-basing. Data-repository management is, thus, now also a consequential UR activity fostering access to and circulation of research. In addition, as big-data research becomes increasingly valuable, the field must create and manage access to major datasets, work that itself must be understood as consequential circulation. It is perfect for a portion of undergraduates invested in writing studies research.

Colleges and universities emphasizing UR experiences in Writing Studies maintain a clearinghouse of local community needs for research-based projects and interventions, likely connected to their offices of engaged learning or undergraduate research. These clearinghouses also circulate past research projects undertaken with local organizations and communities. Such community-engaged research—such as that reported by Simmons and Amidon (2016) and by Simmons (1992, 2018) is devoted to circulation of solutions for community members, rather than simply circulation of publications.

As noted in chapter 1 colleges and universities need to recognize and reward mentorship of UR through release time; credit toward merit, promotion, and tenure; monetary rewards; conference travel funds; research funding; and administrative assistance. Colleges and universities can also develop, foster, and support multi-year mentored processes that enable a variety of opportunities for and modes of circulation. Such support may take the form of curricular sequencing, funding parts of the university (such as writing centers) where multi-year research can take place, and support of nontraditional classroom formats such as independent studies, semi-independent studies, or other structures that allow time for UR processes to be mentored. Research mentorship may be focused on an individual student or a group of students (such as a class), and it may be local or may involve work on a disciplinary journal, conference, or other professional body supporting undergraduate research.

In many ways, the emphasis on circulating consequential UR to invested publics is simply reiterating the longtime call in Writing Studies to have students write to authentic audiences. We have tried, however, to note how UR in Writing Studies can be meaningful in ways that include but go beyond traditional disciplinary forms of publications and presentations. As posited in our three initial recommendations, it is worth circulating new disciplinary knowledge, stories of disciplinary knowledge applied in a particular context, and stories of discovery; such circulation can take more expansive forms with capacious audiences, inside and outside of academic settings; and classrooms, mentorships, and publications can take various forms to encourage such circulation. Embracing such principles allows UR in Writing Studies to have an impact, justify our investments of time and resources, and encourage more work—more research—that matters.

Reflection on Chapter 4

From "Dissemination" to "Circulation" with Consequential Contributions: A Note on Process

Doug Downs

The working group assigned to "Dissemination" at the Naylor Symposium asserted in our pre-symposium framing that it is a troublesome metaphor not simply for undergraduate research (UR), but for research generally. The longstanding image of research findings as "seed," broad-cast through publication, does describe a certain aspect of the nature of research; but it invokes patriarchal and unidirectional resonances that historically have turned the act of circulating contributions into seed-throwing contests. Among the ways of thinking elided by the dissemination metaphor is the conversation metaphor made famous by Kenneth Burke (1941) and broadly adopted by our field. Understanding the sharing of researched knowledge as a contribution to an interactive, unending discussion of questions and issues is foundational to our teaching of research, but lost in the one-way dissemination metaphor.

In our initial work at the Naylor Symposium, the Dissemination group therefore wanted to resist the dissemination metaphor—but did not immediately see good terms to replace it. It is not ironic that our arrival at a *circulation* metaphor was sparked *by conversation*: a moment of recognition gradually catching fire among us, emerging into open enthusiasm for its many ideal resonances and implications, was exactly what a conversational metaphor for knowledge construction predicts. I was the slowest to fully embrace "circulation" as what we should have been talking about for decades—exemplifying Laurie Gries's assertion that the concept was missed among the grounding ideas of our field (2018, 4). For me as one writer, part of what's initially unappetizing about circulation is its (accurate) implication that the life of texts largely falls beyond the direction of their initiating agents (writers, editors, publishers). There is comfort in the (inaccurate) old notion of dissemination that the writer retains agency in the "seeding." But there is a reason for the ascendancy of the circulation metaphor. Indeed, Gries persuasively positions circulation not just as central, but as a threshold concept (5), and our working group now treats it as such in our deliberations on the future of sharing UR.

We arrived more quickly at the idea of *consequentiality*. While reaching for language to convey the validity of contributions besides scholar-to-scholar interchange, we clearly valued work *of consequence* to whatever community it spoke to, for, and with; the traditional narrowness of research lay in which communities counted as having consequence to begin with. We could, then, forward the value of consequentiality to a much wider range of communities and research-related activities simply by using the term itself, directly.

We took a certain pleasure in overturning research orthodoxy by rethinking traditional terms; apart from embodying a healthy scholarly process, we like being able to do for UR what undergraduate researchers do for those for whom their circulated knowledge-making is of consequence.

Reflection on Chapter 4

The Temptation to Privilege Traditional Academic Modes of Circulation

Laurie McMillan

How does one respond to a chapter envisioning a capacious understanding of circulation of undergraduate research (UR) in Writing Studies? Perhaps by not only discussing but also enacting some of the priorities being articulated. With that in mind, I offer reflections on the collaborative writing process that informed the final version of the chapter. As suggested in chapter 4, a focus on process has value in and of itself, and it may also serve as helpful commentary when paired with a research project. In this case, a behind-the-scenes look at process gives a slightly new perspective on circulation, ultimately revealing how easy it can be to privilege academic modes that universities tend to value and, in turn, how intentional we need to be about valuing the wider range of circulation possibilities associated with Writing Studies.

At the start of our writing process, my co-authors and I showed every sign of prioritizing an expansive notion of consequential research that mattered to students and to invested publics. We generated ideas in a series of face-to-face meetings, working inductively by naming various ways we noticed UR in Writing Studies being circulated. Our stories and enthusiasm led to a long list of specific examples, many of these centered in students' local communities. This list helped us gradually identify categories and principles to communicate, though we occasionally felt overwhelmed with how broadly we wanted to think about the topic. When we wrote our initial chapter draft, we focused on capturing this expansive vision of UR designed to meet a wide array of purposes and audiences via a variety of genres and venues, and we offered a series of recommendations to support such work.

You can imagine our surprise when initial feedback from the volume's editors described confusion over the narrow ways we had framed circulation. Our entire goal had been to recognize academic work while calling attention to forms of meaningful circulation that might often be less visible. Once we reread our draft, however, we realized that, although we had posited a capacious vision of consequential undergraduate research, every example we offered focused on traditional modes of academic writing: journal articles, presentations, and posters. As we described such work, we had inadvertently omitted examples of UR being applied in the lives of our students and in the communities to which they belonged, and we similarly minimized stories of process—stories often erased from research traditions that emphasize substantive findings. Once the editors pointed it out, the disconnect between the capacious ways we talked about circulation of research and the limited examples we described was glaring.

How and why did a gap form between the diverse modes of research circulation we conceptualized and the academic examples we discussed in that initial draft? The answer, I believe, is in the disciplinary status of Writing Studies. As Writing Studies slowly becomes recognized as a discipline within the university (Yancey 2018, 23)—and hopefully, eventually, in the wider public domain—the circulation of research in expected academic modes is in itself exciting. Furthermore, circulation of undergraduate voices contributing to disciplinary knowledge reflects student-centered priorities that are foundational to Writing Studies. Thus, as we initially described UR journals in Writing Studies, campus celebrations of writing, and conferences that welcomed undergraduate participation, the examples seemed so diverse that we did not even notice they were all based on traditional academic modes. We were simply impressed with the breadth of opportunities for students to share their research.

At the same time, I believe our oversight in the initial draft reflects an unarticulated fear or worry rooted in the tenuous state of Writing Studies' disciplinarity. The temptation is to frame all or most Writing Studies research in ways that resemble research in established academic disciplines, an instinctive strategy to increase disciplinary recognition and respect. However, that tendency can lead Writing Studies astray in that it prioritizes institutional belonging more than student research and student learning. It is especially problematic because we teach so many students who are not majors and whose needs may not be well met with an emphasis on academic audiences and genres. Rather than capitulate to institutional pressures, our work is to frame and legitimize the capacious and consequential visions of UR that our field—and our students—value.

While the chapter recommendations aim to do just that, it is also up to us to remind ourselves and one another that the disciplinary identity of Writing Studies is rooted in enabling student voices and supporting research that matters—certainly by circulating such work within our field, but also far beyond it.

Part Two

Blazing Future Paths Together: Accessible and Equitable Ways Forward

Moving beyond the recommendations from part 1 on how we might build on the core elements of successful UR in Writing Studies, Part Two turns to critical issues that we must address to extend the impact of UR upon our students, our programs, and our profession.

Each of the chapters in Part Two addresses consequential questions that we face individually and as a field now that we know with great certainty that UR brings significant benefits to the students who participate in it. Knowing the benefits, of course, is not the same as providing them. This part of the report, thus, begins with questions of *access*: who gets to participate, who doesn't, and what might it take to make improvements? The authors addressing these questions do so with an eye to more than "diversity" and "inclusion" in the institutional sense; they also make recommendations designed to open UR to students with the great range of lived experiences and identities of those we advise, teach, and mentor on our campuses. Importantly, their recommendations emphasize practical actions we can take to widen UR's circle of participants along with our own understanding of writing and Writing Studies. Likewise, the chapter on curriculum recommends approaches to creating and sequencing UR curricula that can widen its scope and scale, with an eye toward sustainability. The final chapter on institutional support makes recommendations and provides concrete action steps for working together on our own campuses and as a field to garner the resources needed if we are to collectively forward this high impact practice in ways that are equitable to our students, our colleagues, and our communities.

5 Access to Undergraduate Research in Writing Studies

Alexandria Lockett, D. Alexis Hart, and Rebecca Babcock

As the Introduction to this book suggests, because of the nearly universal presence of required writing courses at post-secondary institutions, "few other fields of study have the opportunity to welcome students with a vast range of interests, abilities, and aspirations into the academy and to play such a crucial role in their post-secondary experiences." But with that opportunity comes the responsibility to acknowledge the diversity and intersectional identities of students who enter campus writing spaces and to make undergraduate research (UR) in writing—as well as its methods and work products—inclusive of those lives and those interests.

This chapter, thus, begins from two premises: First, any student should be able to access UR experiences in Writing Studies. Second, increasing access to UR in our field to students from diverse social and cultural backgrounds and educational affiliations will help us to fulfill the mission of equity that shapes our disciplinary commitments to social justice (Poe, Inoue, and Elliot 2018). Therefore, this chapter overlays the recommendations of part 1 with the question of access, addressing inclusive models of mentoring, suggesting methods of research that are appropriate to a wider range of topics, reminding us of the important contributions to knowledge that can be offered by the embodied experiences of this deeper pool of researchers, and by re-thinking the genres and modes of circulation as universal design. The chapter also anticipates the discussions of curriculum that follow, and reminds us of the institutional support needed to provide full access.

Context: Challenges to Access

The issue of access in higher education presents a definitional challenge when extended to UR. In existing pedagogical research, access is typically framed quite generally as a matter of "student success" (Finley and McNair 2013; Ishiyama 2002; Lopatto 2004). Within that context, UR is framed as one "high-impact practice" (HIP) among others that provide beneficial access to mentors, richer curricular offerings, chances to take part in skill-building and professional development workshops, networking and travel opportunities, paid internships, etc. (Kinzie et al. 2008; Kuh 2008; Collins et al. 2017). These benefits, in turn, impact academic and professional outcomes, including persistence to graduation, employment acquisition, and graduate/professional school admissions. Metrics of success in this context tend to focus on graduation and retention rates and increasing demographic representation of groups (e.g., race, gender, social class, age, dis/ability, etc.) that have historically faced legal and social barriers in education.

Less widely discussed, however is the fact that while participating in UR has been shown to have "a dramatic impact" (Ishiyama 2001, 40) on historically underserved students, those very students have decreased access to HIPs, in large part because marginalized students continue to face serious structural constraints including "invalidation, stereotypes, invisibility, lack of connectedness, hostility, and microaggressions" (Mendoza and Louis 2018, 19). The continued existence of such constraints reinforces the importance of not only making UR accessible in Writing Studies, but providing the support to overcome those structural constraints.

Of course, increasing access to, and support for UR in Writing Studies also raises questions about cost, since it requires significant financial resources (Daniels et al. 2016). Human resources in the form of advising and mentoring are necessary for guiding students, especially those who face financial limitations and/or family obligations that require employment, caregiving, and other temporal barriers that can potentially diminish their ability to engage in UR (Finley and McNair 2013). Our conceptualization of access, therefore, also addresses necessary financial, human, temporal, and academic support.

Recommendation #1: Establish multiple pathways for scaffolding and developing students' research capacities and identities.

Given that "research" as it is understood in traditional academic settings may not be within the lived experience of many of our students—nor among their longer term goals—this section recommends attention to multiple learning sites where a wider range of students can encounter new understandings of *research* and, as a result, broaden their perspective of what constitutes research in ways that they value. (This broadened definition of research is also discussed in chapters 3, 4, and 6 on contribution to knowledge, circulation, and curriculum.) By intentionally scaffolding the experiences of students in ways that acknowledge the multiple sites that spur research, offering methods that can guide their investigations of topics they find consequential, and allowing for genres and modes within which research studies can be circulated, pathways that increase access for underrepresented groups can be blazed. More specifically, we address how access can be promoted within curriculum, in the context of campus employment, during summer research opportunities, and/or as community-engaged research.

Pathways through Curriculum

As is discussed throughout this collection (and in detail in chapter 6), curriculum is often a spur to UR. First-year writing courses (FYW)[1] can offer a pathway for introducing a wide demographic of students to UR, since these courses are one of the first points of access for undergraduates across disciplines to learn how research works. However, the traditional research paper has dominated the introductory college composition curricula for almost a century (Lockett 2017, 240–41), as is also discussed in chapter 6 on curriculum. If, instead, we treat the boundaries of "scholarly writing" as permeable, we can help students to instead access research as an embodied practice of designing an investigation and composing its results in multiple ways. Presenting research assignments in this way prompts a larger and more diverse range of students to find agency as researchers, as people invested in contributing to knowledge-making. By including a wider range of topics, methods, and new genres and modes that resonate with this wider range of students, the "research assignment" often taught in FYW could increase student access. This approach to research as both a highly sociopolitical and intellectually challenging activity is a key part of our disciplinary field and can offer a more inclusive point of entry.

---

1. We acknowledge that some institutions, such as some Small Liberal Arts Colleges (SLACs), may not have explicitly designated first-year writing courses. However, according to the National Census of Writing, 96% of the responding four-year institutions and 75% of the responding two-year institutions stated that they have "a first-year writing requirement whether explicit or embedded" (Gladstein and Fralix, n.d.). While the Census is not a comprehensive survey, it represents a significant sample of 900 institutions of higher education in the US.

Opportunities to broaden conceptions of research also exist within the undergraduate curriculum beyond FYW. Writing across the curriculum (WAC) and/or writing in the disciplines (WID) initiatives provide focused opportunities for research activity. In addition, those institutions that provide or require a for-credit course for writing center tutors often require undergraduate tutors to read various models of Writing Studies research, especially in the area of writing center scholarship. Their workplace experience combined with their classroom learning—when encouraged—can open UR to a wider range of students as well as to a wider range of research questions, providing feedback about the potential of its design as well as instruction in executing research methods and responding to feedback. Instructors may even guide students through the process of identifying the usability of their research and developing materials for its distribution beyond the classroom—whether within their WC, across their campus, or beyond. However, regardless of the availability of courses that explicitly focus on UR and/or UR in Writing Studies, structural barriers such as "lack of student awareness," "lack of a formalized system," and students "[feeling] too intimidated to approach a faculty member to ask about research" (Wayment and Dickson 2008, 194–195; cf. Longmire-Avital 2018) often negatively impact enrollment in these courses and/or the development of research projects that feel authentic to students who are negatively impacted by the academy's structural inequities as well as the microaggressions of individuals within the academy.

Therefore, we recommend that faculty be more intentional about communicating and promoting these opportunities (Moore et al. 2018) by inviting individual students to enroll in upper-division seminar courses, to partake in independent studies, and to complete capstone projects in Writing Studies such as senior seminars and theses. Moreover, faculty mentors should demonstrate that such curricular options can focus on a range of topics that better fit the student body's background and experience. Doing so will not only integrate students more deeply into the Writing Studies intellectual community, but will likely increase their access to mentoring (from faculty and peers) and opportunities for publication, presentation, and networking. As is discussed below, the courses themselves might also more intentionally develop research methods that fit the lived experience and interests of students (for example, a working-class student interested in open admissions policies of the 60s or student movements), making the research process and products more consequential.

PATHWAYS THROUGH CAMPUS EMPLOYMENT

While courses and curricular spaces provide sites to learn about research methods and available modes and genres for research products, consequential topics often arise through students' experiences in the workplace. And as is discussed in several chapters, writing centers often generate worthwhile topics in Writing Studies for students who work as peer tutors. Since writing centers generally serve the entire institution and are highly trafficked on-campus spaces, this undergraduate job opportunity offers a direct pathway to Writing Studies research that reflects the lived experience of both tutors and the diverse set of students who visit the writing center.

If writing centers embrace their role as multicultural[2], multilingual, student-centered learning environments in which students and tutors across disciplines work on developing their writing at any stage, they can also generate UR that fits the experiences of a wider swath of students. Daniels, Babcock, and Daniels (2017) write about how writing centers can use the concept of *inclusion* to remove "socio-economic, cultural, and political barriers" to participation. As such, writing centers can sponsor a wide variety of composing activities to create strategic opportunities for undergraduate researchers to make knowledge about how writing is learned and practiced within diverse communities. For example, UR projects can focus upon serving these diverse populations through data collection for projects in advanced writing courses, independent studies, undergraduate theses, summer research, and research assistantships.

---

2. Writing centers, of course, can be vexed spaces for inclusive practices; the cultural diversity of WC employees may affect UR recruitment and student engagement. That is, when we write, "If writing centers embrace their role as multilingual, student-centered learning environments," we do mean "if" in its fully conditional sense. Towards this end, Valles, Babcock, and Jackson (2017) recommend that WC directors actively recruit a tutoring staff that is "diverse in regards to race, language, and able-bodiedness/disability" and also "encourage administrators and hiring committees to actively recruit PWDs [persons with disabilities], non-native speakers, Blacks, Latinos, and Asians for writing center director positions." See also Boquet (1999), Denny (2010), Garcia (2017), Green (2018), Greenfield and Rowan (2011), Lockett (2019), Jackson (2013), Villanueva (2011).

Displays of research products normalize UR among writing center tutors while also demonstrating to those who visit the writing center the kinds of topics that widen participation. If the writing center displays projects that have consequence to the diverse students who visit, they can generate wider interest in research that demonstrates the social, political, and cultural topics that surround language usage. Further, by giving tutors and writers the opportunity to browse through physical copies of undergraduate scholarship in publications like the *Writing Center Journal* and the *Writing Lab Newsletter* or to see tutors' posters from the CCCC undergraduate poster session, UR in Writing Studies may not only seem more feasible and accessible, but more connected to their lived experience. This opportunity can be enhanced by explicitly asking tutors and writers to consider who and what is not adequately represented in the existing scholarship.

Writing center directors can better provide such on-ramps to Writing Studies research by recruiting, hiring, and training undergraduate tutors who represent the full student body (and do so, ideally, at the end of the students' first semester or anytime during their second semester and retain them as employees throughout their undergraduate education). This consistent employment can, in turn, help to overcome one of the most significant barriers to accessing UR: time for developing a rich project. A tutor who develops a compelling research question and compiles preliminary data and/or completes a literature review in a tutor training course, for example, may have the opportunity to develop that class research project into a more substantial UR experience during subsequent semesters of employment in the writing center. Recruiting a diverse population to act as tutors can help develop a peer-to-peer network of undergraduate researchers, expanding this place of employment into a community of practice that includes faculty, staff, graduate students, and/or near-peer mentors, access to research methods through tutor training courses, opportunities to see the results of their contributions to knowledge, and various means of circulating their research findings, internally and externally. As Elizabeth Kleinfeld has pointed out, "UR disrupts hierarchies and provides opportunities for faculty mentors to question received knowledge about their disciplines and methodologies when they see things through the eyes of an undergraduate researcher. UR also disrupts notions of who is an expert or a scholar" (2018, 1).

Undergraduate Writing Tutors as Researchers

Context: Large, urban comprehensive university where the writing center is staffed by 35 peer tutors, who range from first-year students to seniors and represent diverse disciplines

Snapshot: Two undergraduate peer tutors in the writing center talk regularly during their overlapping shifts about inclusive tutoring practices. Over time, their conversations involve a third undergraduate peer tutor, who identifies as part of a historically underrepresented group, bringing another dimension to the conversations. Around mid-term, the three approach the writing center director to ask for reading recommendations on inclusivity. The director suggests several articles and describes a research project she is currently working on. After doing some of the reading the director mentioned, the three peer tutors talk again with the director, and together, they brainstorm a protocol for a new research study to extend the director's current project. The three peer tutors invite a fourth peer tutor, whose analytical skills they admire, to join the research team. The four peer tutors work with the director to get IRB approval for and begin conducting ethnographic research in the writing center. The director checks in with the peer tutors regularly, both in person and by email, referring to the group of them and herself as a research team.

At the end of the semester, the director suggests that the research team propose a presentation on their research at a writing center conference, with the director providing an introduction and literature review and the peer tutors sharing their data and analysis. As the conference approaches, the peer tutors express apprehension about how they will handle the Q & A portion of the presentation and ask the director if she will answer all the questions. They are worried that they will not be seen as "legitimate researchers" because they feel inexperienced and may not be able to answer all questions. The director assures them that questions at a presentation are a sign of scholarly respect and curiosity rather than a test of a researcher's knowledge and says that she will answer questions related to the literature review and expresses confidence that the undergraduate researchers will be able to address questions about the data collection and analysis. After their presentation, the team receives thought-provoking questions from the audience, with many questions addressed to the peer tutors specifically. Several audience members stay after the presentation to talk more with the team about their research. As they interact with audience members during these conversations, the peer tutors find themselves referring to each other as collaborators and co-researchers. Upon their return to the writing center, the director hears two of the research team members sharing their conference experience with another peer tutor, describing the connections they made with "other researchers" at the conference.

Reflection on Writing Centers as Accessible Sites for Research. What began as a conversation among undergraduate practitioners who may not initially consider themselves to be "legitimate researchers" because they lack prior contact with academic environments can, through thoughtful and informed mentoring, provide them with access to resources, a chance to practice research, and opportunities to share their findings with "other researchers." At the same time, this process of helping them to recognize themselves as legitimate researchers enables undergraduate researchers to present themselves as such to other undergraduates, graduate students, and professionals with whom they work in the writing center—whether fellow tutors or clients.

Other student workplaces that are less directly linked to Writing Studies faculty and staff and/or the practice of writing should not be overlooked as sites for increasing access to Writing Studies research. For example, student workers located in career centers, honors programs, multicultural affairs/equity offices, religious programs offices, teaching and learning centers, international programs offices, residential life, etc. are employed in major spaces on campuses where other students are likely to seek out and exchange information regarding academic and professional development opportunities. Providing information about UR opportunities in Writing Studies to these students and their supervisors can therefore increase the visibility of such opportunities to a larger, and likely more diverse, student population. Moreover, students might work directly on research design, execution, and circulation with faculty as research assistants—an experience that could be inextricably linked to coursework in classes ranging from FYW to independent studies (cf. Kinkead 2011b, 154). Furthermore, students in administrative assistant positions may learn about research by processing fellowship, grants, and admissions paperwork.

Pathways through Summer Research Programs

Summer research programs provide another opportunity to promote and support intensive UR experiences. Conducting research in the summer months might alleviate some of the barriers to accessing UR during the regular academic year because students have time to dedicate their attention exclusively to their research and writing without the burden of a full course load. Furthermore, they are more likely to have extensive access to faculty mentors devoted to assisting with UR if those faculty members are paid a stipend to be available to students. Paid mentorship is essential to expanding UR to underserved students, especially if institutions implement government programs for increasing minority representation among PhDs. Federal programs like the Ronald E. McNair Post-Baccalaureate Program, which serves racial groups historically underrepresented in graduate studies, as well as low-income students, regardless of race, assigns mentors to students throughout the entire academic year and the summer. UR is a major part of this program, which offers students paid opportunities to conduct original research. This experience can play a significant role in preparing humanities students from underrepresented backgrounds to apply to and successfully complete graduate studies, at least an MA and, ultimately, a PhD.

On the other hand, summer research may present barriers to access for other students who may not be able to take the time away from family obligations, and who may need to seek more lucrative employment during the summer. Students may lack resources to travel back and forth to campus multiple times a week for a designated six- or ten-week period. Faculty mentors, therefore, should inquire about how summer research programs might be more inclusive, such as seeking funding for students to conduct two weeks of an intensive research "boot camp," instead of funding one or two students for ten weeks of a more in-depth research experience. Chapter 7 on institutional support and Appendix A to this book address some inroads to seeking such funding.

Beyond individual campuses, faculty mentors might seek ways to offer students the possibility to engage in research with members of the Writing Studies community. For example, the Summer Institute for Writing Center Directors and Professionals and the Council of Writing Program Administrators (CWPA) might invite proposals from undergraduates. Campuses within physical proximity or within existing consortiums such as the Great Lakes Colleges Association (GLCA) or the Associated Colleges of the South (ACS) might fund and sponsor specialized UR experiences in Writing Studies and/or WAC/WID. And the Naylor Workshop on UR in Writing Studies already offers funding for student attendees. If limited institutional support is available, individual Writing Studies scholars could write grants or garner donations to hold a Writing Studies summer institute for undergraduates similar to the Summer Institute for Literary and Cultural Studies, which was a 36-month grant from the Andrew W. Mellon Foundation that supported a four-week summer research experience "especially designed for those from ethnic or racial groups that are underrepresented in the field of English studies, as well as others committed to increasing diversity in the field" (YMV 2012).

Pathways through Community Engagement

Another avenue to increase access to UR in Writing Studies is community engagement. Some organizations work with local higher education institutions to reach out to students across disciplines willing to assist them with their citizen research efforts. For example, in Atlanta, a local environmental organization tests contaminant levels in the Proctor Creek watershed, located in a flood-prone, predominantly black and poor part of the city. Their work, inclusive of cross-institutional writing-intensive work, acquired the attention of local universities who drew on their research methods to further study the health effects of these conditions (Eiffert et al. 2016). Students interested in "real-world" applications for research may be drawn to partnering with community members to conduct research and develop meaningful ways to represent and circulate their findings within the community as it can support skills and competencies more aligned with their own post-graduation goals than other UR projects that have a more traditional academic focus and outcome (e.g., graduate school).

Recommendation #2: Teach students a diversity of research methods and a broad conception of what research is.
While these multiple pathways into potential research topics can draw a wider range of students into UR in Writing Studies, students will also need experience with the methods that can support their inquiries. This section focuses on teaching students multiple concepts of research. As is discussed in chapter 2, and as Crawford, Orel, and Shanahan assert, "a key way to ensure broader undergraduate access to scholarship and creative activities is to show a diversity of effective models" (2014, 3). Because Writing Studies entails a "breathtaking variety of research methods, ranging from humanities-oriented, text-based scholarship to qualitative and quantitative human-subjects research in the social sciences [that] mirrors the methodological variety used by established scholars in the field," it has significant potential to provide access to student researchers from a "range of disciplinary backgrounds" (Fitzgerald 2014a, 95). Providing such access can be achieved through introducing students to writing about writing (WAW), holding open workshops and research sessions, and exposing students to a variety of methods.

LEARNING RESEARCH METHODS THROUGH WRITING ABOUT WRITING (WAW)

Any college writing course, regardless of level, can foster students' introduction to Writing Studies research through WAW, an approach that uses readings, students' own primary research on writing, and the students' literacy experiences as material for some or all writing assignments (Babcock, Cochran and Dean, forthcoming). WAW eschews traditional research papers and "essays" and instead encourages students to both reflect on their own writing process and investigate the processes of others (both professional and amateur writers) and to engage in original rhetorical and genre work. As such, WAW offers one way to introduce a wider array of first-year writers to primary research in Writing Studies, as well as topics related to the socio-political differences among writers.

> ### WAW in a First-Year Writing Program at a Regional Comprehensive University in the Southwest
>
> **Context:** A regional comprehensive university without a writing major or minor where a large dual enrollment program serves hundreds of students, mostly taught in online sections
>
> **Snapshot:** In this first-year writing program, students write personal literacy narratives, in which they conduct primary research on their own literacy histories through introspection, consultation with educators and family members, and by looking back over their own previous writing assignments. The program also assigns an interview with a writer in which students interview a practicing writer in their field or major. By framing this work as "primary research," students can come to value investigations into the practices of writers in varied communities, including their own, and so see research as an investigation of topics related to the lived and embodied experiences of their own communities, making "research" less foreign to them. The next assignment in the series is a genre analysis of some type of workplace or academic writing in the students' chosen career or major. In the next course in the sequence, students compose a rhetorical analysis. All of these assignments engage first-year writers in genuine research practices that can demonstrate how research in Writing Studies is related to their own lived experiences and goals.
>
> **Reflection on WAW in FYW:** Engaging the widest possible swath of students in primary research on writing in their first-year course introduces them both to the research process and to Writing Studies topics. These courses can subsequently provide a foundation on which Writing Studies faculty can recruit students for UR in the field.

Approaches to UR in FYW can also provide students with opportunities to circulate their research. For example, students can upload their literacy narratives to The Digital Archive of Literacy Narratives (DALN) alongside the narratives of established Writing Studies scholars—including some of the scholars whose work the students may have read. Alternatively, the students' research projects can be assembled into a local publication such as an anthology that can serve as a model for future classes. Babcock's Advanced Composition students, for example, created an edited collection in which students submitted their work for consideration through an established editorial process and subsequently published a book (ENGL3340). Similarly, Laurie Grobman (2009b) refers to her students as "Rhetorical Citizen Historians" as they research oral history for her classes and produce published books. Each of these examples instantiates a "more capacious notion of what constitutes a contribution to knowledge," as called for in the chapter 3 of *The Naylor Report*, and demonstrates that through course design and mentorship, faculty and other researchers can bring students into the "inner circle," or, as Mendoza and Louis (2018) call it, the "cultural circle" of scholars and researchers.

Introducing first-year writers to research—as an academic enterprise, a typical aspect of academic thinking and writing, and as a situated institutional, (inter)disciplinary, technological, and writing-intensive processes—may lead to increased engagement in UR in Writing Studies by a greater diversity of students. Many students may find it appealing to know that our field acknowledges the value of student voices through a tradition of including them as co-authors, or publishing UR in journals such as *The Dangling Modifier* (for more examples of the issue of student agency in Writing Studies, see chapter 3 on contributions to knowledge). Taking that research experience beyond the classroom can begin to cultivate a culture of inclusive research at an institution.

Providing Access through Research Workshops

Offering research workshops gives students the opportunity to be exposed to various research topics and methods that they may not otherwise know about. For example, Babcock offers a research workshop with guest speakers on various topics such as "Publishing Your Research" and "Gaining IRB Approval for Your Study." The speakers then join breakout groups and students rotate to discuss various topics such as "Research Ethics" and "What's the Worst Thing That Could Happen?" Such workshops could be tailored to support UR in Writing Studies. For example, Lockett created an entire job position for a writing consultant for the Pennsylvania State University Ronald E. McNair program's summer research program. This job featured weekly writing workshops such as "Genres and Styles of Scholarship," "Basics of Academic Writing," and "Organizing the Literature Review and Presenting Findings." She has also conducted campus-wide research workshops at Spelman College like Multimedia Academic Literacy (Lockett 2015) that focus on navigating databases and crafting search queries to improve the range of possible ways to talk about a subject.

Both Babcock's and Lockett's workshops provide access to many aspects of UR—from institutional policies and student motivation to characteristics of the genre of research and its processes. The sponsors of research workshops can strive to make them more accessible by addressing topics that explicitly address how to do research, as well as major challenges that an undergraduate student may face during the process. Encouraging students to consider their personal relationship to research is integral to building an inclusive UR culture. Considerations about student's racial, gender, and economic backgrounds also presents the opportunity to create positive conditions for continuous participation. To illustrate, workshop organizers and their affiliates should communicate their post-event availability, send personalized invitations (and encourage others to do so), provide remote digital access and recordings of sessions, as well as offer economic incentives such as food and/or childcare.

Recommendation #3: Apply Inclusive Pedagogy to All Aspects of UR in Writing Studies

Since access depends upon students seeing themselves as researchers, and because "college students" no longer connotes a specific demographic, our pedagogies must be inclusive of all students who populate the academy. As such, research opportunities need to be available to all students, regardless of their academic preparedness or status; their age; real or perceived dis/abilities; whether they are enrolled full-time, part-time, or online; whether they are from non-traditional or historically underrepresented groups in higher education; whether they are returning from a hiatus from formal education, sub-baccalaureate, non-degree seeking, and/or taking a non-linear path through college; and despite any personal obligations such as family care, work, or campus activities. Two-year colleges, in particular, present challenges to access, as students' pathways are often less linear and their lived experiences—which ideally can offer many potential topics for UR—can also provide significant challenges to engagement. In all cases, finding the particular points of access for such a diverse group of students is a tall order. But if we are intentional about opening the field to all students by widening our concept of what UR in the field can encompass, access to UR can be improved and the field can benefit by the work a more inclusive group of student researchers bring to Writing Studies.

Universal Design for Learning (UDL) encourages multiple approaches to education, including "flexible means of representing materials" and "allow[ing] students to demonstrate their knowledge in flexible ways" (Johnson and Fox 2003, 13). As with all versions of universal design, the focus should be on finding and removing the obstacles—in most cases, obstacles that institutions have created themselves, even unwittingly. As such, applying UDL to UR can provide undergraduate researchers with a range of modes in which to deliver/present their research, including posters, infographics, written reports, oral presentations, and creative projects like animation, film, poetry, or music. Furthermore, a UDL approach encourages faculty mentors to provide undergraduate researchers with flexible deadlines to complete their activities as well as flexible places to conduct their research (at home or in the field) rather than requiring students to be on campus. Because UDL has often focused on students with dis/abilities, we agree with Waitoller and Thorisu that there is a "need to interrogate and address educational inequities at the intersections of ability, race, language, gender, and class differences" (2016, 367), and inclusive pedagogies may be one way to do so (cf. Hackman 2008).

For example, studying online can be seen as an impediment to UR or as an opportunity to reach out to students who would not otherwise be invited to participate. The sole fact that a student studies online should not hinder their access to UR if mentors are creative, encouraging, and accommodating. Providing access to meetings not only in person/on-campus but also online through voice, video, or text-based options can increase participation—especially if the meetings are recorded and posted for offline access and review.

Building personal relationships in a variety of ways is also important for access. Langley-Turnbaugh, Whitney, Lovewell, and Moeller found that undergraduate researchers with dis/abilities "are more likely to ask for assistance and accommodations if their student-faculty relationships are strong and if faculty members are perceived as being supportive" (2014, 39). Some supportive accommodations include flexible pacing, flexible scheduling, extra time, flexible location (able to complete work at home), help with writing/editing, assistive or adaptive equipment (screen readers, voice synthesizers), and safety equipment (epi pen, cell phone).

Finally, time-intensive activities such as theatre, marching band, athletics, or other commitments that often involve lengthy practice schedules and (sometimes inconvenient) travel should not preclude students from participating in UR. In fact, the time management skills and maturity students often gain through these activities can make them excellent candidates for UR, if mentors are flexible with deadlines and requirements—and if topics can be inclusive of their lived experiences.

Recommendation #4: Strategically use various forms of mentorship.
Building on the recommendations in chapter 1, we encourage UR mentors to develop robust networks of scholars across education levels, disciplines, institutions, cultural backgrounds, and types of embodiedness to exchange strategies for recruiting and working with a wide range of undergraduate researchers. As Ruth Palmer and colleagues argue, "mentored undergraduate research [is] a high-impact learning experience [that makes] available to learners particular versions of what it means to be a person, a learner, an academic person and/or an investigator and member of a specific group" (2015, 418). More specific to our topic, these recommendations about mentoring focus on how developing and training mentors from diverse fields and backgrounds, representing both academic and non-academic networks and communities, can increase access to UR in Writing Studies (Longmire-Avital, 2018). In fact, anyone involved in the UR experience—especially students—can potentially serve as mentors to current and future students, as we discuss in the next subsection.

Peer-to-Peer Mentors

Chapter 1 provides an array for mentoring practices that, when applied to issues of access, can widen participation. For example, peer-to-peer mentors serve a critical role in recruiting students to participate in UR. They simply have more access to multiple aspects of the students' living and working environments (e.g., dormitories, apartments, multiple classes, library, student union building, the workplace, clubs/activities) whereas faculty mentors may only connect with students in "formal" educational spaces and times such as a specific class, office hours, conferencing, or organized mentoring events. Away from the gaze of faculty and staff, student discussions about UR experiences might inspire other students who can better relate to the meaning of research from a peer. Whether the mentor is a close friend sharing in an intimate setting or an acquaintance casually talking at a highly public event like a lecture or an informational grad school panel, students will be more likely to envision themselves realistically completing UR after hearing the testimonies of their peers.

Faculty Mentors

Faculty mentors intensively involved in student work may enable significant UR participation, which is illustrated at Minority-Serving Institutions (MSIs). Faculty mentors for UR should be identified both within and outside of Writing Studies disciplinary networks. They may also be located outside of the students' institution. From teaching research in the classroom to talking about their personal experiences with research during office hours, faculty are positioned to discuss how they negotiated the process, as well as reflect on short and long-term gains from UR. Their involvement, of course, varies. Some faculty mentors will serve as writing coaches from start to finish: helping the student find the opportunity, assisting them with application processes to summer research programs, reading and providing feedback on student works-in-progress, and attending conferences to hear students present the work. Other faculty may enact mentoring by promoting opportunities to students and working with administrators to fund UR and conference travel, as well as graduate studies admission fees (if students pursue that path). Additionally, faculty mentors can work interdependently with student mentors to increase information access to UR in Writing Studies and socialize with other faculty to learn how mentoring works. They might also have formal or casual meetings with colleagues to recruit more faculty mentors for UR, strengthen effective practices among current faculty mentors, and determine additional human and financial support systems. After all, many possible mentors (faculty or student) may not have "extensive training" in teaching or communicating about research methods and therefore may find the prospect of facilitating UR projects "daunting" (Fitzgerald 2014a, 95). The field, then, must commit to preparing mentors. While the CCCC currently sponsors an undergraduate poster session, the annual CCCCs Research Network Forum (RNF) does not actively solicit participation by undergraduate researchers. In the future, the RNF could support UR mentors by expanding access to exceptional undergraduate applicants. The conference could also reserve workshop space and a select block of panels for promoting diverse participants in UR.

Moreover, the field can identify institutions with strong mentoring models, especially those that support historically underrepresented scholars-in-training *as scholars*, such as HBCU and SLAC faculty, who are more likely to invite student researchers to join their projects. According to the 2018 National Survey of Student Engagement (NSSE), 44% of students at baccalaureate institutions with an arts and sciences focus participated in research with faculty; institutions with fewer than 2500 students had the largest percentage (30%) report that they participated in research with faculty (13). Eagan et. al (2011) discovered that HBCU faculty were 17.03% more likely to engage undergraduates in their research than their colleagues at either PWIs or HSIs: "This finding connects to other research that has suggested that HBCUs offer their students a more supportive and collaborative environment than do PWIs and HSIs (Nelson Laird et al. 2007). The finding also connects to work by Allen (1992) and Hurtado et al., which found higher levels of support and engagement among both students and faculty within HBCUs" (2009. 169-170).[3] Professional conferences like CCCCs—and the UR Network proposed in chapter 7—thus should consider providing funding and programming for faculty traveling from these institutions to strengthen mentoring practices among a wide range of institutions.

Recommendation 5: Showcase the Diversity of UR in Writing Studies on an Institution-Wide Basis

While each of the practices above can provide great benefit, changing the overall culture of undergraduate research from an activity for the exceptional student toward full access to these opportunities requires methods to demonstrate its impact. Taking research experiences like this beyond the classroom can also begin to cultivate an institution-wide culture of inclusive research.

---

3. Research suggests that HBCUs offer their students a more supportive and collaborative environment than do PWIs and HSIs (Nelson Laird et al. 2007). This finding also connects to work by Allen (1992) and Hurtado et al. (2009), which found higher levels of support and engagement among both students and faculty within HBCUs.

> **FIRST-YEAR STUDENTS PRESENTING RESEARCH AT AN ON-CAMPUS SYMPOSIUM**
>
> **Context:** Regional comprehensive state university where FYW classes are capped at twenty students and the Office of Undergraduate Research sponsors a campus-wide research conference for first- and second-year students.
>
> **Snapshot:** An end-of-semester project culminates in a presentation at the on-campus undergraduate research symposium specifically designed for first- and second-year students. The faculty member participated in a summer workshop sponsored by the WAC program and the Office of Undergraduate Research to plan and implement this whole-class assignment. All of the students are guided through a carefully curated archival research project in the university archives in order to create a short video-like presentation using a Pecha Kucha or Ignite format. Their goal was to construct an argument in words and images about how campus life has changed and/or stayed the same as seen in the archives. Students learn basic research skills through the use of finding guides and the creation of taxonomic charts. In addition to the faculty member, a peer writing fellow, embedded in the course, works one-on-one with students. She is herself an undergraduate researcher working on her honors thesis in Writing Studies with the faculty member. The Midyear Symposium typically features group projects/presentations by entire classes and individual poster presentations and are the result of modest, course-embedded research experiences that give students an introduction to the process and products of research, typically in general education classes, including FYW. Students have the powerful experience of standing in front of an audience that is not their faculty and classmates and declaiming and defending their ideas. It is an opportunity for them to integrate the skills (speaking, writing, critical thinking) that we value in UR.
>
> **Reflection on First-Year Students Presenting Research on Campus:** Classroom-based research and symposia for early career students allow students who would not otherwise engage in research to begin to identify as researchers and to take on the mindset and habits of researchers. It also makes it possible for students to envision a "research career" in their majors that more closely resembles the one-on-one mentored research we understand as UR. Having presented their projects in the symposium, the language and activity of research no longer feels foreign or reserved for some other sort of student that they do yet see themselves as being.

CONCLUSION

Expanding access to UR in Writing Studies holds promise because the field explicitly recognizes patterns of inequity; that is, access itself is one of the primary research problems in our field. As an interdisciplinary field, we advocate broad conceptions of where research can happen, its favorability to varied means of circulation, and its sponsorship of writing in various groups both within and outside of higher education. This conception of UR, when practiced with access as a method and outcome, therefore has the potential to reach diverse student demographics.

Despite this potential, scholarship on access to UR in Writing Studies remains sparse. We therefore call for intentional efforts to remediate that—and to measure its impact. We need to know not only what happens to undergraduate researchers in Writing Studies during their research process and once they leave our institutions and go out into the world, but specifically how these practices impact underserved populations. For example, programs and departments could develop information systems for sharing data that documents the impact upon these populations of the efforts described in this chapter. WPAs and Writing Studies faculty, as well as department chairs, writing center directors, and other appropriate individuals organized in institution-appropriate faculty committees (departmental or campus-wide) could communicate the kind of work that diverse populations of student researchers do and how it contributes to the study of institutional curricula, assessment, student programming, development of strategic plans, and recommendations for community and corporate or non-profit partners. Beyond individual institutions, Writing Studies scholars could conduct longitudinal studies across institution types of undergraduates engaged in UR in Writing Studies and trace them through their programs to graduation and beyond, similar to the work being done in the Writing Center Tutor Alumni Project. Using this data, perhaps through an Undergraduate Research Network proposed in chapter 7 of this collection and/or a large-scale survey similar to the National Census of Writing to discover how institutions are approaching UR in Writing Studies in general and access in particular, researchers could also apply for cross-institutional grants[4] to expand and continue to work toward universal access to this high-impact practice.

---

4. For example, the National Census of Writing received a grant from the Andrew W. Mellon Foundation and involved undergraduate researchers such as the Swarthmore Writing Associates in the project (https://writingcensus.swarthmore.edu/acknowledgements). Another example is the Great Lakes Colleges Association Oral History in the Liberal Arts project, which issues mini-grants to faculty and student researchers (http://ohla.info/get-involved/).

Reflection on Chapter 5

IMPACT AND ACCESS: OPPORTUNITIES FOR REPURPOSING, LISTENING, LEARNING:

Heather Brook Adams

"We need to know not only what happens to undergraduate researchers in Writing Studies *during* their research process and once they leave our institutions and go out into the world, but specifically how these practices *impact* underserved populations" (emphasis added). This call from Lockett, Hart, and Babcock represents some of the most challenging and some of the most exciting work we can imagine in relation to Undergraduate Research (UR) in Writing Studies. "Impact"—an amorphous, often affective, and typically unspecified aspect of this activity—prompts my commitment to UR. This dedication stems from my sense that UR is not merely a different approach to teaching writing but rather can be a pivotal experience for some students who, through the process of research, recalibrate their own sense of themselves as curious, critical, and capable thinkers and communicators. Of course, UR is by no means the only mechanism for enabling such self-efficacy. But in my own experience, an explicit commitment to UR that situates students *as researchers* and *research writers* can produce appreciable impact. Such an approach can promote access by encouraging all students to become attuned to the possibilities of research as an activity central to the purpose of higher education. Through such attunement building, our field can enable the more equitable application of UR that the access chapter advocates. With greater access can come more wide-spread impacts of UR and greater opportunities to study and understand what impact, writ large, can mean from the perspective of undergraduate researchers themselves and the communities that may be touched by their research.

The five recommendations offered by Lockett, Hart, and Babcock echo Shari J. Stenberg's call to "repurpose" composition so as to "highligh[t] and critiqu[e] existing conditions" in education, "reclaim what has been cast off or suppressed to be used for new ends," and thereby engage "new [and I would add more accessible and equitable] possibilities for teaching and learning, for relating to one another, and for enacting cultural change" (2015, 10–11). A primary repurposing strategy that I have taken when bringing UR to my classrooms involves articulating essential research dispositions and consistently asking students to embrace such dispositions while "doing the work" of research through skills-oriented tasks. For example, I contextualize research as an inquiry-based activity that undergirds the purpose of higher education. With this context in mind, I encourage students to grapple with the notion that quality research might, however non-intuitively, be done *well* while still *appearing to be* or *seeming to be* non-linear and inefficient. A disposition of curious perseverance, then, can replace students' understandable sense that their goal should be to work toward optimal efficiency or to identify time- and resource-saving research "hacks" like those so common in other life activities.

Especially relevant to a discussion of access is my practice of invoking—that is, naming—students as researchers, hailing them as people engrossed in the labor of research that is guided by their own inquiry. This naming practice communicates to each student that I see in them the possibility of pursuing this central activity of higher education and of doing so from a situated place and perspective. Referring to students as researchers as part of this larger commitment to cultivating dispositions has been my strategy for distilling elemental aspects of research and trying to communicate why this activity can be of value to students during and after my course. Similar to the idea of using threshold concepts as a pedagogy of naming, I hope to "clarify underlying assumptions about [my] curricular goals and emphases, revealing places to work toward agreed-upon understandings and practices" (Scott and Wardle 2015, 123). Such "work[ing] toward" represents a collaborative effort, as I intentionally seek to meet each person where they are in terms of their own development as a research writer. Whenever possible, I assign research-based projects that not only require students to compose within a genre related to the course content but also to develop and pursue a relevant research question that is of deep concern to them. I urge my students to see their research not as a task they do for me, the instructor, but as investigation in pursuit of exigences of personal significance. After all, they are researchers.

I have experimented with this practice of disposition naming and cultivation in several of the classes I have taught at two institutions (both public universities serving diverse, mostly working-class, and largely first-generation students). This strategy can be applicable at all levels and in various sites of Writing Studies instruction, and I have used it within a Course-based Undergraduate Research Experience (CURE) model. My course design also includes space for contemplating the attitudes, energies, and behaviors that these and other expectations of research demand. Taking a recursive approach, I ask students to consider and reconsider the tacit aspects of research as an extoled activity, to articulate responses (intellectual, embodied, and felt) to expectations and preferred dispositions, and to express the "impact" of this course-based activity—however they wish to interpret this capacious term.

By focusing on dispositions as a critical component of a research process alongside work toward research products, students are better poised to reimagine the capabilities of research and to pose questions that can create meaning for the communities that matter most to them. While measuring the impact of such work will remain challenging, perhaps in some ways impossible, asking questions about what results come from these efforts is not a fool's errand. Repurposing our approaches to UR and engaging in open-ended dialogue about what impact does and could mean will provide opportunities to listen to students and to consider—from their vantage points—the influences of our shared efforts.

Reflection on Chapter 5

Undergraduate Research and Labor Practices in Writing Studies

Elizabeth Kleinfeld

Lockett, Hart, and Babcock boldly frame access to undergraduate research (UR) in Writing Studies as being not only about making research avenues for students available but also about the bigger picture of knowledge production in Writing Studies: "Fundamentally, the development of new knowledge in Writing Studies depends on creating more UR opportunities." I appreciate this framing of UR as essential to Writing Studies rather than an interesting but ultimately unnecessary add-on. For this reason, I want to consider how our current labor practices limit our ability to implement the most significant recommendation presented by the authors and offer two small remedies.

The authors suggest leveraging First-Year Writing (FYW) as an entry point to UR as a critical opportunity for increasing access. This is an extremely problematic endeavor because of our reliance on our labor practices. Elizabeth Wardle (2013) notes that in many FYW programs,

> we are often caught in a cycle of having to hire part-time instructors at the last minute for very little pay and asking those teachers (who often don't have degrees in Rhetoric and Composition) to begin teaching a course within a week or two . . . . sometimes faculty with little interest in or training to teach writing are nevertheless required to do so. Sometimes entire composition programs are staffed with brand new graduate students, many if not most of whom are graduate students in fields other than Rhetoric and Composition

The issues Wardle identifies seriously limit our ability in Writing Studies to effectively use FYW as an entry point to UR. If a large proportion of FYW instructors hold degrees in other areas and have never conducted writing research or even read Writing Studies scholarship, they may be as unfamiliar as their students are with writing research.

These realities call into question how effectively we in Writing Studies can count on FYW as a location for engaging students in UR. The authors discuss the importance of facilitating identity formation as researchers for students; I want to highlight that access to UR in Writing Studies depends upon us also facilitating identity formation as writing researchers for FYW instructors. All students will not have "equal opportunities to participate in UR in Writing Studies" as long as some students' FYW instructors are unprepared as teachers, unexperienced themselves as researchers, and unfamiliar with Writing Studies as a discipline. Because, as the authors note, access to UR provides access to other benefits, such as networking and internships, if access to UR is hindered by certain labor practices, access to these other benefits is also hindered. Instructors who don't know about UR or don't know how to conduct research in Writing Studies are unable to make opportunities to engage in UR available to students.

Even the happier scenario of a FYW instructor who is steeped in Writing Studies is fraught. Imagine an adjunct instructor or TA does know about research in Writing Studies and wants to mentor an undergraduate researcher. Quality mentoring is time and energy intensive and involves a tremendous amount of emotional labor. These efforts are largely invisible and uncompensated, and instructors may do the intense work of mentoring undergraduate researchers at the expense of developing their own research agendas, unaware of how little value their mentoring may receive on the job market. While research in the sciences suggests that graduate students benefit from mentoring undergraduate researchers (Dolan and Johnson 2009; Horowitz and Christopher 2013), my point is that the work is generally uncompensated. Many adjunct and graduate instructors are motivated enough to mentor that they are willing to do it on their own time, which means the opportunity for the student depends upon an instructor's willingness to do high-level, complex work for free. What a terrible irony: participating in UR in Writing Studies can increase social equity but it may depend upon the exploitation of labor.

Solving the problem of FYW programs' dependence on contingent labor is beyond the scope of this piece, but I do want to suggest two small remedies that can help us in Writing Studies implement Lockett, Hart, and Babcock's recommendation without further exploiting vulnerable workers. To help foster identity formation as writing researchers in TAs and adjunct instructors, WPAs can adopt textbooks that feature writing research, such as Wardle and Downs's *Writing about Writing*, and provide professional development opportunities to support instructors in integrating UR into their courses. To support instructors who are mentoring undergraduate researchers, WPAs can offer explicit guidance about program expectations for mentoring, including how to protect one's own research time. And, of course, WPAs can continue to look for ways to carve out stipends and other forms of compensation to demonstrate the value of all instructors' work to mentor undergraduate researchers.

I raise these concerns in the hope that others inspired by Lockett, Hart, and Babcock's arguments will understand that our labor practices impact not only the experience of students in the classroom but also knowledge production in Writing Studies. As the New Faculty Majority website notes "faculty working conditions are student working conditions." As long as access to UR in Writing Studies requires us to rely on instructors who themselves lack access—to identities as Writing Studies scholars, to support for mentoring, to fair wages, and more—our students, and our very ability to produce knowledge as a discipline, will be restricted.

6 Curriculum; or If You Build It, They Will Do It

William FitzGerald

This chapter addresses how undergraduate research (UR) in Writing Studies might be more fully imagined, enacted, and supported as *curriculum*. Central to the recommendations that follow is the principle that UR is *taught* as well as conducted, that instruction is a necessary complement to mentoring, and that, while UR goes beyond the classroom and traditional coursework, its roots are in curriculum. Indeed, UR is integral to Writing Studies as a "teaching subject" (Harris 2012). Not only does UR begin in the classroom, it in turn can contribute to curriculum design in our field when integrated into the learning goals of courses and programs in ways that the Boyer Commission had in mind in its call to put research at the center of undergraduate education. I identify opportunities and challenges in designing curricula that anticipate and advance UR in light of its transformative effects on students, teachers, and the field as a whole.

At the same time, as is discussed throughout this book, UR in our field is not fully transformative when simply derivative of professional or even graduate-level research. Indeed, it should reflect the interests and experience—and perhaps even the naiveté and amateur status—of a diverse set of undergraduates, with their goals, level of experience, and intersectional lives factored in. More than "meeting students where they are," teachers and researchers in Writing Studies can support UR by accommodating students who may lack formal preparation in methods, who often do not come to us as the eager, gutsy inquirers of our imagination, yet who bring with them a wide range of interests that can help to advance both their own work and the work of our discipline. To teach them, we must also listen, adjust, and value what they do bring with them. We must also design curricula that can help them launch their research.

From Serendipity to Design

I use *curricula* here not in a monolithic sense to refer to a standard set of courses that define Writing Studies, but as a generative concept in dialogue with other sites of UR as a mode of learning. I emphasize the applied, experiential character of UR in our field as distinct from a body of declarative or procedural knowledge.

As a field, Writing Studies is evolving and capacious, encompassing many sites, subjects, and practices, including rhetoric and composition, professional and technical communication, writing centers, literacy and media studies, and many other areas of knowledge-making. Because UR follows the contours of the field where it is cultivated, curricula can be the sites where habits of inquiry are fostered, where methods of research are introduced, where subjects and contexts for research are first encountered, and where students model processes and practice genres. With attention to curricular design, UR is not an adjunct to Writing Studies; it is *built into* our field's mission and ethos. At the undergraduate level, Writing *Studies*—research on writing as a cognitive, social, and mediated practice—can substantially overlap with writing *arts*——studio models of text production in civic, creative, and professional contexts (DelliCarpini 2007; Balzhizer and McLeod 2010; Giberson and Moriarty 2010). In any particular program, UR will thus depend on institutional history. Even so, research is critical to what we teach. Through recent curricular models, teachers and researchers in Writing Studies expose students to theories and histories of writing and forms of writing practice and introduce them to modes of research. Beyond that, undergraduates advance the field through *their* contributions to knowledge and fresh insights to disciplinary conversations (Kinkead 2011b; Downs and Wardle 2010).

Given this fluid, multidisciplinary character, its curricula can also vary across institutional contexts at the level of course and degree program (e.g., majors, tracks) and in their mix of curricular, co-curricular and extra-curricular components. UR can be a vital part of this mix.

As Writing Studies has matured and become institutionalized in degree programs, in journals and conferences, and in research agendas, it has also opened new areas of research for undergraduates; indeed, the development of research experiences for undergraduates is a major sign that Writing Studies has evolved into a distinct field. At earlier stages, say a decade or two ago when Writing Studies was synonymous with Composition or subsumed under English, opportunities for UR were largely a matter of serendipity—a ready student and a willing teacher exceeding conventional boundaries of learning. In multiple fields, pathways from classroom-based instruction to forums for presenting research were ill-defined or non-existent. This is not to say that undergraduates weren't *doing* research, only that such research was often invisible in institutional terms.

The landscape changed with the emergence of distinct sites for undergraduates to present their research, locally in campus-based poster fairs and journals as well as nationally, and the creation of offices and programs to support UR. Writing Studies has arguably come of age in an era of UR and other "high-impact" practices (Kuh 2008). The establishment in 2003 of *Young Scholars in Writing* as a venue for UR serves as a benchmark of our field's progression from UR being primarily an *ad hoc* arrangement, historically, to where it is today—a matter of curricular *design*. The *exceptional* has become *expected* practice. But to activate this productive cycle of instruction and UR at the level of curriculum, and to do so mindfully, we must first consider matters of *sequence, scope, scale*, and *sustainability*.

Programmatic Concerns, Pedagogical Commitments

Writing Studies is a field with multiple points of entry for undergraduates. Student learning experiences include not only courses, but also co-curricular and extra-curricular sites such as working in a writing/media center and various forms of engaged and experiential learning. As is also discussed in chapter 5, UR in our field benefits from these diverse sites of applied learning (e.g., a student volunteering at a neighborhood literacy center connecting his experience to theories of genre in a survey course on writing studies) (Hummel 2012).

Writing Studies curricula can, thus, be built as diverse *local* responses to an expanding and evolving field. As there is no "one size fits all" curriculum, there is also no *best* approach for integrating UR into curricula. The question is how teachers and researchers might articulate and align learning goals so that not only is there "room" for UR in an institution's courses, programs, and degree requirements but also so that UR is an effective *curricular* response to those goals.

To advance conversation at a local level, we might address four intersecting *challenges-meet-opportunities* in developing curricula in which a culture of UR can flourish: *sequence, scope, scale*, and *sustainability*. These criteria, pertinent to curriculum design in any field, serve as shorthand to frame a set of recommendations for advancing UR in Writing Studies.

Sequence: Envisioning a trajectory of learning opportunities in Writing Studies that can support students in UR.

While all four of these factors are interdependent, I begin with sequence because I understand curriculum as a required or recommended set of courses and related co-curricular learning opportunities taken in a reasonable, while iterative, order. In the context of a curriculum and co-curriculum that supports UR, and vice-versa, what comes before what? By contrast with experimental or computational sciences, there is little agreement in Writing Studies on a formal sequence for structuring curricula. As regards UR, a "vertical" approach is not the only available or plausible model, nor must UR be regarded as the necessary *culmination* of coursework. It can occur at all stages from introductory to advanced, both within courses and in conjunction with field-based learning such as internships. Indeed, we see what undergraduate researchers, working with their mentors, can achieve, not just in contributing to *scholarly* knowledge (see chapter 3) but, as important in broader civic terms. As chapter 4 notes, we also should attend to the metacognitive processes and "narratives of discovery" produced by undergraduate researchers. Still, we need to sequence learning from foundational research experiences and exposure to key concepts in the field all the way through fully realized forms of UR. This involves bridging a gap between students *learning* about a field and researchers *contributing* to the key priorities of that discipline. Well-designed curriculum can form that bridge.

Scope: Considering who participates and who is afforded opportunities to do so.

A core question is whether UR is (or should be) an exceptional practice, taken up by the relatively few, or something expected of all students. By contrast with disciplines in the humanities that regard UR as primarily for the most ambitious or talented students, Writing Studies aspires to an egalitarian mission, to give all students opportunities for inquiry, exploration, and a meaningful contribution to the field. Further, as is discussed in chapter 5, forming pathways that can make UR accessible to the widest possible range of students needs to be considered, especially in a field that professes (but does not always attain) full access for underrepresented groups and students in a variety of institutional types, including two-year colleges. As such, questions of scope need to take into account the broad range of students we serve rather than making it only the province of those who aspire to academic fields.

SCALE: RIGHT-SIZING UR EXPERIENCES WITHIN THE INSTITUTION'S MISSION AND TYPE.

The place of Writing Studies in UR, as compared with STEM fields, has up to the present been marginal. While easily overlooked at a national or even local level, Writing Studies nonetheless plays an outsized role in transforming undergraduate education in the twenty-first century. Like its counterpart in digital humanities, Writing Studies directs students in non-STEM fields to forms of experiential learning to advance both the field and the prospects of undergraduates—preparing them for *what comes next*. It is in our interest, and theirs, to provide such experiences at the broadest possible scale. With growth, however, comes challenges. What works for a handful of undergraduate researchers and mentors does not for a score. To avoid becoming a victim of its own success, Writing Studies needs curricular models that lead students to robust sites for research but avoid "industrial" approaches that constrain inquiry or place students in merely subsidiary roles. We need to be wary of claims made within neoliberal institutions to this "high-impact practice" meant more as a marketing ploy than rich curricular experiences.

SUSTAINABILITY: ASSESS AND PLAN TO MAINTAIN UNDERGRADUATE RESEARCH BASED ON AVAILABLE RESOURCES.

Matters of *sequence*, *scale*, and *scope* in UR depend on *sustainability*. UR is labor intensive and difficult to sustain even in the best of circumstances. It is, thus, necessary to address factors that promote or inhibit our efforts, matters taken up in chapter 7 on institutional support. Curricular efforts have the potential, if planned carefully, to increase sustainability without creating unrealistic expectations of faculty. As such, building a sustainable model within the priorities of any given institution, as well as within the field writ large, can keep UR in our field from becoming just a short-lived trend and instead make it a hallmark of our discipline.

Building from these four key priorities, institutions wishing to advance UR through curricula might consider the following recommendations:

Recommendation #1: Introduce broad and relevant definitions of research early, including in first-year writing (FYW)

Due to prior experiences, the term *research* itself can be alienating for undergraduates—evoking drudgery and the monolithic "research paper" and feeling like something beyond present ability (FitzGerald and Midiri 2011; Allan 2018). If UR is to take root, we must be responsive to students' *potential* attraction, but also to their potential wariness, decoupling formative experiences with research from the school genre of the "research paper" (Fister 1993). Rather than zealous attention to citation, students can be exposed to habits of inquiry that undergird all research and offered "bite-sized" practice with methods of data collection and analysis. If introductory courses in writing, rhetoric, and literacy allot sufficient time to consider the various activities that can constitute research in the discipline, if only on a small scale, students can experience first-hand how the creation of knowledge is something within their range.

Bridging this gap requires accessible "on-ramps" from early, generic experiences of research, typically pre- or pan-disciplinary in nature, to research specific to Writing Studies. For example, instead of a full research-based paper, students might engage with various elements and modes of research (e.g., primary and secondary, qualitative and quantitative). Beyond the gathering and vetting sources on a topic (what many novices *think* "research" means), students might learn to pose questions and consider what types of data and methods might serve to answer those questions. They might try their hand at interviewing and surveying, counting and coding as exercises in research. Formative encounters with research at early stages are crucial for future transformative work.

Most students, if not all, pass through FYW where there are opportunities at a pre-disciplinary stage for exposure to and practice with modes of research beyond the traditional research paper. To the extent that faculty in Writing Studies shape these foundational courses, they can orient students to the "craft of research" (Booth et al. 2016). At a minimum, students can begin to see research as a process of inquiry rather than exploring a topic or defending a pre-disposed thesis, and they can start to explore notions of method and methodology, genre, and discourse community (Adler-Kassner and Wardle 2015). Above all, the first-year writing classroom is where students can begin to experience writing to audiences beyond their instructor. The expectation of addressing an audience that will value their work, which can include a classroom of peers, is *the* threshold to cross in UR.

Recommendation #2: Develop Curricular "Maps" to Support UR
Beyond establishing a foundation to support UR, attending to sequence values identifiable pathways for students entering the discipline. For students to engage in UR in Writing Studies, consider where and how students will assemble and integrate the components of research and, thus, how curricula might function as building blocks (or as impediments). Attention to sequence and to institutional type can help us to acknowledge that our students come from many places and navigate diverse paths.

No single course can address the multiple learning goals supported by UR, including: how to frame meaningful questions, how to employ methods and identify appropriate methodologies, how to conduct research in all its unpredictability and messiness. UR depends on integrating multiple domains of declarative and procedural knowledge together with requisite "habits of mind" for undertaking research practices (Council of Writing Program Administrators et al. 2011). Since it is critical to know where in a curriculum the various elements that enable and enact UR may be found, a curriculum "map" is a valuable tool for planning and assessment. As part of such mapping, Writing Studies curricula can consider how UR contributes to a program's capstone experience. For example, a writing studies degree that culminates in a portfolio could include research in some form (report, poster, etc.) Insofar as UR makes learning experiences of students, it shines an affirming or reforming light on the curricula it supports.

Recommendation #3: So that all students can access UR, create levels of participation (and support) within curricular and extra-curricular frameworks.
A *perception* exists that UR is exceptional and of limited scope given the investment it demands from both sides of the student-mentor relationship. Students who attend elite institutions or who are members of select cohorts are typically expected or encouraged to engage in UR: write a thesis; conduct lab work or fieldwork; contribute to ongoing, multi-stage projects. Often, this research involves close interaction or even collaboration with faculty mentors and can extend beyond curricular bounds of semesters and credit hours, including in summer internships.

> ## Research Methods and Vertical Curricula
>
> In certain contexts, a dedicated course in research methods might follow (or precede or be taken concurrently with) courses centered in key readings in the field or offering specialized content. For example, at York College of Pennsylvania, a 200-level course, Research Methods in Writing Studies, is "designed to lay the groundwork for future research in academic and professional settings" (York College of Pennsylvania Course Catalog). Though required for the major in professional writing, the course is not a pre-requisite for other courses. Even so, its numbering suggests that exposure to quantitative and qualitative methods used in writing studies is best experienced earlier in one's studies. By contrast, a different course at York College at the 400-level, Research in Teaching and Tutoring of Writing, has for a pre-requisite a 200-level course, Teaching and Tutoring Writing. In this case, a research experience is designed to follow exposure to key readings and field experience in tutoring.
>
> In other contexts, research methods may be integrated with topical or thematic content to support undergraduate research experience. For example, students in a course on Literacy and Community at Rutgers University-Camden were introduced to the Digital Archive of Literacy Narratives (DALN) as a resource for conducting field-based, collaborative research and taught to use the DALN for *their* research, including analyzing archived materials and emulating its recommended practices for data collection (FitzGerald and Kairis 2019). Indeed, archival research is a productive point of entry for undergraduate and graduate students in writing studies moving from, for many, more familiar text-analytic to field-based modes of research (Buehl et al 2012, Hayden 2015, Hayden 2017, Enoch and VanHaitsma 2015).

As valuable as such opportunities are, expectation does not guarantee participation in the presence of constraints, real or imagined. As is discussed in chapter 5, expectation may itself be an impediment where access and equity are concerned if students assess the cost of *their* participation in UR as too high. Time constraints are especially keen, with only so many semesters, courses, and hours available and for students who are attending two-year colleges and/or working to support themselves and their families. Beyond a reasonable scope, which varies across contexts, we can't expect undergraduates to invest in research. Some students *can*, of course. But if we want UR to be accessible to as many students as possible, we need to build into our curricula appropriate degrees of investment.

Increased participation in UR requires that we thread a needle between low-risk and "high-impact" practices (Kuh 2008). For some students, engaging in research outside the system of credits and courses is unrealistic. For example, apart from bringing UR *into* courses, credit can also be given to forms of experiential learning like independent studies, internships, labs, and writing seminars. With variable levels of participation and flexible approaches to credit, more students can benefit from what otherwise may be considered elite forms of education.

Recommendation #4: Imagine a broad array of sites and tools for UR to encourage the particular insights and interests of undergraduates.

Expanding the scope of UR is not just a matter of *who* participates but *what* they do. Even novice researchers can contribute to understanding "what writing does and how it does it" (Bazerman and Prior 2003). Our curricula can welcome and advance the distinct contributions of undergraduates to the field, working alone or with fellow students and faculty (Downs and Wardle 2010, Kinkead 2011b, Toth et al. 2015).

Indeed, we can welcome the diversity in the research of undergraduates because of the nature of our discipline. More than other fields, Writing Studies allows researchers to pursue *their* interests, often in fresh and *un*disciplined ways. Our students enrich this pluralism. At the same time our curricula can help to adjust the scope of research so that it is within reach of our students. We can leverage our expertise in methods and project management to maximize the learning experiences of undergraduates in the available window.

At the least, we can identify diverse *sites* for UR, from writing centers (Fitzgerald 2014b, Ervin 2016a) and classrooms to local discourse communities and modes of print and digital literacies. We can likewise identify diverse *tools* for data collection and analysis, including rhetorical and computational analysis as well as ethnographic and archival research (Kinkead 2015). Each institution can engage matters of scope by inventorying available spaces and sites of disciplinary work, considering how expansive, intensive, and inclusive to make UR, consistent with an institution's character and mission and the lived experience of its students.

Part of scope is also recognizing limits. Programs can avoid scattershot approaches to UR by committing to a few signature points of focus, such as archival or qualitative research (based partly on the institutional culture and experience of faculty[5]). At the same time, students introduced to and experimenting with various types of research can be given choices as they learn to research independently. By integrating learning *about* with learning *how*, students can explore how particular methods map onto inquiry and assess the respective virtues and limitations for *their* work. For example, in researching instructor feedback on writers' affect in first year writing, a student might conclude that a focus group is preferable to a survey. Or a student might choose to apply insights and practical skills learned through methods of archival research to unofficial archives of digital or physical materials of personal significance, perhaps a family collection of letters or photos. The opportunity to contribute to knowledge is important but ultimately secondary to what UR affords in the discoveries students make about their subjects and themselves.

Finally, as a field committed to access and social justice, we should also support curricula that encourage students to do work in areas that align with their identities, lived experience, and social conscience. Curricula can extend to sites of civic and political engagement so students may link their academic work to broader social concerns.

We should also acknowledge that without mindfulness, UR can widen existing gaps of privilege. To close such gaps, teaching practices, curricula, and institutional frameworks must address systemic inequities and impediments. How do teachers and researchers in Writing Studies do that in the context of UR? For one, by a commitment to democratizing the learning that flows from UR with curricular sites and pathways benefitting all students. In particular, the needs of students who find themselves on the periphery of academic life must be considered: those in online courses, those who work as much as they study, non-traditional and first-generation students. For some students, what might be celebrated as innovative and transformative experiential learning can seem more a barrier than a breakthrough.

---

5. As discussed in chapter 7 on institutional support, a network of undergraduate researchers and mentors can also help students access advice beyond their own campus.

Undergraduate Research, Two-Year Colleges, and Transfer

The availability (or lack) of opportunities to engage in UR is of particular concern at two-year and community colleges, where so many undergraduates begin their path through higher education. Writing Studies can look to curricular models such as those advanced by the Community College Undergraduate Research Initiative, or CCURI. This STEM-oriented program promotes the incorporation of UR into community-college curricula through case-study methods of instruction in first-year courses followed by additional research experiences in course-based or summer projects, all of this before students move on to four-year institutions.

On the receiving end of college transfer, four-year institutions can be pro-active in facilitating opportunities for UR for their transfer students. An exemplary curricular model in our field is the Writing Studies Scholar Program at the University of Utah, where an articulation agreement allows students majoring in Writing and Rhetoric Studies to complete twenty-five percent of their degree requirements while attending Salt Lake Community College (SLCC). A distinctive feature of this bridge program is a course, Writing Across Locations, that allows students to "critically examine what it means to transfer writing knowledge across locations in their home communities, SLCC, and the U[niversity of Utah]" through the integration of "scholarly readings, class discussions, and primary research projects" (University of Utah 2019). Indeed, this curricular "on ramp" recognizes that students transferring from community colleges to four-year institutions are often at a disadvantage. Such courses and programs prepare students for additional UR experiences.

Recommendation #5: Identify economies of scale to expand opportunities for UR.

As is discussed in chapter 7 on institutional support, our default model for UR has been a single student working with a mentor on a project that grows out of classroom-based learning, perhaps through an independent study (Grobman 2007). Valuable as this model is, it is also difficult to scale up given limitations on time for and availability of mentors. With only so many *individual* projects that can be realistically supported, at a certain point it is necessary to work with *cohorts* of students. Instead, UR in our field should be considered not an afterthought, but a distinctive feature of our curricula, indeed a reason to choose Writing Studies for its rich possibilities for discovery and impact. Scaling up UR so that more students can benefit requires additional resources but also modes of research that are also scalable.

In some classes, including many designated writing-intensive, course-based UR experiences (CURE) are possible with either individual or small group projects. For example, a course in technical or professional writing may let students engage in various modes of inquiry that address writing *qua* writing, presenting their research through papers, posters, proposals, or recommendation reports. A course in visual rhetoric might allow students to bring critical analysis to bear on cultural artifacts in the past or present. Such courses can offer below-the-radar research experiences for undergraduates. Yet, it can also prove difficult to move projects past their initial stage and keep momentum going through the arc of research, including modes of circulation beyond the immediate sphere of the classroom. And once such classes hit a certain size, it can prove difficult to maintain a culture conducive to UR.

Here, matters of *sequence* and *scale* intersect. Given the challenge to both learn methods and apply them in one semester, the value of longer-term, collaborative research projects becomes clear (Toth et al. 2015). These projects include those that welcome periodic cohorts of students who can cycle on and that do not necessarily end as particular students graduate

---

SCALING UR IN THE ARCHIVES

Archival research offers ample opportunities for scaling up, much like archeological digs allow for many hands and variable degrees of training. A case in point at the crossroads of writing studies and digital humanities is the "Suffrage Postcard Project" at the University of South Florida. There, several undergraduates each year serve as research assistants along with graduate students and faculty leads, contributing to the collection, curation, and dissemination of findings on historical postcards associated with the women's suffrage movement. Closer to home is the Digital Archive of Literacy Narratives (DALN), which allows large numbers of students to engage in literacy studies both in and out of the classroom through projects that contribute to or analyze this digital repository.

Recommendation #6: Think beyond curricular silos to cultivate a culture of UR.

Opportunity at a scale sufficient to impact all students requires going beyond curricular silos to engage in campus, regional, and national initiatives that support UR. These initiatives may include research grants to support travel or funds for summer study. Beyond what we do as teachers and researchers in Writing Studies for students, we can also contribute to larger efforts by our expertise in writing across the curriculum and our stewardship of writing centers. Indeed, we are in a position to identify factors that allow for scaling up UR in multi-disciplinary ways. For example, we might explore ways to coordinate the teaching of methods courses across academic programs or offer writing courses that support students engaged in UR in multiple fields.

Finally, concerns of scale acknowledge that students shift from being learners to becoming researchers for different reasons (Hunter et al. 2007; Morrison 2012). Expanded numbers bring trade-offs in the kinds of UR we support as well as broaden the range of motivations for doing research, including admission to graduate school and practical skills for employment. Even so, nothing is more crucial to the endeavor than cultivating essential habits of mind such as curiosity and persistence whereby students gain soft skills and broaden their horizons (Council of Writing Program Administrators et al. 2011).

Recommendation #7: Identify conditions that enable and constrain UR, leveraging resources and incentives to align UR with institutional initiatives and mission.

For UR, *the* critical resource is faculty prepared to teach research methods, foster essential habits of mind, and mentor. These practices go beyond disciplinary expertise and solid classroom pedagogy. And these practices take time to develop in early-career faculty. Moreover, they require an environment in which UR is valued. They require a shared commitment to stewardship to ensure that curricular efforts, undertaken, can carry on. These issues, as is discussed in chapter 5 on access and chapter 7 on institutional support can be exacerbated by the lack of faculty who bring intersectional experiences to their work, in contrast to the many identity issues that will engage students.

Curriculum is not just courses; it is also personnel. An over-reliance on adjunct faculty or curricular "bottlenecks" when only one faculty member can teach a required course can impede momentum or even reverse gains. Long-term success depends on confronting logistical challenges to delivering a curriculum and thinking strategically about resources.

Gains in UR may be solidified by aligning program goals with institutional initiatives and mission. UR is not the answer to every problem, but it is a sound curricular response to challenges institutions face in making the case for college as a healthy return on investment. The more UR contributes to institutional narratives, the more programs such as Writing Studies can advocate for scarce resources. Indeed, UR is a tool for outreach and entrepreneurship, a means for engaging diverse audiences and making alliances within and beyond institutions. UR can be an effective calling card—a way to make clear that a program has something to offer students, among other stakeholders. For Writing Studies, UR contributes to brand identity. The actual research produced by undergraduates in Writing Studies is the best argument for the impact of these efforts. But for that work to contribute to sustainability, it must be publicized and cited in arguments advocating for resources. Teachers and researchers in Writing Studies benefit from hearing those experiences and from sharing the good news with others.

Of course, UR must be appropriately incentivized so that students see their efforts not as a roadblock to a degree but a vital and valuable experience. In making that case, part of any effort toward sustainability, there is a need for ongoing assessment of the impact UR has on students and faculty. Can benefits be measured and documented? To assess such impact, students—those most impacted by UR—should be heard.

Increasingly, CURE offer an alternative to labor-intensive mentored research in co-and extra-curricular settings like internships and independent studies. (Dolan 2016, Hensel 2018). The extent to which UR occurs *within* courses or coursework serves as training for mentored research in extra- and co-curricular settings will vary across settings, based on the kinds of research undertaken and resources available to support independent inquiry.

One Student's Curricular Journey as an Undergraduate Researcher

UR has a positive and lasting impact on the vast majority of students who participate in it. A compelling testimonial to that effect comes from Brynn Kairis, a former student of mine. In a co-authored contribution with the whimsical title "Year of Living DALNgerously: Breakthrough Encounters with Archival Pedagogy" to *The Archive as Classroom: Pedagogical Approaches to the Digital Archives of Literacy Narratives*, Kairis recounts her experience of collaborative undergraduate research in a course on Community and Literacy taken as a junior transferring to Rutgers University-Camden from a community college (FitzGerald and Kairis 2019). Further on a curricular arc, Kairis recounts a deeper engagement with research in a second course on Research Methods in Composition and Literacy offered to a mix of undergraduate and graduate students. As Kairis describes, these courses led her to write "D/deaf Writing Does: An Investigation of D/deaf Literacy Theory and Narratives," later published in *Young Scholars in Writing* in 2015. For that to occur, however, she needed a paradigm shift:

> This experience with the DALN unsettled previous notions about what it meant to "do research." In the past, I learned that "research" meant picking a topic that I found vaguely stimulating, reading several related pieces of scholarship, and then reporting what they said. In this course, I learned that research is driven by genuine inquiry, informed by theory, and governed by methodology. Most importantly its primary goal is the creation, not recirculation, of knowledge. Diving deeper into the DALN, I truly became a "researcher." (FitzGerald and Kairis 2019)

Such are the insights about learning and the joy of discovery that drive UR. Indeed, they sustain *us* in our efforts to make these experiences possible now and for a long time to come.

Conclusion: A Few Words about Serendipity

With considerations of sequence, scope, scale and sustainability in mind, I have offered seven recommendations that might factor into deliberations and decisions on curriculum with respect to UR. As a whole, they speak to matters of design and intentionality in thinking about a process that begins in a classroom and ends in concrete effort by students to have an impact through acts of inquiry, discovery, and circulation. Collectively, these recommendations articulate the ways that we, as teachers, support their efforts through careful instruction and creative responses to challenges in delivering quality education. We build on-ramps and pathways. We stage learning experiences. We remove obstacles. We risk facing uncomfortable facts about we might do better even as we swap stories of success. In particular, we ask who we aren't serving as well as we might so that UR might be the agent of change we profess it to be.

A profundity at the heart of UR is the realization that at a certain point we must simply get out of the way if our students are to advance. To these four S's we might perhaps add one more: *serendipity*. For all our designs and plans, some of the most powerful, transformative moments arrive unexpectedly. At best, we only partially anticipate them, though we may just as easily miss them if we aren't paying attention. Our course doesn't go as planned; it goes better. Our students don't disappoint; they surprise us by their willing spirit. That new thing we try, almost by accident, works. UR reminds us of the possibilities that lay ahead despite blind curves and unpredictable outcomes.

A parting recommendation I thus offer regarding curriculum is that besides engaging in what Kenneth Burke calls "the bureaucratization of the imaginative," we allow for serendipitous moments to emerge, moments in which UR reorients us and leads us where we did not expect to go in our teaching, in our research, in our programmatic commitments (Burke 1984, 225).

Reflection on Chapter 6

SERENDIPITY AND BUREAUCRATIZATION: LOOSENING THE GORDIAN KNOT

Dominic DelliCarpini

Chapter 6 concludes with a benediction that highlights the vast opportunities offered by undergraduate research (UR) in Writing Studies, tempered by some cautionary words. On one hand, it reminds us that despite "all our designs and plans, some of the most powerful, transformative moments arrive unexpectedly." On the other hand, building curriculum to support UR, as William FitzGerald points out, necessarily contributes to what Kenneth Burke calls "the bureaucratization of the imaginative" (1984, 225). The challenge with which FitzGerald leaves us is one that has been on my mind for many years. When we increase scale and scope, when we sequence learning, and when we strive for sustainability, what becomes of the serendipity from which UR projects often emerge?

For many of those engaged in this work, the path to UR originated with students' desire to be contributors to a field of knowledge as both *recipients* and *practitioners*. As I wrote over a decade ago, "the growth of research projects arising from students' work in our writing center . . . . demonstrates how occupational experience has begun to create [a] type of group consciousness among our undergraduate peer fellows within this new disciplinary space. This growth in UR at least until we started to notice it, was not part of the plan." Indeed, many of us who now support the UR of our students entered that space because we started paying attention to their "research impulses that, like our own field's scholarship, moved from praxis to gnosis" (DelliCarpini and Crimmins 2007, 192, 194).

I also concur with FitzGerald's beliefs that "UR in our field is not fully transformative when simply derivative of professional or even graduate-level research" (a point raised also in chapters 3 and 4) and that "it should reflect the interests and experience—and even the naiveté and amateur status—of a diverse set of undergraduates, with their goals, level of experience, and intersectional lives factored in." Indeed, he reminds us of the reticence many of us feel when we build albeit necessary curricular structures, when we wish to increase scope and scale, when we wish to sequence learning (which is, by definition, what curriculum does), and when we want systems that provide sustainable programs. These are all necessary, but can bureaucratize the imaginative impulses of students. I am also mindful of the limits and romanticizing of the ideal—as FitzGerald puts it, "a ready student and a willing teacher exceeding conventional boundaries of learning." Lovely, but that vision is at the same time largely unsustainable, is often unethical in terms of rewarding labor, and is not likely to provide wide access.

This is the Gordian knot we face as we attempt to productively systemize UR while accounting for students' natural research impulses in writing centers, writing majors, writing about writing, and community-engaged writing. Students joined us in this work and in our discipline because they loved being part of it. They loved the community it brought them, they loved what authors in this collection call the "capaciousness" and "consequentiality" of this work, and they loved the generosity of their mentors. In that idealized space, all is well.

But as FitzGerald also reminds us, we must accommodate students who are often not the "eager, gutsy inquirers of our imagination." After all, the alternative is to limit their ability to enact their vision, and to offer this high-impact practice to only those who come to us with backgrounds that support academic inquiry. As Michelle Grue argues in her response to chapter 7, this can restrict access to those who most benefit from high-impact practices but who least often have opportunities to engage in those practices.

Thus, the Gordian knot grows tighter, and looks like this: Without intentional curricular support, sequencing learning in ways that increase scope and scale and access is not likely nor sustainable. Nor is the learning of reliable and valid methods, as argued in chapter 2. At the same time, curriculum, by its very nature (and the nature of time) needs to be sequenced in ways that are linear, that prioritize systemization over serendipity, and that provide training in methods that are sometimes separated chronologically from the (lived and embodied) impulse to learn.

I am aware, of course, that this Gordian Knot describes all curricular efforts, at least to a degree. But since we are about the work of building the future of both UR and undergraduate researchers in our discipline, I believe that we can still be mindful of the dangers of bureaucratizing our students' imaginations. Indeed, FitzGerald's chapter and the scholarship of UR (such as that of Kinkead 2011b as well as Downs and Wardle 2010, both of which FitzGerald cites) consistently asks for that mindfulness in ways that "look to undergraduates to advance the field through *their* contributions to knowledge . . . . for evidence shows they bring fresh insights to disciplinary conversations." To do so, as FitzGerald reminds us, "we might recognize Writing Studies is a field with multiple points of entry, including for undergraduates."

Among the many features of this chapter that might resonate with those of us supporting the growth, then, is its underlying cautionary tale about becoming victims to our own disciplinarity in ways that limit our students' ability to re-write our field as its newest entrants. While I cannot delve deeply into solutions, let me conclude with a few possible principles we might keep front of mind as we develop curricular pathways:

- *Try not to separate gnosis from praxis.* This can be accomplished, for example, by developing community-based learning courses that apply methods to real needs, rather than creating artificial situations to teach methods. Real projects, with external clients who can benefit by the proposed research, can be an exercise for students to choose methods that best fit the research question—or even develop new methodologies. Indeed, this is the theory underlying the Naylor Workshop on Undergraduate Research in Writing Studies: come with an area of inquiry, find pertinent methods and mentors there.
- *Include student researchers in developing curricular pathways.* As the end-users of the curriculum we create, the insights of undergraduate researchers are instrumental. I would suggest focus groups or "empathy interviews," whose main focus is to uncover the deeper human needs that draw students to act as researchers. These conversations can help us to create or innovate curricula that resonate with students.
- *Design locally.* Begin the process of curriculum design by first considering deeply the local conditions that impact your program of UR. Many of the questions asked in the Self-Study Heuristic included as Appendix A to this book can be helpful in surfacing the local conditions not only for institutional support, but for curricular development.
- *Subvert, as far as possible, the impulse to imagine sequencing as fully linear,* instead valuing elements of iterative design. This principle, which is especially important in institutions with non-tradi-

tional students or students who must of necessity do coursework outside an idealized order, suggest that curricular connections among courses are as much horizontal as vertical. With this in mind, instructors can make connections based not wholly on prior knowledge, but with the needs of individual student projects—and of serendipity—in mind.

Taken in sum, these principles acknowledge FitzGerald's fifth "s," (serendipity), the capacious and consequential nature of our research, the desire to be as accessible as possible, and a commitment to retaining the energy that led to the growth of UR in our field—energy that after all, was generated by our students' natural impulse to learn, to do, to make, and to act on the topoi that defines our discipline.

7 Beyond "Cosmetic Surgery": An Action Plan for Institutional Support

*Dominic DelliCarpini, Michael Mattison,
Andrea Rosso Efthymiou, Gabriel Cutrufello,
and Michelle Grue*

Just over twenty years ago, the Boyer Commission issued its critique of the US research university and its *ad hoc* approach to involving undergraduates in substantive research:

> For the most part, fundamental change has been shunned; universities have opted for cosmetic surgery, taking a nip here and a tuck there, when radical reconstruction is called for. Serious responses to complaints about undergraduate teaching have generated original and creative pedagogical and curricular experiments. But too often bold and promising efforts have vanished after external grant support disappeared, have withered on the fringes of the curriculum, or have been so compromised that their originality has been lost. (Boyer Commission)

Much has changed since this report was issued, not only for the "research universities" to which it was addressed, but also for institutions with a primarily teaching mission. Undergraduate research (UR) is now almost universally valued as a high-impact practice to which all types of institutions wish to lay claim, at least in principle. What has often not changed, however, is the "nip and tuck" approach to supporting that work, despite the promise it holds for driving a wide range of consequential research for students across disciplines, backgrounds, and levels of expertise. Given that writing programs are already often over-burdened and under-resourced, the lack of institutional support can be particularly constraining.

This chapter builds upon the many "bold and promising efforts" represented throughout this collection and provides practical suggestions for seeking the resources necessary to develop sustainable UR initiatives in Writing Studies at both the local and national levels. Undergirding our sense of the best way forward for UR in our field is a shared conviction that we too often fail to articulate to our institutions: *Resources are not gifts; they are what we need to do our jobs.* We recognize this belief will not immediately produce the specific resources we need, whether tangible (e.g., funding, space) or intangible (e.g., goodwill, recognition). Still, there are ways to access necessary support, and in this chapter, we address concrete steps that can guide that process. Specifically, we suggest ways for UR advocates, both individually and together, to inventory campus resources, build and sustain relevant campus relationships, and collaborate cross-institutionally to establish a network for UR in Writing Studies. The bulk of this chapter describes possible action steps in detail. In addition, recognizing the particular challenges involved in networking UR nationally and even internationally, we conclude with a list of recommendations that could guide collective action in our field.

INVENTORY CAMPUS RESOURCES

On one hand, no set of action steps can address all local conditions that support, or fail to support, UR in Writing Studies and the teacher/mentors who do this emotional and physical labor. On the other hand, reiterating our general need for more time, more money and more recognition does not help stakeholders identify priorities or pathways to obtaining those things.[6] Hensel and Paul's 2012 collection *Faculty Support and Undergraduate Research: Innovations in Faculty Role Definition, Workload, and Reward* addresses this problem. They highlight specific needs, including the need to manage both students' and mentors' workloads and the need to align resources and institutional goals with our work with undergraduate researchers. Similarly, the Conference on College Composition and Communication (CCCC) Position Statement on Undergraduate Research is even more specific, naming policies (e.g., hiring, annual evaluation, tenure, and promotion) that recognize and reward involvement in undergraduate research" (CCCC 2017).[7]

---

6. In particular, see Mitchell Malachowski (2012) and Doug Downs and Gregory Young (2012) for thorough discussions of the need to workload balance and support mechanisms necessary for supporting faculty work with undergraduate researchers.

7. The statement lists infrastructure, scaffolding (curriculum needs), and resources as the three main areas an institution must create and maintain to sustain UR in Writing Studies.

But to bring about real change, position statements must be activated at the local level, beginning with a detailed and realistic inventory of the circumstances that we encounter on individual campuses. As Joyce Kinkead has argued, "writing administrators can see where their own goals intersect with those of the larger institution" and "fitting the activity to the mission can be a good way to demonstrate the [UR] program's value to the institution" (Kinkead 2016, 35). That is, in order to advocate effectively for UR in Writing Studies, it is important to find points of intersection between UR in our discipline and the priorities, programming, and public rhetorics of our home institutions. Whether we conduct formal or informal inventories, advocates for UR would do well to uncover the potential in three topoi: sites, personnel, and campus standards and guidelines.

Sites that can support UR include not only formal coursework but also the many co- and extracurricular sites (or potential sites) of UR in Writing Studies—including the physical, digital, and hybrid locations where UR can take place. *Personnel* encompasses not only the people under contract to teach writing courses, but also the great range of individuals who contribute to writing education when they support undergraduate researchers in our field. And both for equity and for sustainability, we suggest an examination of relevant *campus standards and guidelines* that contribute either directly or indirectly to the success of UR in Writing Studies over time. If you move forward with assessing resources, the list of questions collected in Appendix A to this book can guide you through an in-depth self-study.

Curricular Sites of Undergraduate Research

Seeking institutional support begins with a global look at the landscape of writing within your institution, mapping not only where writing is taught, but also where resources for formal and informal writing instruction (including UR) may be available. As is discussed in hapter 6, the depth and breadth of curricular and related co-curricular sites offer many opportunities to seek support.

As is also discussed in several chapters in this collection, First-Year Writing (FYW) is increasingly becoming a point of entry for UR. Its methods (for example, through writing about writing pedagogy) can provide access to a wide swath of students. We of course must acknowledge the limitations of this site—after all, FYW is treated quite differently on various campuses (and there are campuses where no formal program exists), FYW programs are often underfunded and understaffed, and FYW pedagogy is often seen as "mere service" that does not require disciplinary expertise.[8] Even so, FYW is still often one of the more stable and visible campus entities, and it can offer essential support to UR efforts—and vice versa.

FYW, for example, has the potential to support what is described in chapter 4 on Circulation as "consequential research." By connecting the knowledge, concerns, and interests of increasingly diverse students (see chapter 5 on access) to Writing Studies research, UR-enriched FYW courses can deepen and expand students' knowledge, address their vital concerns, and engage them in activities that ignite a new understanding of "research."[9] It can also buttress students' community development (Kinkead 2003, 9), which is of particular concern to first-generation college students, students of color, multilingual students, veterans and other non-traditional students, to name only a few.

These multiple sites of support and alignment through FYW can, in turn, drive arguments about the value of UR in Writing Studies to a wide swath of students at the institution. In many cases, UR advocates will find deep alignment with the institutions' general education mission and learning outcomes in FYW learning objectives, syllabi, and course materials. By triangulating the points of connection between FYW, UR, and the institution's educational priorities, arguments for support can be made both more visible and more viable.

---

8. See Nancy Welch and Tony Scott (2016) for compelling cautionary tales about how de-funding and under-funding is affecting our disciplinary work.

9. See, for example, Carr et al. (2013), which discusses the Keck Scholars Program as an example of drawing on peer mentors in introductory courses.

> ### Connecting UR with FYW
>
> **Context**: Tuition-driven private university on the East Coast serving approximately 4,000 students
>
> The capacious nature of UR in Writing Studies offers multiple inroads to alignment with college mission and priorities. For example, the Foundations Communication program at York College of Pennsylvania (which also hosts the Naylor Workshop) has begun to align its work with the college's focus upon project-based learning (PBL). By demonstrating how research projects in First-Year Communication (a combination of oral, written, and visual communication) can serve community needs, the program was able to access grant funding available for PBL courses. This approach, which extends the traditional "service-learning" model, includes FYW among other courses that produce research and work products that are of value to a community. For example, one section of FYW worked with a local Underground Railroad site to revise the ways that this place could be marketed to the local community, accessing resources in a project-based learning program (the Graham Innovation Scholars). The course also received notice in local press, opening further philanthropic support.

Looking beyond FYW, it is also useful to identify locations where writing throughout the curriculum happens at your institution, as this provides additional sites for seeking institutional support. For example, First-year seminars are increasingly important within many institutions as ways to engage students in academic culture. They therefore offer opportunities to highlight ways that higher education is itself a discourse community, helping students from across different areas of study to contribute to their own and others' knowledge of writing both in general and, as chapter 3 illustrates, within specific campus contexts. Likewise, UR advocates might seek alignment with general education courses that are designed to provide entry points not only to content knowledge, but also to the discourse communities of those disciplines. In this way, UR advocates can find allies in other disciplines by demonstrating how rhetorical knowledge across fields produces more effective practitioners, and how that goal can be served by Writing Studies research.

In addition, as we collect and assess key sites for UR (and potential support), we might look to outcomes derived from courses in digital writing, professional writing, business writing, technical writing, and/or writing for advocacy that often exist both within and outside of undergraduate majors/minors. As these sites are inventoried, faculty can seek ways to scaffold assignments that employ Writing Studies research methods within these curricular spaces, helping students develop UR projects. More specifically, we can seek sites of research activity that have the potential to contribute to knowledge in Writing Studies, further defining our field's value to both insiders and outsiders of the field, and actualize the field's stated equity and inclusion goals.[10] These sites can then serve to identify potential funding for initiatives that bring mutual benefit to our disciplinary work and that of other programs, as is discussed later in this chapter.

Writing centers provide another physical and intellectual site with co-curricular (and often curricular) components and a ready source for UR by motivated, informed students. As argued by DelliCarpini and Crimmins (2010), research questions that emerge as tutors do their work provides fertile ground for UR. Christopher Ervin has likewise noted that "tutors exist in a liminal space, one that places them squarely among peers and professionals simultaneously" (2016b)—a space that mirrors the space occupied by undergraduate researchers. In her review of tutor-authored work in *Young Scholars in Writing*, Lauren Fitzgerald discovered that undergraduate writing tutors are "the most likely authors of [UR] scholarly and researched essays that use composition methodologies" (2014b, 21). Further, by considering the call for "consequential" research described in chapter 4 and the work done by community-focused writing centers, value can be found in developing and assessing the research opportunities—and sites of support—that emerge when these centers serve community needs. (See, for example, Dan Singer's work with the "Clinic for Writing and the Public Good" at the University of Denver, which provides "open-access, writing-centric resources to advance public good causes.") In addition, the collaborative nature of these places makes WCs a natural fit for the types of "mutual mentoring" described in chapter 1 among directors, graduate students, and professional tutors. Working together, writing centers and UR efforts can form strong arguments for shared, tangible support.

---

10. See, for example, Laurie Grobman (2017b); Mary E. Hocks (1999); Stacy M. Perryman-Clark (2013).

> ### Undergraduate Research in a Writing Center
>
> **Context**: Community college serving over sixty thousand students.
>
> Salt Lake City Community College Student Writing & Reading Center (SWRC), which employs students as peer tutors, offers insights into both available and needed institutional support. On the positive side, in addition to their time meeting with student writers, peer tutors are paid to identify and work on research projects during their SWRC shifts under the mentorship of the Center's Director. However, the director does not receive additional funding or reassigned time for this mentorship, and so offers an example of why support for faculty and administrative labor is also needed. Another important issue that this example offers regards sustainability of programs built on soft money. While once supported by a Carl Perkins Grant, funding to send peer tutor researchers to conferences now must be sought on an ad hoc basis. The SWRC thus offers both a wealth of good examples and some cautionary tales. See also Clint Gardner's article about the SWRC's work in *Praxis*.

Personnel for Undergraduate Research

While the frequently ad hoc nature of mentoring UR is often the genesis of work on individual campuses,[11] it can also lead to labor inequities and under-informed mentoring. So, while we acknowledge that efforts of visionary faculty champions can be a catalyst for larger efforts, we also must acknowledge that this work is largely unsustainable without consistent institutional support. Indeed, while UR often begins in one class or with one faculty- or student-generated research project, reliance upon individual faculty champions also requires "extra-role behavior" in which mentoring can be undervalued in traditional teaching and advising roles usually assigned (DeAngelo et al 2016. These inequities exist not only for WS faculty and administrators, but other campus personnel such as librarians, those who provide IT support in digital scholarship labs and other sites, and those who consult informally with our students about projects across discipline. This work can be largely invisible and under-supported when UR is treated in this "nip and tuck" way.

---

11. As Kinkead has suggested, the genesis of UR most often "derives significantly from faculty enterprise and effort rather than from institutional movement" (2003, 9).

To develop sustainable and programmatic efforts, as is argued throughout this book, it is important to inventory those sites of labor, looking more deeply at what exists but is often not acknowledged. For example, a program may have several or no tenure and tenure-track Writing Studies faculty, the majority of courses may be taught by contingent faculty (here, we mean any faculty member, part or full time, who is not on tenure-track and whose contract is semester-to-semester or yearly), and there may or may not be graduate students teaching writing. The often-precarious employment status of participants in our discipline, as well as the educational pathway that led them to the teaching of writing, also affect the kinds of support needed to create systematic resourcing and appropriate reward systems. It is of benefit to consciously chronicle how the status of our colleagues affects their access to resources on and off campus to conduct research with students, to travel to conferences, and to share their work through publications or other venues. The challenges, including physical and emotional labor, of mentoring undergraduate writers make it especially necessary to inventory resource needs within a variety of specific mentoring models and to consider curricula that balance faculty workload (Paul 2012).

For example, the calls for wider access addressed in chapter 5 cannot succeed without support. Consider the implications of enacting an often-neglected element of the Boyer Commission's recommendation to provide opportunities "to interact with people of backgrounds, cultures, and experiences different from the student's own and with pursuers of knowledge at every level of accomplishment, from freshmen students to senior research faculty" (1998). Achieving this important goal can place new burdens upon those already called upon to address an increasingly wide need. Indeed, attention to the needs for support of UR generally is exacerbated by the intersectional lives of faculty: race, gender, class, contingency of security of contract, sexuality, and ability all add additional challenges to mentoring UR. As Jackson and Guerrant argue, faculty of color are often "pressed into service due to institutional expectations of high visibility" and that they "provide mentoring to students of color" (2012, 58). Just the sheer number of students who seek to work with faculty of color because they are the "only" in their department is not tangential, but must be an essential part of any inventory of resources at your institution. See Michelle Grue's reflection following this chapter for more detail on this topic.

Keeping these human resource issues in mind can help program leaders to address practicalities in implementing programmatic efforts alongside the theoretical and intellectual concerns—to ask not only what is best, but what is possible, sustainable, and ethical. This information may be available in hiring documents, union agreements, and faculty handbooks, and can be assessed with UR research in mind. Some of these possibilities are examined below. You can also draw upon the self-study questions in Appendix A to this collection to begin this process.

Institutional Standards and Guidelines for Undergraduate Research

Not only practically, but ethically, institutional support for UR must align with the policies under which faculty and program administrators work and are evaluated and rewarded. This section can help inventory the support that exists (or does not exist) for UR within institutional expectations. As you collect this information, you should consider the institutional landscape that shapes the cultures and reward structures of research, professional development, and achievement for both undergraduates and various personnel (as discussed below).

Because faculty who occupy administrative positions have a particularly important role in integrating and supporting UR into their programs, duties related to their work should also be examined and inventoried. This assessment may also be conducted by individuals who support UR, keeping track of and making visible the day-to-day activities in which they are engaged to support undergraduate researchers. To what degree are WPAs, coordinators of writing majors, and department chairs responsible for the curriculum, staffing, budgeting and assessment (among a host of other responsibilities) of their programs? How much time do mentors spend supporting students in projects outside of the classroom? Since WPAs already often have difficulty articulating the intellectual work and disciplinary knowledge needed for administrative work, (Council of Writing Program Administrators 1998), it is important to examine the policies that exist to support their claims in reviews and promotion and tenure. How is assessment of program-learning outcomes of this high-impact practice (White 2018) valued by the institution as part of the acculturation to college and college retention?[12]

---

12. Small and Waterman (2017) suggest that first-year writing classrooms and other early college experiences of HIPs help students transition successfully to college.

> **ADDRESSING UR IN TENURE AND POMOTION MATERIALS**
>
> **Context**: Application for tenure-track reappointment at a mid-sized, private university
>
> For reappointment at Hofstra University, Andrea was asked to discuss her research agenda. Because it explicitly involves assessing the impact of UR on her students she mentors in the writing center, Andrea foregrounded her UR activities and their value. Here is an excerpt that demonstrates how Andrea connects her investment in UR to her college's mission statement:
>
>> My interest in assessing the value of undergraduate tutors' research is in line with my institution's learning objectives. Moreover, I am committed to making the work that undergraduate tutors do more visible within our institution to demonstrate that UR positively impacts retention. My work as a mentor and scholar of UR has been accepted at two upcoming conferences: the Naylor Workshop on Undergraduate Research in Writing Studies at York College and the State University of New York Council on Writing (SUNY CoW) at SUNY Farmingdale. It is my hope that making this work more visible through scholarship will offer inroads for other writing program administrators to create more sustainable practices around undergraduate mentorship. I have been awarded a Faculty Research and Development Grant, the third such award in my time at Hofstra, along with a Presidential Research Award that will serve to support this work.

How does UR support underrepresented and first-generation college students?[13] How does the intellectual work of curriculum design and development, especially as related to UR in Writing Studies, add to the work of partners across campus (GenEd, Registrar, Academic Advising, etc.)—and where is this important intellectual labor reflected in policies and evaluation? As you assess not only what your college does in terms of UR in Writing Studies, but also how you would like to see it develop, it is important that you know how this administrative is supported in institutional policies—and that you demonstrate how this work aligns

---

13. Dickter et al. (2018) also argue that programmatic assessment and development of UR opportunities can successfully support underrepresented students in the academy.

with priorities of the institution. It (and those who do this work) can otherwise remain invisible.

While program leaders play an essential role in setting an agenda for UR, institutional expectations for engaged faculty are also central. It is, thus, crucial that you examine the ways that expectations and rewards for mentoring and service are articulated in contract, promotion, and tenure language to support faculty buy-in (Free et al. 2015, 55). While definitions of "service" vary from institution to institution, it is important that the expectations of faculty and opportunities to engage in the work of the institution are clearly articulated in your inventory of available—and needed—resources (Jackson and Guerrant 2012, 58). For instance, you might make note when writing faculty sit on institutional review boards or serve as part of funding or planning committees for UR. You might also assess the degree to which policy support for contingent and untenured faculty members, whose contributions are crucial, exists or is needed. And you might pay special attention to chronicling the labor of minority faculty, who are often tasked with additional service (Jackson and Guerrant 2012). The sustainability of UR programs in Writing Studies as well as the imperative to support equitable practices requires that current policies are carefully inventoried.

Likewise, a full assessment of the sustainability of UR efforts requires careful attention to the documents and guidelines that delineate annual reviews and tenure/promotion. This area is often the most fraught for faculty members as it is often least defined (Chapdelaine 2012). Building upon Day et al.'s (2013) call to rethink and advocate for expanded understandings of scholarship in tenure and promotion materials for Writing Studies faculty, your inventory should include documentation of the degree to which UR mentoring and scholarship is explicitly situated and valued in an institution's documents for scholarship, teaching, and service. Other documents to examine include official reappointment letters, WPA contracts, and contingent faculty contracts; as they *drive* institutional culture as well as reflect it, knowing how UR is valued in those documents is crucial. Look also to program or department's guidelines, and the degree to which they explicitly state how faculty/student co-written scholarship is valued, whether mentoring is valued as a form of teaching, and how serving on institutional committees that support UR constitutes important service. In the process of collecting this information, you can also be asking whether the types of structures and labor required in your program to put UR into a position of prominence exist.

> ### Using College Credit to Track Undergraduate Research and Support Mentoring
>
> **Context**: Mid-sized, private liberal arts university
>
> Elon University's writing center consultants regularly undertake original research related to their writing center work. Consultants, who are also undergraduate students, register for an independent credit with the writing center director. This system helps Elon track and support the mentoring of UR. Students first learn about this opportunity when they take the writing center workshop course, also taught by the writing center director, and they are reminded regularly through their work as consultants in the writing center. Since consultants' projects engage diverse questions about writing, faculty mentors are recruited and supported through Elon's Office of Undergraduate Research; you can learn more about this program at Elon's Center for Writing Excellence site.

Develop Campus Relationships

Once the landscape of your own program has been mapped, a next step is to assess ways that other entities on campus might support UR in Writing Studies. Again, conditions will differ from campus to campus, but there are also some similarities in academic institutions that offer possible sites for your investigation and planning. We use some of those sites below to offer suggestions that should be applicable to most readers. Cultivating sponsorship of UR in Writing Studies from different campus offices is a process that will unfold over time, following the rhythms of the academic and fiscal years. In general, it is important to discern the best contact person in any given office and how to get on his/her schedule, whether for an initial meeting or a regular, annual or semester conversation. It is also helpful, as a UR advocate, to develop a pattern of stewardship for these relationships (e.g., invitation to UR event, annual report on UR activity).

Advancement Office

Offices of college advancement are often not only the key to fundraising for UR efforts, but also act as gatekeepers for contact with donors. As donor relationships are usually tightly held and centralized within the full institution or within units of larger institutions, going directly to donors is ill-advised. But a relationship with fundraisers in collaboration with advancement professionals can be crucial to building a case for support, and requires that you first learn about the advancement office's priorities, active campaigns, and philanthropic prospects. At the same time, program leaders can work with their advancement officers to make suggestions that fit institutional priorities. Keep in mind that advancement officers value new ways to raise funds. For example, program administrators might:

- Supply examples of UR in Writing Studies and ask how these might be advertised to donors.
- Ask about adding a "giving" page or button/link for your writing center, first-year program, writing fellows program that would allow donors to earmark gifts directly to your program through the advancement or alumni office.
- Suggest donation possibilities: a travel fund for conferences, an endowed "chair" in the writing center for an undergrad, a named research position in a first-year program. Create a range of gift amounts to include both endowments and funds that accrue smaller gifts.
- Align possibilities for supporting UR in Writing Studies with active campaigns.
- Peruse available alumni directories (which often exist within advancement offices to facilitate alumni giving) of students who have participated in and benefited from UR in Writing Studies. Send out notices to those alumni, in collaboration with the advancement office, highlighting recent accomplishments.

Office of Marketing and/or Communications

As with fundraising, internal and external communications are usually tightly controlled, and so require relationship building. But these offices also regularly seek and value stories about student and faculty achievement. To make UR in Writing Studies visible as part of the institutional marketing, WPAs, writing center directors, and/or other champions of UR should have regular meetings with the communications team. At such meetings,

> ### UR through Alumni Donation.
>
> **Context**: Mid-sized public, Hispanic-Serving Institution
>
> The Raab Writing Fellows Program at the University of California, Santa Barbara is a UR fellowship program funded by a gift of university trustee Diane Raab. Students of any major and in their first through third years at UCSB are welcome to apply, as long as the project is rooted in Writing Studies and students have found a faculty mentor who agrees to work with them.
>
> Once accepted, students enroll in a year-long, four-credit course that supports and connects the cohort of Raab Writing Fellows and receive up to $750 for project needs. Students are required to present a representation of their work at the year-end showcase. Expectations of faculty mentorship include: helping the student develop an original project proposal, facilitating said projects execution during the fellowship year through quarterly independent study courses. Faculty mentors are compensated for teaching in this program. Learn more about this program at the Raab Writing Program site.

- Inventory the types of materials that are produced through your communications and marketing offices, including alumni magazines, recruiting materials, social media, press releases, etc.
- Establish a contact person in the communications office so that whenever a student presents at or attends a conference, publishes a piece, or does any substantive work with UR in Writing Studies, that person can be notified.
- Ask to have products of UR in Writing Studies promoted on the college website and in other college publications.
- Work with the marketing and communications office to develop regular press releases and social media presence for UR in Writing Studies.

Human Resources

The expectations for both faculty and administrative positions begin with the drafting of job advertisements and continue through performance reviews. It is therefore important to first assess whether UR in Writing Studies is included in job advertisements—and then to advocate for the inclusion of mentoring UR in those ads to attract apt candidates and to help guide their work. For example, UR champions might:

- Assess the degree to which job ads reflect the value of UR mentoring as part of the institution's teaching mission.
- Advocate for adding "mentorship" to job descriptions, yearly reviews, and any other documents that work their way into the institutional stream.
- Advocate for new roles on campus for UR in Writing Studies mentorship with appropriate compensation and/or course release, perhaps modeling upon the institution's internship coordinators or independent study supervision.

Enrollment Management and Financial Aid

An oft-overlooked source of institutional support exists within enrollment management and financial aid strategies. As these offices are increasingly pressed to find new ways to attract and enroll students, and as discount rates and incentive packages increase, recruiters are often open to creative funding packages. That is, since recruiting students is increasingly tied to available scholarship dollars and as financial aid programs are one of the few areas of budget growth within institutions, you might work with Enrollment Management to create scholarships earmarked for UR in Writing Studies. Funds for recruiting through scholarships are often already available, so making the case for using those funds in targeted ways can help attract students interested in UR without the need for new budget lines. Students and parents are particularly interested in scholarships that demonstrate personal attention to students' interests and that identify their work as significant—so this strategy can also help you to recruit students already excited about UR in WS. As such, you might:

- Establish relationships with the enrollment management teams to learn their priorities for attracting students.
- Suggest incentive packages linked to Writing Studies majors or UR in Writing Studies that can bring in students who are interested in doing UR, perhaps creating a "Writing Scholars" designation.
- Investigate community research opportunities related to Writing Studies that can be linked to incentive packages for students

with interests in the kinds of consequential research discussed in chapter 4 and that offer "community networking" to students. In some cases, Federal Work-Study dollars can be allocated for community research.

> **UNDERGRADUATE RESEARCH THROUGH FINANCIAL AID**
>
> **Context**: Private, four-year liberal arts college in the Midwest
>
> Wittenberg University's First-Year Research Awards (FYRA) offers a $2000 award applied to the cost of tuition. Students are expected to meet regularly with faculty and spend approximately six hours each week on their research project. Participants convene monthly to meet with the entire FYRA mentor-researcher group to discuss everything from IRB procedures to strategies for presenting research. Student researchers are recruited in promotional materials to incoming students encouraging them to apply for the award.

OFFICES OF RESEARCH AND/OR UNDERGRADUATE RESEARCH

Though UR plays an increasingly central role in institutional mission and marketing on many campuses, our field has not had the visibility it might within administrative units that offer financial and human resource support for research activities. If an Office of Undergraduate Research exists, spend time with its leaders; if not, find out which administrative division administers this work. If your campus does not have a specific unit devoted to UR, similar work can be done through other units that oversee and/or support research on your campus. In any case, program leaders can:

- Inventory the kinds of financial and other support available for research activities through these campus sites, paying attention to the kinds of work that tends to be supported.
- Assess whether faculty research grants can be used to support student researchers.
- Inform the office of ongoing work and your interest and objectives so that when opportunities come to them, they can notify you.

- Find advocates for the types of research your writing faculty (and others involved in Writing Studies work) tend to produce, so that students and/or student/faculty teams can made aware of specific programs and resources.

> ### Institutional Support for Student/Faculty Research Partnerships
>
> **Context**: Mid-sized private undergraduate and graduate university
>
> At Pace University, the Office of Undergraduate Research sponsors a year-long Undergraduate Student-Faculty Research Program to which students and faculty apply in pairs. If accepted, they work together over a summer or two semesters on a research project that culminates in a poster presentation at the Annual Undergraduate Research Showcase. Each winning pair is awarded up to $2000 if their work is accepted for a conference presentation in their field. Learn more from Pace University's Office of Student Success.

Connecting with an office responsible for resourcing research, both by undergraduates and faculty, can also help to place the work of undergraduate researchers in Writing Studies among other fields in national organizations. The sciences have been active (and pro-active) in seeking funds for student research development and presentation; our field has been less so. An informal search of the National Council on Undergraduate Research (NCUR) conference program for 2018 with the word "writing" leads to only eleven presentations, out of hundreds, and "writing studies" is not even a listed topic in the program (while linguistics and creative writing do have designations).

Program directors, thus, might

- Begin by finding the best site for making known your interest in the opportunities for external grants that can support Writing Studies research. Depending upon the institution, grants are facilitated through advancement, offices of institutional research, individual colleges, or other units. In any case, UR in Writing Studies is infrequently seen as holding potential for grants, and so you may need to change that perception by demonstrating the kinds of research Writing Studies faculty and students do. For

example, ask to be alerted to any grant opportunities that speak to research in broad terms, including requests for proposals that are usually STEM-focused, such as the National Science Foundation and the National Institutes of Health. Demonstrate to grant officers how technical communication, science writing for the public, medical rhetoric, etc. support those fields of knowledge.
- Seek out funding for summer UR research assistantships normally associated with other disciplines. For example, summer work is done in science labs, but there are usually no restrictions on which disciplines can apply for funds to support summer research. Work with undergraduate researchers to propose possible funded projects. See chapter 6 for an example of how this might also support underserved populations.
- Check if your institution funds travel to the NCUR conference and encourage students to apply for such funding if available.

FEDERAL SUPPORT FOR UR ACROSS THE CURRICULUM

Context: Mid-sized public, Hispanic-Serving Institution

UC Santa Barbara partners with the McNair Scholars Program, which helps undergraduates enter PhD programs across the curriculum. McNair Scholars Program aims to diversify the faculty in colleges and universities across the country. The program is currently established at 151 institutions across the United States and Puerto Rico. The UC Santa Barbara McNair Scholars Program is funded by a five-year grant from the US Department of Education with additional support from the institution. UR in Writing Studies has been increasingly represented in the program, which provides undergraduates with opportunities to participate in academic year and summer research activities. Students complete a research project under the guidance of a faculty mentor and then present their research at local, regional, and national conferences. They also attend courses, seminars, and workshops on topics related to graduate school preparation and application. Students at UCSB have the opportunity to submit their papers to the UCSB McNair Scholars Research Journal. The McNair Scholars program funds and facilitates faculty mentorship and dissemination of research.

Offices Overseeing Community Service, Community Engagement, and Project-based Learning

Research opportunities related to Writing Studies abound in the community, both on an individual and curricular level. Though not included in the high-impact educational practices validated by Kuh's research [2008], project-based learning—and the offices and programs that support it—can also serve as allies. Because this work often takes place on an ad hoc basis, it is less often systemized so as to receive regular support. Program directors can therefore:

- Work with offices of Community Service, Community Engagement, and Project-based Learning (among others) to identify opportunities for writing-based projects that might involve one or more undergraduate researchers.
- Work with local schools, literacy centers, and other similar institutions to identify and address community needs that might be met through programming and projects with a UR component.
- Seek support from relevant offices and administrators on campus, in the community, and through relevant national organizations.

Establish an Undergraduate Research Network

While assessing and acting upon local opportunities is central to developing UR programs, aligning and maximizing opportunities at a national level is also necessary. Our work as individuals needs to be supported by the group as a whole. An Undergraduate Research Network in Writing Studies (UR Network) can bring together scholars who are driving this work and the many organizations that support it intellectually and financially. It can also support efforts to complete needed research on the impact of UR in Writing Studies, attempts at widening access, and discipline-wide support for the varied types of circulation of the "capacious" and "consequential" products that are recommended throughout this volume.

There are many organizations and scholars who have brought us to what we envision as a watershed moment for UR in our discipline, and we believe that connecting those entities would make all of us stronger. Contributors to this book have not only demonstrated interest in UR across Writing Studies; the work they have chronicled suggests that we have a critical mass of active participants or practitioners. Some have been involved in UR efforts for decades, giving shape to UR activities as we know them; some have become involved in UR more recently, contributing fresh perspectives and invaluable insights. Along with numerous campus examples, including those offered throughout this volume, we also have an unprecedented range of national professional resources, including publications and platforms for sharing UR sponsored by our national professional organizations. We do not overlook nor do we fail to value these resources when we call for the creation of a UR Network. Instead, our call is an effort to build the resources we have established to advance UR in specific ways. In the following two sections, we want to first make a case for why and how such a network would benefit all of us, and then second highlight some of the allies that might participate in the UR Network toward a coordinated, sustainable effort for UR in our field, and the functions that they serve.

RATIONALE AND RECOMMENDATIONS FOR A UR NETWORK

Establishing a network can, first and foremost, combat the isolation of the "champions" who initiate this work on the local level—especially (as noted above) for the often sole champion tasked with mentoring diverse groups. The UR Network can formalize a community committed to the priorities identified throughout *The Naylor Report*: steadily improving students' equitable access to mentored opportunities for learning about and contributing directly to knowledge in Writing Studies. It can promote consequential research that circulates widely and, in so doing, helps widen as well as deepen our field. The UR Network can also support and promote ongoing scholarship on the impact of UR on student learning, as discussed throughout this volume and which undergirds each of the chapters.

To guide a network with these aims, we propose the following mission statement: "The UR Network connects undergraduate researchers and mentors in Writing Studies with relevant resources and showcases pertinent scholarship about the practice and impact of undergraduate research in our field." Alongside this broad statement, we offer four specific recommendations. They are initiatives that reflect immediate priorities for UR in Writing Studies. We believe that by working on them in concert—in ways that connect our individual efforts, our campus programs, and our national professional organizations—we can advance UR in our discipline significantly.

Recommendation #1: Develop the UR Network to increase the public visibility of our students' "consequential" research.

At present, the products of UR are mainly collected and distributed at individual institutions and local showcases. Even regional and national conferences and scholarly publications have limited, scholarly circulation. We see a need for resources that will enable us to collect and make available artifacts of research created by undergraduate researchers. A national database of UR publications in Writing Studies would allow us to link to additional resources sponsored by individual institutions and organizations. Through crowdsourcing or other means, the UR Network might also create and maintain a bibliography of UR and related materials as well as a clearinghouse of conferences and other opportunities for undergraduate researchers to share their work.

Recommendation #2: The UR Network can catalyze and coordinate efforts to document the impact of UR in Writing Studies.

The UR Network can do a great deal to demonstrate the impact of UR in Writing Studies to both academic and non-academic audiences. To begin, it can act as a clearinghouse for scholarly research on this topic, and it can translate that research into related public statements intended for audiences outside the discipline, including administrators, media, funders, and so on. The UR Network can also help individual researchers connect so they can share research designs and protocols as well as research findings with one another. In addition, the UR Network can seek ways to support inter-institutional research teams that can work together—and perhaps attend research institutes and workshops offered by Elon University, AAC&U, and others—toward enriching the scholarship on impact.

Recommendation #3: The UR Network can be a vehicle for seeking extra-institutional support.

By amassing this wealth of documentation described above, the UR Network could also bring together UR champions to write compelling inter-institutional grants and make strong appeals for philanthropic gifts. In this way, the UR Network would do more than increase our collective ability to procure financial resources for UR in Writing Studies. It would also help raise the profile of Writing Studies on individual campuses. To support this goal, the Network site can regularly publish opportunities and facilitate cross-institutional grant writing. To drive forward the potential for external grants and gifts, the network might obtain its own 501(c) (3) (non-profit) status, or align itself with an institutional home that can provide that status.

Recommendation #4: The UR Network Can Develop Consulting and Evaluation Services.
Over time, the UR Network can lead field-wide efforts to develop criteria and procedures for consulting and evaluation services akin to those offered by the Council of Writing Program Administrators and the Coalition for Community Writing. Such services might be of value to campuses first developing UR programs and curricula and campuses seeking to better understand and sustain established opportunities for UR in our discipline. Whatever the case, consultations might begin with a self-study (working from protocols such as the institutional inventory included in Appendix A) and would include a visit by an experienced UR Network team prepared to help colleagues across the country do strategic planning and delineate needed resources. The UR Network's Consulting and Evaluation services might also offer short- and long-term mentoring tailored to colleagues' site-specific projects and needs.

To establish this network, we can bring together the various organizations that already support some of the key recommendations of this report. Appendix B provides a useful, if necessarily limited, inventory to draw upon and a call to imagine what these groups could accomplish in aligning efforts.

Conclusion: Towards "Radical Reconstruction"

A rich array of resources already exists for undergraduate researchers in our field. In suggesting ways to inventory and support that work locally, and by proposing a UR Network in Writing Studies, we demonstrate that we believe that more can be done by connecting resources than by trying to create a new entity or organization. Many of the chapter contributors in this volume are already engaged in work that the UR Network would highlight—heading UR committees and special interest groups, editing UR journals, sponsoring research seminars and workshops. We invite readers of this volume to also consider how their work might be a node within this larger network. Conversations among stakeholders to develop such a network are in progress, led by leaders of the

Naylor Symposium and of some of the organizations discussed above and in Appendix B.

In any case, impressive, high-impact work has already been accomplished by the visionary individuals, institutions, and organizations that have led us to this tipping point in the field. But as the Boyer Commission's work reminds us, efforts like these—especially in an age of austerity—can tip either way. Our recommendations are thus meant to help transform aspirations into action, to celebrate all we value, and to discover new and successful ways to ask others in our institutions and elsewhere to value it as well.

As academics, we sometimes neglect, even denigrate, self-promotion. While that may be a noble sentiment, in the end it does not help us garner the support we have earned. This chapter, with its action steps and concrete recommendations for advancing UR, affirms our previous good work while orienting us toward a bright future full of new successes.

Reflection on Chapter 7

Institutional Support for Emerging Scholars in Undergraduate Research in Writing Studies

Michelle Grue

As an emerging scholar in the field of Writing Studies, the challenging path I see before me is sketched out within this book and chapter. Prevailing among these challenges are the physical and emotional labor involved in mentoring undergraduates, especially as a minoritized woman (Charity-Hudley 2017). Concerns about this mentorship lead to questions about what the field is actually doing in service of first-generation and other underrepresented students (Perryman-Clark and Craig 2019) and the sustainability of the field as a whole. While *The Naylor Report* still leaves some of my concerns unresolved—it can only do so much—it does speak to many of them. It acknowledges them as concerns, but it also articulates a way forward. It speaks to funding and cooperation between first-year writing (FYW), upper-division writing classes, and the writing center.

As a graduate student teaching first-year composition courses, I am often the first person to tell undergraduates that they can, in fact, do "consequential research" as we perform rhetorical analysis, rummage through archives, collect tweets, and construct arguments based on the data. I am sure that many of the readers of this chapter recognize themselves doing similar work. Further, because FYW is a required course at my minority-serving institution, each of my classrooms are a microcosm of the beautifully diverse students who learn and research there. Despite the importance of this threshold into UR in Writing Studies, the course is often relegated to graduate students, contingent faculty, and others in precarious positions at the university. Writing program administrators (WPAs) can take advantage of the advice within this chapter to support teachers of FYW, so, in greater security, they can water the "fertile ground" that is the first-year writing classroom.

WPAs often have the authority and standing to make asks that are difficult for emergent Writing Studies scholars. They can create structured mentorship systems for graduate students and new faculty, providing not just guidance on how to do it well, but training junior scholars on how to access the support and compensation they need for their emotional, intellectual, and physical labor (De Mueller and Ruiz 2017). The chapter above provides several specific strategies to both increase funds for UR in Writing Studies and create more structural supports for the labor required to mentor faculty and students engaged in UR. My hope is that with such a clear set of options, WPAs can begin implementing these enriching and empowering changes, in ways that are appropriate to their specific situations, to make the field better in substantive ways. Indeed, in the proposed network, the Council of Writing Program Administrators might consider this one of its key tasks.

But, for many people invested in UR in Writing Studies, the suggestions in this chapter and the rest of *The Naylor Report* are not enough. We need more than a book to carry this work into fruition. The field must continue to improve the realities for contingent faculty and graduate students, hire more minoritized scholars, provide all faculty with more support, and reduce the precarity and austerity of writing programs. Establishing a UR Network in Writing Studies could help those of us committed to UR in Writing Studies in responding to these charges. The network, from its inception, will be formed and led by a diverse range of scholars with the explicit goal of furthering UR in Writing Studies and the people involved in making it happen. Indeed, as far as possible, the Naylor Symposium worked to include those voices, as does this report. Similarly, the UR Network can help mitigate isolation, provide a repository for resources, a space for the circulation of UR in Writing Studies research, and ample evidence of the value of the work we do.

Graduate students have spoken to the need for research networks that straddle the digital and physical environments as resources, opportunities to deepen and practice our engagement in the field, and places to connect with other scholars (Alvarez, Salazar, Brito, & Aguilar 2016; Coad 2017; Eyman, Sheffield, & DeVoss 2009). Given the ways in which online and in-person networks in the field of Writing Studies have been revealed as insufficient to serve all its members, creating and supporting the network suggested herein becomes increasingly important, especially with regard to meeting the needs of the most vulnerable in our field. The UR Network could work to ensure that no one is left out by operating as a clearinghouse of sorts, providing a means through which existing formal and informal professional groups can communicate with each other. A UR Network could also provide a host of new resources, including a website that might open new kinds of conversations and resource sharing. In this way, a UR Network would allow for a richer and deeper, more multi-faceted pool of resources for UR in Writing Studies. The changes described in my reflection and in the chapter as a whole would not negate the need for digital and physical counter-publics that enrich and empower graduate students and others in precarious positions. However, they would relieve the burden from existing digital counter-publics needing to do this work. Staring in the face of an otherwise daunting future, these possibilities also provide some of the assurance I and others like me need in order to support UR in Writing Studies.

Reflection on Chapter 7

THE IMPACT OF THE RAAB WRITING FELLOWS PROGRAM AT UCSB

Ljiljana Coklin

The Raab Writing Fellows Program (RWF) at the University of California, Santa Barbara (UCSB) presents a good example of a contribution to undergraduate research (UR) that a predominantly teaching unit can achieve through a hybrid model of institutional support and philanthropic giving. Created in 2016 through a donation from Diana Raab, a university trustee, the program was broadly defined as an opportunity to "further [students'] engagement with writing" (raabwritingfellows.com/about.html). In the first two years, interested students worked with mentors on a year-long project, and then presented the findings of their research at a year-end showcase. In the third year we introduced a year-long research mentoring seminar in an effort to create a stronger support system for the students, build community, and increase retention. The number of fellows completing the program has been steadily on the rise, from eleven in 2017 to twenty-five in 2019. In all, the RWF Program has emerged as a unique cohort-based space for collaborative learning and multi-mentoring for UR in Writing Studies.

While a more systematic study of impact of the RWF is yet to be undertaken, some trends emerge. Anecdotal student comments frequently describe the work done in the RWF as "the most important thing I've done throughout my college career" (Garcia n.d.). Such strong endorsements of UR projects tend to fall into two categories: "meaningful to me" and "meaningful to my community." Students have described the value of their projects in terms of personal growth, acquisition of relevant knowledge (e.g., transitioning to the work force), healing, self-expression, or development of agency and voice. The strong affective value of these projects is further reflected in the connections students see between their projects and their communities. Students perceive those contributions in terms of reinforcement of community ties and belonging, raising visibility of a community and related issues (e.g., undocumented immigrants), and attempts to define, strengthen, and build a specific community.

Students also connect their participation in RWF with the development of their identities as writers and researchers. They report that their projects enabled them to write new media and styles, gain time management skills and appreciation for editing, and expand their writing portfolios. A year-long immersion in a research process in a cohort setting also familiarized students with different research methods while introducing them to the IRB process and ethical dimensions of research. By providing resources and continued guidance from mentors, the program actively fosters students' membership in a research community while also promoting the circulation of their research. As a result, students have participated in national conferences as well as in a range of campus-wide events associated with undergraduate research and creative activities (URCA). In addition, students are increasingly gaining awareness of more situational opportunities for impact as they discover the many ways in which research-based information can be circulated within interested groups, organizations, and communities.

The Raab Writing Fellows Program is leaving a mark on the Writing Program (WP) as well. By providing matching institutional support and securing teaching credit for the seminar leader, the WP demonstrates commitment to UR and creative expression. The RWF is emerging as a welcome and exciting opportunity for non-tenured teaching faculty to engage in one-on-one and multi-mentoring of UR. That in turn is helping create stronger bonds between faculty and students and is catalyzing important discussions about issues like successful mentoring, curriculum design, or diversification of disciplinary research methods. Moreover, the fellows' participation in campus-wide research related events brings greater campus visibility to the WP and strengthens its connections with other academic and non-academic units. In an effort to provide a greater access to UR for under-represented, first-generation, and non-traditional students, the WP has also actively reached out to organizations like the McNair Scholars Program.

The continuity of UR opportunities like the RWF would benefit from more formal impact research, both short-term and long-term, quantitative and qualitative. A case study of the RWF already offers evidence of short-term quantitative impact as it is, for instance, possible to track a number of literary journals sold or record a number of visitors to community-specific websites (on Montecito mudslides or campaign contributions in the Santa Barbara county). Introducing year-end surveys and reflective writing would help us gain a better insight into the personal and professional impact of UR. Collecting stories of alumni would shed more light on the transfer of research skills to other disciplines, workplace, communities, and the development of a capacity for lifelong learning. While case studies like the one of the RWF provide insight into isolated opportunities of UR, it is only through more formal impact research that we will be able to secure bigger and more sustained institutional support.

A Reflection on Chapter 7

Institutional Support for Investigating the Impact of Undergraduate Research in Writing

Jenn Fishman

In response to this chapter's call to action, my own first act is to concur. I agree that we must not only cultivate but also strategically marshal support for undergraduate research (UR) in writing from different institutions, including not only our campuses and national professional organizations but also our journals and archives, our community partners, and our private sponsors (i.e., businesses, foundations). I also appreciate the authors' suggestions regarding mapping and relationship building, and I endorse the formation of a UR Network. As a participant in and leader of UR efforts sponsored by the Conference on College Composition and Communication (CCCC) and the Rhetoric Society of America (RSA), I see great need as well as desire for the increased connectivity a UR Network promises. As a scholar who has written and edited works explicitly concerned with research methods and circulation, I also recognize our collective need and desire to "showcase pertinent scholarship about the impact of undergraduate research in our field." However, as a writing researcher, I believe we will benefit even more if the UR Network helps us not only publicize the impact of UR in Writing Studies but also build our capacity to study it.

To this end, let's take the actions this chapter suggests. Let's commit to mapping our campuses and discovering present and future resources for investigating impact. Along with writing programs and centers, let's canvass additional units, including departments, colleges, and schools where writing is studied. Let's also partner with offices of institutional research and colleagues tasked with self-study for other purposes (i.e., reaccreditation) to discover who engages in UR in our field and how they fare. Likewise, let's marshal our national professional organizations and their capacity for impact inquiries. The CCCC Committee on Undergraduate Research (active since 2011) has conducted member surveys in 2013 and 2020, and in 2015 the committee also advocated successfully for collecting registration data from undergraduates who participate in the annual convention. In the future, a UR Network could coordinate similar efforts across organizations. As a result, we could learn actively about UR across Writing Studies, discovering gaps in our knowledge as well as sites and partners for future collaborations.

We need to make concerted efforts to study the impact of UR in our discipline, and we need institutions that support them. A UR Network represents a way forward. It will enable us to extend discussions begun at the Naylor Symposium, particularly discussions about the importance of diversity in where, when, and how UR is practiced and studied. A UR Network will also enable us to develop an ethics for impact research, including guidelines for working with undergraduates as co-researchers and models for adopting and, where appropriate, adapting strategies that writing scholars already use to prevent the misrepresentation of the writers whom they study. Above all, a UR Network will enhance our ability to come together as a community of practice so that we can regularly deliberate priorities, share protocols and data, and circulate findings in a variety of ways.[1] By doing so, we will be better able to conduct robust and multi-perspectival assessments of the impact UR is having, and we will enrich our ability to communicate with others, whether students first learning to see themselves as researchers, cross-disciplinary colleagues, or higher education policy makers.

Ten years ago, Laurie Grobman opened discussion about UR as a pedagogical movement (2009a). Scholars who study social movements typically identify four stages of development, which extend from initiation and early growth to formalization and, ultimately, transformation into a social institution (Christiansen 2009). If the same is true of educational movements, then this chapter along with the Naylor Report and the wealth of activities it indexes confirms that the third stage, the formalization of UR in Writing Studies, is well underway. Typically, social movements at this stage establish an official organization, and so it is fitting for one of our next steps to be the founding of a UR Network.

---

1. At the Naylor Symposium, these priorities for studying the impact of UR in writing emerged through intensive discussion with Heather B. Adams, Lilijana Coklin, and Enrique Paz.

May the support it provides include robust resources for investigating the impact of UR in our discipline and for engaging in related, consequential conversations both within and beyond our field.

Afterword

Being Bold: Undergraduate Research in Writing Studies

Joyce Kinkead

In this Afterword, I honor several bold moves within Writing Studies and undergraduate research (UR) and also add my voice in looking to the future. The focus to *The Naylor Report* is to put writing itself at the center of study and research. I concur. Too often, we focus almost exclusively on writing as academic writing. We should boldly look at writing writ large.

My enlightenment about the enormous impact of writing across time and place first dawned when my anthropologist husband offered a course on the Origins of Writing. I realized that I was largely ignorant about what Charles Bazerman (2002) calls the "large, important, and multi-dimensional story of writing" in his essay "The Case for Writing Studies as a Major Discipline" (33). Over the last two years, I have traveled around the globe to visit sites of historic importance to writing and museums that exhibit artifacts. Cuneiform clay tablets, oracle bones from China, chained books, printing presses, quill pens, and hand-made paper are just a few examples of the material culture that have defined writing through the ages.

Others are looking at writing in this way. Laura R. Micciche, writing in *The Atlantic*'s Object Lessons series, examines seventeenth- and eighteenth-century writing boxes in "Writers Have Always Loved Mobile Devices." The goal is to uncover the "hidden lives of ordinary things," and I daresay that much about writing is taken for granted, simply because it is so ubiquitous and integrated in our daily lives. Our students often see writing in ways that we do not. I think of my research methods students who are curious to investigate the rise of expensive hand-written calligraphy on wedding invitations or the effect of laptops-for-all programs in secondary schools on the quality and quantity of writing. As teachers and researchers, we can expose them to the long story of writing through the ages and also engage them in important contemporary questions.

Laying the Groundwork

Undergraduate research has been a part of higher education for a long, long time, predating the founding of the Council of Undergraduate Research (CUR) in 1978 and the National Conference on Undergraduate Research (NCUR) in 1987. As early as 1912, the University of Chicago handed out awards to students engaged in UR (Kinkead 2012). And what about the history of Writing Studies? Although Harvard inaugurated the first required writing courses in higher education in the 1870s, it was not until the 1960s–1970s when research in English, funded nationally, began to focus on the cognitive process of composing. Before then, writing classes emphasized mechanistic approaches and relied heavily on literary texts. A paradigm shift changed the instructional approach from product to process. Writing centers became commonplace on college campuses. In the 1990s, standalone programs and departments in Writing Studies began to appear fueled by a CCCC address by Maxine Hairston (1985). As several chapters in this report note, rhetoric and composition gained disciplinary status in the late twentieth century, although a clear starting date is debated. The National Census on Writing has gathered data from hundreds of these departments and programs.

By the turn of the millennium, an increasing number of undergraduate degrees in Writing Studies (under a variety of names) appeared. As with almost every subject area, the focus on inquiry and research came to the fore and made significant impact on curricular decisions as well as policy and practice locally and nationally. The Naylor Workshop anticipated the demand for increased attention to UR in Writing Studies and provided a home for incubating and mentoring these activities, increasingly drawing students from the national and even international landscape. The fifth annual convening drew on expertise among faculty to pause, reflect, analyze, and look to the future. This volume is testament to that symposium. It is yet another bold move to solidify what has come before and to take an activist and forward-looking view.

Allow me to offer a quick summary of UR initiatives in Writing Studies that has led to this moment. In 2003, Laurie Grobman and the late Candace Spiegelman fearlessly created *Young Scholars in Writing: Undergraduate Research in Rhetoric and Writing*. The peer-reviewed journal publishes high-quality work and is guided by the beliefs that "research can and should be a crucial component of rhetorical education and that undergraduates engaged in research about writing and rhetoric should have opportunities to share their work with a broader audience of students, scholars, and teachers through national publication." In volume 5 of *YSW*, a section dedicated to scholarship produced in first-year writing classes was added.

Professionals in the field increasingly have turned to UR in Writing Studies as the subject of their work. Amy Robillard's article in *College English* (2006) suggested that UR has the potential to transform how compositionists conduct research. The following year, Laurie Grobman argued in a *CCC* article, "The Student Scholar: (Re)Negotiating Authorship and Authority," that by viewing UR production and authorship along a continuum of scholarly authority, student scholars obtain *authorship* and *authority* through participation in research, and she addressed several implications of this continuum for the discipline. *Undergraduate Research in English Studies* (Grobman and Kinkead 2010), which includes descriptions of projects from across the nation, has been called "trailblazing."

Grobman, an astounding activist in the service of UR and community-based research, proposed to CCCC the establishment of a Task Force on Undergraduate Research in Composition and Rhetoric; it met first in 2010, evolving to committee status along with a Special Interest Group (SIG). The group produced a *Position Statement on Undergraduate Research in Writing: Principles and Best Practices* (2017). In 2012, Jessie L. Moore organized the first UR poster session at CCCC, a conference for which this medium was largely unfamiliar. Moore's home institution, Elon University, has hosted important summer workshops in faculty development that have explored topics such as mentorship through its Center for Engaged Learning. The multidisciplinary journal, *Perspectives on Undergraduate Research and Mentoring (PURM)*, launched in 2011.

Other journals dedicated to student researchers have appeared: *TheJUMP: The Journal for Undergraduate Multimedia Projects* (founded 2010; rebranded *TheJUMP+* in 2017); *Xchanges*, a student journal in technical communication (founded 2001); *The Oswald Review* (for criticism and research in English, founded 2003); *Queen City Writers* (for all English fields, founded 2012); and *RhetTech* (for rhetoric and technical communication, founded 2018-2019). Some professional journals have made space specifically for undergraduate researchers. *Kairos* dedicated an issue to undergraduate scholars in writing and rhetoric in 2011. A year later, *The Writing Center Journal* devoted a special issue to "Peer Tutors and the Conversation of Writing Center Studies: An Undergraduate Research Issue." Likewise, textbooks that feature instruction in research methods have been published. Lauren Fitzgerald and Melissa Ianetta's *The Oxford Guide for Writing Tutors* includes a robust section on conducting research. (See also Fitzgerald, "Undergraduate Research in Writing Studies.") Kinkead's *Researching Writing: An Introduction to Research Methods* (2015) is the first methods book specifically targeting undergraduates. The 4th edition of Wardle and Downs's textbook *Writing about Writing* (2019) includes a primer on research methods, indicative of the growing interest in authentic research at all levels.

This catalog of innovation and advancement over the last twenty-plus years tracks the advancement of UR throughout all campuses and disciplines, spurred by the Boyer Report, *Reinventing Undergraduate Education: A Blueprint for America's Research Universities*; George Kuh's work on high-impact educational practices; and AAC&U's LEAP initiative. Whew! It's an exciting time. Undergraduate education truly has been reinvented with an increased commitment to students and their development. As the Boyer report proclaimed, "inquiry, investigation, and discovery are at the heart of the enterprise" (1998, 9).

What Next?

The authors in this volume lay out recommendations to move ahead and advance the state of UR in Writing Studies. These intentional strategies will help institutionalize UR in academic programs and professional organizations. The case is clear: student research, undertaken collaboratively or independently, may take many forms and provide new insights. The field can be strengthened by student research that adds to the scholarly knowledge base. I add that mentoring such researchers and scholars can be one of the most rewarding facets of a faculty member's career. I know that is true for my own career, which has stretched over forty years.

Readers responding to these recommendations may find themselves evolving in their approaches to undertaking student inquiry. Certainly, my own thinking about engaging students in authentic research has matured over the decades. I have administered writing centers, a writing fellows program, and a vertically-sequenced university writing program. The power of students engaging in real writing for real audiences hit home during the seminar for writing fellows that I created and taught in the early 1990s. A qualitative difference in their final projects became manifestly clear when I asked them to write a "Tutor's Column" for the *Writing Lab Newsletter*. They were lively and thoughtful, such as the column by a nontraditional student who wrote about tutoring students similar to her and their challenges (Hirschi 1996). Another Fellow took on a collaborative research project to investigate the architecture of writing centers (Hadfield, et al. 2003).

That early experience with students conducting authentic inquiry contributed to my own growth as a teacher and scholar of UR. For the last few years, I've taught a full-on research methods class that requires students to see a project from concept to completion. We scaffold their independent projects by beginning with a whole-class project (described in Kinkead 2019). During one semester, the class members focused on the Blue Book, the long-standing format used for essay examinations (Duersch et al., 2019); in another, they analyzed more than three hundred syllabi that had been approved as Communication Intensive (Kinkead 2018); in yet another, they compiled a history of writing at the institution from 1890 to the present day to be housed in university archives. These group projects allow students to practice using various research tools: interviews, surveys; graphics that depict quantitative data, and an IRB proposal. Their individual projects have been accepted to the campus UR day, our State Capitol research event, and state and national UR conferences. As one of my students from this immersive, intensive class said of her transformational experience, "I see research questions everywhere now."

In addition to my role as a faculty member in Writing Studies, I have also served as a dean, a vice provost for undergraduate education, a director of university undergraduate research, and a councilor of the Council on Undergraduate Research (CUR). In each of these roles, I came to understand the enormous value of public relations, communications, and fundraising. This Naylor Report helps tell our story.

Our collective goal is to offer students "opportunities to learn through inquiry rather than simple transmission of knowledge" (Boyer 1998, 10). As the editors of this report underscore, UR in Writing Studies also reflects "our field's constant striving to contribute to the public good." At the heart of the UR initiative is the belief that engaging in this activity means that students graduate with skill in problem-solving, communication, teamwork, and a deep curiosity as well as an increased capacity to contribute to civil society. We help them map their journey of discovery through reflective work that also reveals to them how the attributes that they have added or enhanced to their portfolio have also led to increased employability, further educational study, and greater participation in the world around them.

We expect students to make big gains in all aspects of their knowledge and skills through active participation. For students in first-year writing programs, transfer of skills is essential. They should depart with behaviors that adapt to their disciplinary field. Be bold enough to recognize the possibility of first year students—whether in FYW or a program for majors—producing work that is of a quality for circulation or dissemination. Think of the confident move of *YSW* to include a Spotlight on First-Year Writing students.

Students seeking certification and expertise in Writing Studies should encounter increasingly sophisticated research tasks that are carefully mapped onto the curriculum. I concur with the Boyer Report and this Naylor Report that immersion in meaningful inquiry must begin with the first year. Engaging in UR must not simply be a capstone or Honors experience. It's only by going through the entire research process that a student can proclaim, "I am a researcher." Certainly, not all products will be worthy of circulation as research findings or what report authors call "discovered stories." But some certainly will be, while UR will also yield valuable "stories of discovery" or narratives about conducting research that underscore a truism: it is the *doing* that matters. It is an essential step on the pathway to becoming a competent researcher—what Grobman called making progress on the continuum of becoming a scholar (2009a, 177). As Kuh (2008) found, research is a high-impact educational practice that makes a qualitative difference in an undergraduate's experience.

Finally, some additional aspects to consider for undertaking research in Writing Studies. Echoing the authors of chapter 2, I urge readers to embrace both humanistic and social scientific approaches, along with emerging, multi-disciplinary methods for digital inquiry. This is how I ask the students in my research methods course to approach their questions. Archival research or textual analysis draws on our humanities legacy while the case study and ethnography borrow from other fields. Often a mixed methods approach reveals dimensions that the researcher had not considered. As engaged and active citizens, students may work with people as "human subjects" (the Federal term), which requires training in responsible conduct of research (RCR) to protect the rights of participants, particularly vulnerable populations. Likewise, I hope readers will welcome quantitative analysis and the graphic visualization of data into their repertoires. A simple activity introducing descriptive statistics, such as keeping a log of all writing over a week, reveals to students what tasks they invest in, such as the person who counted over 1400 text messages within that time period. It also helps them consider how work can be quantified: volume, time, instances. Turning these data on a spreadsheet into charts or graphs then reveals the power of graphic depiction. As researchers, we want to employ and interrogate the evidence to develop replicable, aggregable, and data-supported (RAD) evidence that can bolster results and appeal to a broader audience. As teachers and mentors, we must not only be statistics skeptics; we must also teach undergraduate researchers to collect and deploy quantitative data both intentionally and ethically. We can think of numbers as a language that helps communicate research results.

Building a Culture of Undergraduate Research

We must not only engage in teaching and researching in Writing Studies with our students, but we must build a culture of UR that permeates the profession. The authors of this report have made this case, emphasizing the importance of creating an inclusive culture that affords all students and all Writing Studies educators an opportunity to participate. The UR Network proposed in chapter 7 is a step we can take together toward this goal. We can also tell our stories, employing the power of narrative. I'm fond of saying, "If it's not written, it didn't happen." Documenting our work through print, visual, and oral modes is essential.

With expertise in communication, we and our students have the power to tell the stories of UR in Writing Studies, bringing attention to students, their contributions, and their mentors. We should not forget the importance of telling our stories to each other. Graduate students and colleagues, whether faculty or staff, need to know what UR in our field has to offer. However, our prime audience is students themselves. They may initially have naïve notions of research and its role in Writing Studies. However, a culture of UR can make research as well as students' work as researchers visible and concrete. The many examples featured in this report remind us that stories of UR can be told on bulletin boards, digital venues, admissions brochures, newsletters, blogs, campus newspapers, radio stations, social media, and many other places. At every turn, students can be partners in telling these stories. In every instance, we should look to our own students for insight and production; we should also look for opportunities to partner with them as coauthors, co-editors, and co-designers. We should also become partners with our institution's public relations and development units and help them see stories of UR in Writing Studies as university assets with high value.

This report is not only an account of UR in our discipline but also an effort to advance it. As such, it can be read as a handbook, the recommendations included in each chapter forming a guide to cultivating UR in disparate educational spaces. The Institutional Inventory that follows (in Appendix A) provides an additional resource: an instrument for analyzing how a campus includes UR in its faculty roles and reward structures, what funding opportunities exist for student inquiry, and what awards are given for achievement. To continue building a culture of UR in our field, we can conduct such inventories on our campuses. We can develop course-based UR experiences (CUREs) as well as independent research projects. We can create opportunities for students to work with and learn from faculty, and we can create partnerships that bring together undergraduates, graduate students, faculty, and staff to learn from each other. Working together, within and across our campuses, we can enact projects for the good of our communities and our world.

IMPACT WRIT LARGE

The authors in this volume have no doubt about the transformational potential for students who engage in authentic research that adds to our knowledge base. They are not only staunch advocates for UR; they also offer clear evidence that there has been a sea change over the last twenty years in how undergraduates are viewed as *knowledge makers*. In Writing Studies, those experiences should be accessible to all, extending from first-year composition courses to Writing Studies degree programs and writing across the curriculum.

Scaling up UR in Writing Studies and engaging a more diverse and inclusive group of practitioners is the goal of *The Naylor Report*. Let's recall that the study of writing occurs in multiple places. On one hand, this is much in evidence in this volume, from lower-division writing courses (typically required for general education) to writing-centric degree programs. That's good news. On the other hand, research on writing is not limited to any one curriculum or campus location. Writing is a hallmark of our culture. It is not something we are born with but must learn, starting with honing the fine motor skills required for using writing implements. The subject of writing is enormous and complex. We can boldly engage with this topic on many, many levels; we can leverage campus partnerships to address the complexity of our topics from multiple disciplinary perspectives; and, we can borrow from other disciplines to improve our own practices.

Enacting UR initiatives in Writing Studies has the potential for exciting results. I commend the participants in the 2018 Naylor Symposium, endorse recommendations they make, applaud data collection and assessment of our various UR activities, and anticipate the impact of this significant and important report.

Appendix A: A Guide for Assessing Institutional Support for Undergraduate Research

Chapter 7 of this collection suggests ways to move beyond the "nip and tuck" approach to supporting undergraduate research (UR), and the entire collection focuses upon developing a sustainable, cohesive, structured, accessible, and equitable program for UR. Since local conditions can provide both opportunities and challenges, the first stage of that planning is often a self-study to produce an inventory of available, and needed, resources.

This document is meant to act as a heuristic for undertaking that self-study. Based on the needs identified throughout this collection, this document can guide program leaders in this process. Beginning with some fundamental, team-building questions, this document suggests key areas of inquiry that can help you determine the feasibility of a program of UR in Writing Studies. Individuals and program teams can customize the action steps and questions below to their local conditions.

One crucial and overarching point to remember: You are looking for units and individuals who will also benefit by supporting your efforts in UR. Think of it as enlightened self-interest and the search for a framing rhetorical situation. Advancement professionals are looking to raise funds—you can help them do that. Your Communications division is looking for good stories to advance the name of the institution—you have many. Enrollment divisions are seeking selling points for students—and UR can be that. Rather than see your role as just seeking institutional support, see your role as providing it in return for the resources you need to do that work. And always remember to do this work proudly, remembering the central reminder of chapter 7: *Resources are not gifts; they are what we need to do our jobs.*

I. GETTING STARTED
   A) **Build a Leadership Team**
      - *Invite Collaboration.* Who are the current and/or potential "champions" of UR in Writing Studies (and perhaps in related fields)? What are they doing already that can form a base from which to work? Where are there opportunities for interdisciplinary collaborations?

   B) **Assess Institutional Contexts and Conditions**
      - *Locate and share your institution's mission with the team.* What specific parts of the college mission align with your leadership team's goals and provide opportunities for alignment with UR efforts? How does the institution characterize its learning goals for students, and how can those goals be advanced by UR? What kinds of initiatives tend to be supported/funded by your administrators? What common elements emerge from that list?
      - *Locate and share your institution's most recent strategic plan.* What parts of the institutional plan align with your writing program goals and provide opportunities for alignment with UR efforts? What parts of the plan are supported by financial and/or human resources? You might also consult results from the National Survey of Student Engagement (NSSE) if your institution participates.
      - *What current internal or external conditions affect budgeting decisions at your institution?* What financial opportunities and threats are communicated from upper- and mid-level administrators, especially those related to your writing program? Consider institutional goals for recruitment, retention, advancing high-impact practices, career placement, fund-raising, diversifying, and so on that might align with the goals of an UR program in Writing Studies.
      - *What changes (or desired changes) might you observe in your student body?* In what ways might the kinds of "consequential" research done in Writing Studies support those students?
      - *What institutional units seem to have been most successful in receiving needed resources?* Are there any areas of shared mission or potential partnerships with those units that could also align with UR efforts in Writing Studies?

II. WRITING PROGRAM ADMINISTRATION AND STRUCTURE

A) Inventory and Map Curricular and Co-curricular Spaces

- *Name as many curricular locations where writing is taught at your institution as you can.* (Consider locations such as FYW, WAC/WID/WEC, upper division writing, majors, minors, writing centers (WC), discipline-specific writing programs). Seek information about the source and relative stability of institutional support for each, especially as it might support UR. What administrative structure is in place for each initiative or program? To whom do faculty administrators report? What committees govern or advise how writing is taught?
- *Describe and/or draw a map of your "writing program" as it is seen by those outside the program.* Would it be recognized as a single program, or are courses distributed across several administrative units/departments? Chart the channels of communication across the various pieces of the institution's "writing program," as well as silos where units fail to communicate. It is often best to represent this visually.
- *Describe or map the ways that students encounter writing opportunities (especially those that could support UR efforts) on your campus.* What resources and/or constraints exist for students in finding time, opportunities, motivation, and support for UR? Where in your program might students encounter disciplinary research methods?
- *Describe the staffing model of key divisions.* For example, since writing centers often generate many research opportunities, you might your document the level and areas of scholarly expertise and involvement in writing center disciplinary activity, as well as types of tutors (peer, graduate student, professional, interdisciplinary, intersectional) that serve there. In addition, you might:
    ◦ Describe the degree to which other faculty are engaged with peer tutors.
    ◦ Describe your tutor training model (required for-credit course, workshops, etc.), considering the degree to which the course/workshop discusses (or might discuss) scholarly work and methods?

- Describe any formal or informal occasions for tutors and mentors to discuss possible research projects. If none exist, envision how those occasions could be created.
- Describe existing budget lines for tutor professional development, including conference travel and/or presentation. If budgets exist, describe how those budgets are used, and/or how they might be used to support UR.

Consider how this model could be customized, depending upon local conditions, for other apt programs such as FYW (especially with Writing about Writing), WAC, Service Learning, etc.

B) **Inventory Policies and Procedures Governing Labor and Reward**
- *Create a spreadsheet showing individuals who teach writing, their job titles and current ranks, and their working conditions.* Create a full list of the "Writing Faculty" that goes beyond the official list. Consider, for example, WAC/WID/WEC courses, writing center personnel, faculty in other disciplines that teach writing, etc. Consider a variety of possible taxonomies: required educational background, disciplinary/department identification, contract status, teaching load variances, the types of degrees and training faculty have in the field (English, Rhetoric and Composition/Writing Studies, Communication, etc.). To what degree do human resources mirror and/or support the diversity of the student body? Where are there areas of need to support full access to UR?
- *Research and describe how the reward system differs for each group in the spreadsheet above.* Describe the expectations for teaching load for each group of faculty, considering needs for course releases, stipends, and/or course cap adjustments. Describe the processes that govern course scheduling and teaching load management. Include who has the authority to offer course re-assignments, reduced course caps for special initiatives such as UR, etc.?
- *Describe the degree to which your institution recognizes and provides incentives for teaching and mentoring undergraduate research in annual reviews, pre-tenure, and tenure and promotion materials.* Seek both explicit and implicit statements that recognize UR and mentoring, noting where those implicit statements might be made more explicit for all levels of faculty. Describe the service expectations/opportunities that exist and/or are encouraged at

the program, departmental, school, and institutional level, considering levels of faculty inventoried in the previous section. List points of alignment between these service expectations and/or opportunities to support undergraduate research in Writing Studies. The suggestions below show how you might approach this for different groups of faculty:
- *Inventory and show the value of the labor that supports UR. More specifically,*

For Program administrators and other academic staff, inventory and make visible their labor:

- Name the writing administrators and staff at your institution, including program directors or coordinators, writing center staff, and others.
- Name the responsibilities of those individuals, to whom they report, how their work is supported with financial and course release benefits, and their own involvement in intellectual work in the field.
- List ways in which the leaders and academic staff in the program might draw upon existing duties, connections, and available resources to support undergraduate research in Writing Studies.
- Consider ways that contracts articulate the value of supporting undergraduate research, or absent that, how they could;
- Review the expectations for teaching excellence at your institution and find points of alignment (or potential alignment) with work in mentoring undergraduate research.
- Describe the degree to which co-authoring and/or co-presenting with student researchers is valued (or not).

For tenure-track and tenured faculty, seek sites of alignment with labor related to UR within:

- Institutional expectations for teaching, service, and scholarship;
- Departmental expectations for teaching, service, and scholarship;
- Annual review policies and expectations;

- Pre-tenure review procedures and expectations;
- Structure of Tenure and Promotion applications.

For full-time continuing contract faculty (NTT, Visiting Positions, Teaching Track faculty, Lecturers, etc.), seek sites of alignment with labor related to UR within:

- Institutional expectations for teaching, service, and (when applicable) scholarship, especially as related to renewal and advancement;
- Departmental expectations for teaching, service, and scholarship especially as related to renewal and advancement;
- Annual review policies and expectations especially as related to renewal, advancement, and salary adjustments.
- Access to funding for travel, course releases, internal grants, etc.

For part-time and adjunct faculty seek sites of alignment with labor related to UR within:

- Departmental expectations for, definitions of, excellence in teaching;
- Departmental support or reward for part-time faculty who mentor students;
- Institutional or departmental support made available to part-time faculty for conference travel and scholarship, as well as internal grants.
- Inclusion of part-time faculty in departmental events, faculty development, department or program meetings, committees, etc.

III. LOCATE UR IN WRITING STUDIES WITHIN BROADER INSTITUTIONAL CONTEXTS

- *List other units or individuals who are stakeholders and/or decision-makers in curricular decisions for each part of your "writing program" writ large* (consider using the map you created earlier). Focus upon stakeholders who would benefit by an enriched UR program and what resources might they offer.
- *Name the (tangible) ways that your institution supports high-impact educational practices.* List sources of funds are available (eg., faculty development funds, internal grants, course-releases) to de-

velop curricular innovation. Consider how those resources and guidelines for using them might intersect with the UR in Writing Studies.(See Kuh's *High-Impact Educational Practices: What They Are, Who Has Access to Them, and Why They Matter* for a complete list.)

- *If your institution has a writing center or writing tutors within a larger unit (i.e., Center for Student Success), describe the administrative and funding structure of that center as related to the broader institution.* For example, is it part of the writing program, academic support, office of student retention, etc.? Describe the external administrative structures that set the WC agenda and their priorities. In what ways can UR serve those priorities?
- *List the committees or offices on campus that regularly support or interact with undergraduate research work.* Consider, for example, curriculum committees, promotion and tenure committees, honors programs, etc.
- *List events (UR presentations, showcases, enrollment events) that your institution sponsors,* and for which faculty might serve as planners to be sure UR in Writing Studies is included.
- *List ways that research and inquiry in FYW supports stated goals of General Education in both internal and external documents* (such as accreditation reviews and strategic plans), and how an emphasis on UR in Writing Studies serves those goals.
- *Research and list the types of institutional resources that might advance UR in Writing Studies*—faculty development funds, student showcases, curricular innovation funds, speakers or visiting experts. Research the pools of funds or other faculty support (course releases, faculty development, speakers, etc.) that exist beyond department or program resources that could support UR in Writing Studies enacted in required, upper division writing courses.
- *Work on framing possible arguments for upper administrators.* For example,
    - The FYW program generates "X" FTE hours, and its per-student cost of delivering credit hours is "Y." (Often, this is a very favorable metric).
    - NSSE suggests students need access to more high-impact practices involving writing.

- ° FYW assessment data demonstrates how UR in Writing Studies advances institutional goals for undergraduate research, and that further funding can provide a high return on investment.
- ° Our FYW program forms a bridge into higher-level inquiry and thinking, making support of UR is instrumental in the following ways. . . .
- ° Students' work in UR has tangibly supported students' recruitment and/or retention within in a writing-related major, enhancement of career skills, or acceptance into graduate programs by . . . .
- *Research the kinds of UR that is being conducted in other disciplines.* Find points of intersection with topics in Writing Studies (considering the capacious and consequential forms of research discussed in this book)—eg., through rhetoric of science, marketing communication, civic and community engagement, project-based learning.
- *Seek information on the disciplines at your institution that command solid resources for generating UR*—both for its production and its circulation. Align with goals for UR in Writing Studies. Locate faculty in other disciplines that might advocate for UR that links Writing Studies with disciplinary knowledge.

IV. EXPLORE AND ESTABLISH POTENTIAL RELATIONSHIPS FOR INSTITUTIONAL SUPPORT

 A) **Advancement Office**
- *Research the personnel in Advancement.* Who has a record of advocating for UR, Writing Studies, or work in the Humanities generally? (Hint: Have a look at their CVs—you'll often find individuals with Liberal Arts backgrounds.)
- *Research the institution's recent and longtime donors and/or have a conversation with Advancement personnel about possible prospects.* Provide a list of outcomes that can help them envision potential donors.
- *Consider naming opportunities* (writing research lab, endowed professorships, etc.) Remember that Advancement officers are always looking for such opportunities to find opportunities that interest untapped donors—so ask them if they know of prospects.

- Offer to present to the Advancement team about success stories in UR and/or invite them to your events.

B) **Office of Communications.**
- *What kinds of stories about impact* might resonate with the institution's public relations efforts? What success stories can you tell about students to highlight on the college website or in publications?
- *How does UR demonstrate the kinds of faculty/student relationships* that your institution tends to highlight? In what other ways does UR serve the institutional mission?
- *How can you feature UR examples* that resonate with mission? How could you tell their stories for the website or alumni magazine.
- *How might you feature successful alumni* who benefited by UR in Writing Studies?
- *What press releases might you write* about student projects, presentations, publications, etc.?

C) **Human Resources**
- *How are decisions made about how job advertisements are written and search teams formed?* Consider department level as well as higher administration input, and ways that mentoring can be included in job ads/job descriptions.
- *What policy documents exist that govern hiring?* What language in those policies can be correlated with your goals for undergraduate research?
- *How can diversity initiatives support broad access to UR opportunities?* What language is needed?
- *What is the process for revising hiring standards?* How might advocates for UR find their way into these processes?

D) **Offices of Enrollment Management and Financial Aid.**
- *What are key recruiting strategies and messaging?* If possible, obtain and read marketing plans, then align with the goals of UR. In what ways can UR be framed in ways that fit Enrollment Management strategies?
- *How might aid that is given as part of recruitment effort be tied to support for UR? Can specific scholarships be established for UR in Writing Studies?* Keep in mind that funds that are used to attract students can often be earmarked for specific initiatives without

additional budget needed; you can target funds already allocated for these efforts.
- *What kinds of activities might you create for open houses and other recruitment events that highlight UR?* How might you involve successful students in these efforts? For example, an institution scheduled its UR showcase during a college open house, then collected reactions of parents.
- How might student presentations at conferences of publications become a recruiting tool?
- What kinds of "consequential" research can show the college's engagement with the local community?

E) **Office of Undergraduate Research**
- *Does a specific office of UR exist,* and if not, is there an administrative division that has funds and resources for this work?
- *Consult faculty in other disciplines* (especially the sciences) to see how their efforts are supported and funded.

F) **Community Service, Community Engagement, and Project-based Learning**
- *What challenges does your local community face?* What are its points of pride? What kinds of UR might lend support to those challenges and/or highlight community assets through the kinds of "consequential" research discussed in this collection?
- *What kinds of Writing Studies UR can support community service initiatives?*
- *What for-profit industry exists in the area?* How might UR in Writing Studies serve the needs of those industries through individual projects or course-based project base learning?
- *What are the demographics of your community?* How are they changing? What kinds of research on literacy, for example, might support the community in addressing those changes? What governmental agencies of NGOs might have need our disciplinary research?

As this document makes clear, the process of finding institutional support for UR in Writing Studies requires building a base of institutional knowledge, locating the work of UR in Writing Studies within broader institutional and community contexts, and building arguments that align this work with institutional priorities. In many cases, untapped funding and support mechanisms already exist; as a rule of thumb, it is usually easier to access existing budget lines and work within existing structures than to ask for new ones, especially in our current age of austerity.

In all, it is important to remember that self-study is the first step to building and sustaining institutional support for UR in Writing Studies. Alignment is also a crucial tactic, so look for institutional partners that will benefit in some way by becoming champions of UR in our discipline. Along the way, consider the value of benchmarking your institution in relation to referent (e.g., peer, aspirational) schools, and consider securing outside consultants from one or more of those institutions. As the UR Network proposed in chapter 7 develops, a UR consultant evaluator service may become available. The Council on Undergraduate Research can also be a useful resource.

Appendix B: Available Resources for Undergraduate Research in Writing Studies

While this appendix makes no claim to be exhaustive in its presentation of some of the organizations that have advanced the work of UR in Writing Studies, it does provide an overview of some of the many resources that exist and can help us to consider ways that our work could be further networked. As the Network for UR in Writing Studies develops, it will become resource for continuously gathering and updating this kind of information.

Promoting Faculty Research and Scholarship

The Association of Rhetoric and Writing Studies serves all teachers and scholars in rhetoric and writing, especially those affiliated with stand-alone departments and programs. Founded to "to encourage inquiry and experimentation in the teaching of rhetoric and writing" and "to identify and support new areas of inquiry that need to be explored," it stands to be a strong ally to the UR Network.

The Coalition for Community Writing, founded in 2018, brings together students, teachers, academic administrators, and community members from across the country and around the world to build capacity for community writing work, including UR.

The Coalition of Feminist Scholars in the History of Rhetoric and Composition offers feminist undergraduates and graduate students as well as colleagues of all ranks and roles a professional home. A potentially powerful ally to the UR Network, the CFSHRC has hosted mentoring tables on UR, and its journal, *Peitho*, and its biennial conference, Feminists and Rhetorics, offer regular opportunities for circulating consequential research.

The Conference on College Composition and Communication (CCCC) has emerged as a leader in promoting UR in the discipline, largely through its Standing Committee on Undergraduate Research and the annual Undergraduate Researcher Poster Session.

The Council of Writing Program Administrators (CWPA) is a potential ally to which the Network can provide support as the central advocate for program administrators, equitable labor conditions, development of learning outcomes, and articulation of the intellectual work of program administration.

The Council on Undergraduate Research "supports and promotes high-quality undergraduate student-faculty collaborative research and scholarship." While this organization is membership-driven and multi-disciplinary, UR Network can coordinate efforts with this crucial national organization to promote the place of Writing Studies research as part of larger national efforts.

Dartmouth's Institute for Writing and Rhetoric: As this Institute promotes "systematic or replicable inquiry in response to a research question that can generate interpretable data," NURWS can help to coordinate research teams to attend this Institute and work together to produce such data—data that can then be used on individual campuses and toward grant and philanthropic opportunities.

Elon University's Center for Engaged Learning, as part of its mission, "brings together international leaders in higher education to develop and to synthesize rigorous research on central questions about student learning." It has sponsored a Research Seminar devoted "Excellence in Mentoring Undergraduate Research" which continues to breed important scholarly activity.

The Rhetoric Society of America regularly includes sessions on UR at its biennial conferences, and it has hosted both research networks for undergraduate researchers and workshops for mentors.

SIGDOC is the Association for Computing Machinery's Special Interest Group (SIG) on Design of Communication (DOC). The Undergraduate Division of SIGDOC hosts an annual student research competition for undergraduate researchers. The SIG also maintains a database of research and teaching tools.

Promoting Student Learning of Disciplinary Research Methods

The **Naylor Workshop on Undergraduate Research in Writing Studies** was designed to fill the gap between efforts to support disciplinary research methods on individual campuses and national venues for presentation and publication of student scholarship. It helps students to place their work within ongoing scholarship and to learn methods of research that are well-suited to their topic of study.

The Conference on College Composition and Communication's Annual Convention provides an annual poster session and "various forms of support for undergraduates attending the convention."

The International Writing Centers Association (IWCA) and The **National Conference on Peer Tutoring in Writing (NCPTW)** have long fostered undergraduate contributions to writing center scholarship.

Appendix C: Conference on College Composition and Communication Position Statement on Undergraduate Research in Writing: Principles and Best Practices and Bibliography

Originally published in March 2017 by the Conference on College Composition and Communication, this position statement was authored by Jenn Fishman and Jane Greer with Dominic DelliCarpini, Doug Downs, Laurie Grobman, Jonathan Hunt, Joyce Kinkead, and Jessie Moore. The following colleagues contributed feedback: Hillarie Ashton, Dev Bose, Gay Brookes, Julie Christoph, Janine Chitty, Randall Cream, Marion Dillahunt, Bradley Dilger, Jeremiah Dyehouse, Jessica Enoch, Jason Esters, Leonard Ferry, Sergio Figueiredo, William Garrett-Petts, Cristina Hanganu-Bresch, Lyra Hilliard, Anne Kozak, Brian Larson, Benjamin Lauren, Laura Mangini, Ben McCorkle, Deborah Mutnick, Patricia Nereim, Cornelia Paraskevas, Steven Price, John Pruitt, Jim Purdy, Cristina Ramirez, Clancy Ratliff, Shelley Reid, Veronica Richard, Bryna Siegel, Glenn Southergill, Rachel Stumpf, Howard Tinberg, Janice Walker, Shane Wood, and at least three anonymous commentators.

Executive Summary

Undergraduate research is a widely recognized, high-impact educational practice that offers student researchers and their mentors unique opportunities to engage in shared, discipline-based intellectual inquiry. For undergraduate research in writing studies and rhetoric to flourish at two- and four-year institutions, whether it is embedded in curricula or located in co- and extracurricular opportunities, it must be well-defined and well-supported by relevant campus units (e.g., departments, programs, campus policies) and by the allocation of available campus resources.

Introduction

Part educational movement, part curricular innovation, undergraduate research is now widely recognized as a "high-impact educational practice":[1] a method of teaching and learning known to substantially benefit students from a variety of backgrounds across a range of instructional contexts, including curricular, co-curricular, and extracurricular activities. On one hand, undergraduate research in all subject areas involves written communication. On the other hand, undergraduate research in writing creates unique, discipline-specific opportunities. Students who become undergraduate writing researchers obtain knowledge of writing that can be learned only through direct participation in full-fledged creative or critical inquiries. As undergraduate writing researchers, students also have the unique experience of contributing actively as subject experts to one or more communities (e.g., department or program, campus, discipline). Likewise, faculty, staff, and graduate students who teach and mentor undergraduate writing researchers gain distinctive opportunities for student-centered instruction, collaboration (e.g., coresearch, coauthorship), and professional development.

This position statement reflects CCCC members' growing commitment to undergraduate research. It also supports members' efforts to foster undergraduate research in writing at their home institutions, whether two- or four-year colleges or universities. To that end, this statement affirms undergraduate research in writing as a distinctive activity, and it outlines principles and best practices for mentoring undergraduate writing researchers, developing curricula that support undergraduate research in writing research curriculum, and building and sustaining campus infrastructure that can sustain undergraduate writing research activities.

Recognizing Undergraduate Research in Writing

At its most robust, undergraduate research includes the following elements: the formation of one or more mentoring relationships, preliminary study and project planning, information gathering and analysis, and the feedback loop of peer review and revision associated with the dissemination of findings, whether through publication or public presentation.

In writing studies, undergraduate research reflects the breadth of available methods and methodologies developed and used by professional writing researchers, including textual, archival, and digital scholarship; quantitative and qualitative empirical research; and creative inquiry. Undergraduate research in writing also reflects the full range of students, faculty, and staff involved in college writing. Undergraduate researchers can be first-year students, two-year college students, English language learners, writing or English majors and minors, writing tutors, supplemental instructors, and/or students from any discipline who engage in Writing Across the Curriculum (WAC), Writing in the Disciplines (WID), or Writing in the Major (WIM). Mentors of undergraduate researchers in writing are similarly diverse. They can be full-time and part-time faculty members, graduate students, staff, administrators, and/or community members affiliated with relevant campus programs. Mentoring relationships, whether formal or informal, benefit from various forms of institutional support calibrated to mentors' roles and status.

No single model for integrating undergraduate research in writing into postsecondary education exists. Instead, undergraduate research in writing can be curricular, co-curricular, or extracurricular. It can take place during a single quarter or semester, over a summer, or across a period of years. Whatever the case, undergraduate research in writing follows established ethical standards for inquiries of different kinds, including archival work, community-based projects, studies that involve online or digital media, and studies that involve human participants.[2]

PRINCIPLES AND BEST PRACTICES FOR UNDERGRADUATE RESEARCH IN WRITING

For undergraduate research in writing to flourish, it must be actively cultivated and sustained through individual relationships; through scaffolding provided by campus initiatives and strategic plans; and through infrastructure provided by campus units (e.g., programs, departments), policies, and resources. Specifically

FOR STUDENTS

Undergraduate research in writing starts with well-supported undergraduate researchers or students who have one or more opportunities during college to work formally or informally with one or more mentors on well-defined, well-scaffolded projects that align with both institutional learning outcomes and students' own educational goals.

Good mentors

- Can be faculty and instructors of any status or rank, graduate students, or staff.
- Have relevant knowledge of not only writing practices and processes but also writing research methods and methodologies.
- Are willing and able to communicate regularly with undergraduate researchers, offering guidance and feedback over time, at every stage of a project.
- Connect undergraduate researchers with available experts (e.g., librarians, statisticians) and relevant disciplinary and institutional resources (e.g., data collection and analysis software, funding opportunities).
- Help undergraduate researchers comply with ethical standards for writing inquiries, including (but not limited to) certification and project approval procedures specific to research with human participants.
- Guide researchers through dissemination in various media and offer a conduit to disciplinary and institutional support.

Well-defined projects

- Have exigence, addressing a research question of pressing interest and importance to the student researcher and the field.
- Make a genuine contribution, however modest, to public knowledge of writing, whether academic (e.g., disciplinary knowledge), professional, or community-based.
- Fit into students' schedules over a set period of time.
- Follow relevant ethical standards.
- Have concrete and realistic goals for dissemination.

Well-aligned projects

- Reflect relevant learning outcomes, whether for a single course or course of study.
- Advance students' individual college-level educational goals.
- Are eligible for support from available sources (e.g., course credit, travel funding).
- Reinforce students' post-graduate plans.

FOR MENTORS

Whether mentors work one-to-one with undergraduate researchers, in small groups, or in teams involving multiple mentors and mentees, mentoring undergraduate research in writing can enliven teaching, enrich research and scholarship, and enhance professional development in alignment with mentors' own job responsibilities and career goals.

Pedagogically, mentors

- Draw on and expand existing instructional expertise to focus holistically on mentees' interests and needs.
- Draw on and expand existing scholarly expertise to help students move through the research process from identifying a research question through to relating project findings to the larger scholarly, professional, or community conversation.
- Promote knowledge transfer by helping undergraduate researchers recognize how they are using previously acquired knowledge and how they are building skills and abilities they will be able to apply subsequently in their academic, professional, and personal lives.
- Help students build networks of connection on campus and within broader local and disciplinary communities through relationships forged in conjunction with their projects.

As researchers and scholars, mentors

- Draw on existing disciplinary expertise in rhetoric and composition/writing studies and adjacent fields.
- Expand their disciplinary knowledge to engage student researchers' interests and needs.
- Develop research and workflow protocols for effective and ethical collaboration with undergraduate researchers.
- Collaborate with students on the coconstruction of knowledge and the coauthorship of scholarly publications and presentations.
- When appropriate, draw from existing scholarship on undergraduate research and also contribute to it.

As members of campus, local, and disciplinary communities, mentors

- Foster and contribute to the development and ongoing delivery of curricula that support undergraduate research in writing.
- Participate actively in building and sustaining campus capacity for undergraduate research.
- Identify opportunities for undergraduate researchers to collaborate with community and workplace partners.
- Connect campus efforts with regional, national, and international initiatives for undergraduate research.

For Institutions

To build and support a culture of undergraduate research that includes writing studies, individual colleges and universities must provide infrastructure, scaffolding, and sustaining resources.

Infrastructure consists of

- Campus leadership informed about how writing, as a discipline that draws on humanities, social sciences, and fine arts methods and methodologies, fits into the larger campus picture of undergraduate research.
- Inclusion of writing scholars on campus committees related to undergraduate research.
- Attentiveness to the needs of undergraduate researchers in writing by relevant campus units (e.g., IRB, libraries, stats centers).
- Policies (e.g., hiring, annual evaluation, tenure, and promotion) that recognize and reward involvement in undergraduate research.
- Scaffolding comprises
- Support for lower- and upper-division courses that incorporate research or elements of research and thus require special accommodations (e.g., equipment, location, credit hours).
- Professional development opportunities for mentors.
- Inclusion of undergraduate researchers and their mentors in relevant campus events and publications.
- Awards that recognize and celebrate excellence in undergraduate research.
- Mechanisms for assessing the impact of undergraduate research on campus.

Resources include

- Funding to support undergraduate researchers through the full arc of undergraduate research, from data collection and analysis to dissemination.
- Funding to support undergraduate research mentors' involvement in all stages of their mentees' work, regardless of mentors' ranks and campus roles (e.g., adjunct, non-tenure- track, and tenure-track faculty members; staff; administrators).
- Access for spaces and tools for completing undergraduate research, including software licenses, storage for physical and virtual data, poster printers, and so on.

SELECTIONS FROM THE BIBLIOGRAPHY

The complete Bibliography can be found on the CCCC website:

https://cccc.ncte.org/cccc/resources/positions/undergraduate-research

Journals that regularly publish scholarship by undergraduate researchers in writing:

Inquiries Journal (formerly *Student Pulse*): http://www.inquiriesjournal.com/

The JUMP+: The Journal for Undergraduate Multimedia Projects: https://jumpplus.net/

Queen City Writers: https://qc-writers.com/

The Undergraduate Research Commons: A Showcase of Undergraduate Research: https://undergraduatecommons.com/

Xchanges Journal: http://www.xchanges.org/

Young Scholars in Writing: https://arc.lib.montana.edu/ojs/index.php/Young-Scholars-In-Writing

Special issues that feature scholarship by undergraduate researchers in writing:

Undergraduate Scholars in Writing and Rhetoric. *Kairos: A Journal of Rhetoric, Technology, and Pedagogy*, vol. 16, no. 1, 2011. http://technorhetoric.net/16.1/

Peer Tutors and the Conversation of Writing Center Studies. *The Writing Center Journal*, vol. 32, no. 1, 2012. http://www.writingcenterjournal.org/find/

Scholarship coauthored by undergraduate researchers in writing and their mentors:

Anderson, Worth, Cynthia Best, Alycia Black, John Hurst, Brandt Miller, and Susan Miller. "Cross-Curricular Underlife: A Collaborative Report on Ways with Academic Words." *College Composition and Communication*, vol. 41, 1990, pp. 11-36.

Balzhiser, Deborah, Mandy Grover, Evelyn Lauer, Sarah McNeely, Jonathan D. Polk, & Jon Zmikly. Cade Holmes, Ellen Porter, Corey Saucier, & Tiffany Swearingen. "The Facebook Papers." *Kairos*, vol. 16, no. 1, 2011. http://kairos.technorhetoric.net/16.1/praxis/balzhiser-et-al/index.html

Boles, Jacoby, and Julianne Newmark. "*Xchanges Journal* - Web Journal as the Writing Classroom: On Building an Academic Web Journal in a Collaborative Classroom." *Kairos*, vol. 16, no.1, 2011. http://kairos.technorhetoric.net/16.1/praxis/boles/

Brown, Renee, Brian Fallon, Jessica Lott, Elizabeth Matthews, and Elizabeth Mintie. "Taking on Turnitin: Tutors Advocating Change." *The Writing Center Journal*, vol. 27, no. 1, 2007, pp. 7-28.

Conzo, Crystal, and Karen Gabrielle Johnson. "Undergraduate Research Survey: Students Satisfied but Desire More Mentor Guidance in Managing Projects and Accessing Secondary Sources." *Keystone Journal of Undergraduate Research*, vol. 4, no. 1, 2016-17, pp. 56-63.

Downs, Doug and ZuZu Feder. "Undergraduate Research on Writing: Benefits to Faculty and Curriculum Development." *CUR Quarterly*, vol. 31, no. 1, 2010, pp. 9-13.

Fishman, Jenn, Andrea Lunsford, Beth McGregor, and Mark Otuteye. "Performing Writing, Performing Literacy." *College Composition and Communication*, vol. 47, 2005, pp. 224-52.

Fitzgerald, William and Natalie Midiri. "But Is It Really Research? Undergraduate Anxieties in the Humanities." *PURM: Perspectives on Undergraduate Research and Mentoring*, vol. 2, no. 2, 2013, pp. 1-13.

Godbee, Beth, Jessica Bazan, Megan Glise, Ariel Gonzalez, Katelyn Quigley, and Brittany White. "Stretching Beyond the Semester: Undergraduate Research, Ethnography of the University, and Proposals for Local Change." *PURM: Perspectives on Undergraduate Research and Mentoring*, vol. 3, no. 2, 2015, pp. 1-15.

Godbee, Beth, Katie Ellington, Megan Knowles. "Why Inquiry Matters: An Argument and Model for Inquiry-Based Writing Courses." *Wisconsin English Journal*, vol. 58, no. 2, 2016, pp. 7-21.

Halbritter, Bump, Noah Blon, and Caron Creighton. "Big Questions, Small Works, Lots of Layers: Documentary Video Production and the Teaching of Academic Research and Writing." *Kairos*, vol. 16, no. 1, 2011. http://kairos.technorhetoric.net/16.1/praxis/halbritter/index.php

Mallory, Angie, and Doug Downs. "Uniform Meets Rhetoric: Excellence Through Interaction." *Generation Vet: Composition, Student Veterans, and the Post-9/11 University*, edited by Sue Doe and Lisa Langstraat, Utah State UP, 2014, pp. 51-72.

Mina, Lillian, Megan McAfoose, Megan Moulden, and Shannon Zilavy. "Class-Based Research in the English Composition Class." *PURM: Perspectives on Undergraduate Research and Mentoring*, vol. 3, no. 1, 2013, pp. 1-13.

Notes

1. See George D. Kuh, *High-Impact Educational Practices: What They Do, Who Has Access to Them, and Why They Matter* (Washington, DC: AAC&U, 2008) Kuh's analysis of data from the National Survey of Student Engagement (NSSE) demonstrates that high-impact practices, including undergraduate research, not only improve retention and graduation rates but also promote deep learning and gains in general, personal, and practical knowledge. Kuh traces the value of high-impact practices to the ways in which they require students to invest considerable energy in purposeful intellectual activities; to be engaged with faculty and peers in substantive work and to receive feedback on that work; to connect with people from diverse backgrounds; and to transfer their developing knowledge and skills across contexts, including classrooms, campus organizations, the workplace, and the wider community.

2. See *CCCC Guidelines for the Ethical Conduct of Research in Composition Studies*.

Works Cited

About Our Marathon. 2019. https://marathon.library.northeastern.edu/home/about/.
"About the CCCC UR Poster Sessions." 2019. Undergraduate Research in Writing Studies. www.writingfaculty.net/undergraduateresearch/about-the-cccc-ur-poster-sessions.
Adler-Kassner, Linda, and Elizabeth Wardle, eds. 2015. *Naming What We Know: Threshold Concepts in Writing Studies.* Boulder, CO: Utah State University Press.
Alim, H. Samy. 2007. "Critical Hip-Hop Language Pedagogies: Combat, Consciousness, and the Cultural Politics of Communication." *Journal of Language, Identity, & Education* 6, no. 2: 161–76.
Alim, H. Samy, and Geneva Smitherman. 2012. *Articulate While Black: Barack Obama, Language, and Race in the U.S.* New York: Oxford University Press.
Allan, Elizabeth G. 2018. "'Real Research' or 'Just for a Grade'?: Ethnography, Ethics, and Engagement in the Undergraduate Writing Studies Classroom." *Pedagogy* 18, no. 2: 247–77.
Allen, Walter. 1992. "The Color of Success: African-American College Student Outcomes at Predominantly White and Historically Black Public Colleges and Universities." *Harvard Educational Review* 62, no. 1: 26–45.
Alvarez, Nancy, Cristina Salazar, Francia N. Brito, and Karina Aguilar. 2016. "Agency, Liberation, and Intersectionality among Latina scholars: Narratives from a Cross-Institutional Collective." *Praxis: A Writing Center Journal* 14, no. 1.
Archibald, Jo-ann (Q'um Q'um Xiiem). 2008. *Indigenous Storywork: Educating the Heart, Mind, Body, and Spirit.* Vancouver: University of British Columbia Press.
American Library Association. 2015. "Framework for Information Literacy for Higher Education." http://www.ala.org/acrl/standards/ilframework.
Babcock, Rebecca Day, Cynthia Cochran, and Aliethia Dean. "Writing about Writing: The State of the Art." Manuscript under submission.
Babcock, Rebecca Day, and Therese Thonus. 2012. *Researching the Writing Center: Towards an Evidence-Based Practice.* New York, Peter Lang.

Baker, Vicki L., Jane Greer, Laura G. Lunsford, Dijana Ihas, and Meghan J. Pifer. 2018. "Supporting Faculty Development for Mentoring in Undergraduate Research, Scholarship, and Creative Work." In *Excellence in Mentoring Undergraduate Research*, edited by Maureen Vandermaas-Peeler, Paul Miller, and Jessie L. Moore, 131–53. Washington, DC: Council on Undergraduate Research.

Bakke, Abigail, and Kira Dreher. n.d. "Written Communication in the Classroom: Resources for Teaching Method." Accessed June 18, 2019. https://journals.sagepub.com/page/wcx/collection/classroom/introduction.

Balzhiser, Deborah, and Susan H. McLeod. 2010. "The Undergraduate Writing Major: What Is It? What Should It Be?" *College Composition and Communication* 61, no. 3: 415–33.

Bastian, Heather, and Lindsey Harkness. 2008. "A Look Back from Two Young Scholars." *Young Scholars in Writing* 5: 4–6.

Bazerman, Charles. 2002. "The Case for Writing Studies as a Major Discipline." *The Intellectual Work of Composition*, edited by Gary A. Olson, 32–38. Carbondale: Southern Illinois University Press.

———. 1988. *Shaping Written Knowledge: The Genre and Activity of the Experimental Article in Science*. Madison: University of Wisconsin Press.

Bazerman, Charles, and Paul Prior, eds. 2003. *What Writing Does and How it Does it: An Introduction to Analyzing Texts and Textual Practices*. New York: Routledge.

Beaufort, Anne. 2007. *College Writing and Beyond: A New Framework for University Writing Instruction*. Logan: Utah State University Press.

Beckman, Mary, and Nancy Hensel. 2009. "Making Explicit the Implicit: Defining Undergraduate Research." *CUR Quarterly* 4: 40–44.

Belmont Report. 1979. https://www.hhs.gov/ohrp/regulations-and-policy/belmont-report/read-the-belmont-report/index.html.

Berlin, James A. 1984. *Writing Instruction in Nineteenth-Century American Colleges*. Carbondale: Southern Illinois University Press.

———. 1987. *Rhetoric and Reality: Writing Instruction in American Colleges, 1900-1985*. Carbondale: Southern Illinois University Press, 1987.

Bird, Barbara, Doug Downs, Moriah McCracken, and Jan Rieman, eds. 2019. *Next Steps: New Directions for/in Writing about Writing*. Logan: Utah State University Press.

Bizup, Joseph. 2008. "BEAM: A Rhetorical Vocabulary for Teaching Research-Based Writing." *Rhetoric Review* 27, no.1: 72–86.

Blum Center for Global Poverty Alleviation and Sustainable Development. n.d. Accessed June 1, 2019. https://www.blumcenter.ucsb.edu/.

Booth, Wayne C., Gregory G. Colomb, Joseph M. Williams, Joseph Bizup and William T. FitzGerald. 2016. *The Craft of Research*. 4th ed. Chicago: University of Chicago Press.

Boquet, Elizabeth H. 1999. "'Our Little Secret': A History of Writing Centers, Pre- to Post-Open Admissions." *College Composition and Communication* 50, no. 3: 463–82. JSTOR, www.jstor.org/stable/358861.

Borowitz, Alex. 2019. "Le Processus d'Ecriture." *The JUMP+* 8, no. 2. jumpplus.net/issues/issue-8-2/le-processus-decriture-8-2/.

Boyer Commission on Educating Undergraduates in the Research University. 2001. *Reinventing Undergraduate Education: Three Years After the Boyer Report*. Carnegie Foundation for the Advancement of Teaching.

—. 1998. *Reinventing Undergraduate Education: A Blueprint for America's Research Universities*. Stony Brook, NY.

Boyer, Ernest L. 1990. *Scholarship Reconsidered: Priorities of the Professoriate*. Princeton, New Jersey: Carnegie Foundation for the Advancement of Teaching.

Bradley, Evan D., Michelle Bata, Heather M. Fitz Gibbon, Caroline J. Ketchum, Brittany A. Nicholson, and Meagan Pollock. 2017. "The Structure of Mentoring in Undergraduate Research: Multi-Mentor Models." *Scholarship and Practice of Undergraduate Research* 1, no. 2: 35–42.

Brent, Douglass. 2013. "The Research Paper and Why We Should Still Care." *WPA: Writing Program Administration* 37, no. 1: 33–53.

Brew, Angela. 2013. "Understanding the Scope of Undergraduate Research: A Framework for Curricular and Pedagogical Decision-Making." *Higher Education* 66: 603–18. doi:10.1007/s10734-013-9624-x.

Brew, Angela, and Lilia Mantai. 2017. "Academics' Perceptions of the Challenges and Barriers to Implementing Research-Based Experiences for Undergraduates." *Teaching in Higher Education* 22, no. 5: 551–68.

Buddie, Amy M., and Courtney L. Collins. 2011. "Faculty Perceptions of Undergraduate Research." *PURM: Perspectives on Mentoring Undergraduate Researchers* 1, no. 1. https://blogs.elon.edu/purm/2011/10/11/faculty-perceptions-of-undergraduate-research-purm-1-1/.

Buehl, Jonathan, Tamar Chute, and Anne Fields. 2012. "Training in the Archives: Archival Research as Professional Development." *College Composition and Communication* 64, no. 2: 274–05.

Burke, Kenneth. 1984. *Attitudes Toward History: With a New Afterword.* Berkeley: University of California Press.

—. *The Philosophy of Literary Form.* Berkeley: University of California Press.

Carr, Katy S., Stephen D. Davis, Stella Erbes, Constance M. Fulmer, Lee B. Kats, and Melissa Umbro Teetzel. 2013. "Developing First-Year Students as Scholars." *CUR Quarterly* 33, no. 4: 8+.

Carter, Sarah E. 2018. "It's Time to Make a Push for More Primary Research in First-Year Composition" (blog). May 28, 2018. National Council of Teachers of English. http://www2.ncte.org/blog/2018/05/its-time-to-make-a-push-toward-more-primary-research-in-first-year-composition/.

Center for Engaged Learning (CEL). 2018. "Students as Partners." https://www.centerforengagedlearning.org/doing-engaged-learning/students-as-partners/.

Chapdelaine, Andrea. 2012. "Including Undergraduate Research in Faculty Promotion and Tenure Policies." In *Faculty Support and Undergraduate Research: Innovations in Faculty Role Definition, Workload, and Reward*, edited by Nancy H. Hensel and Elizabeth L. Paul, 115–32. Washington, DC: Council on Undergraduate Research.

Charity Hudley, Anne H., Cheryl L. Dickter, and Hannah A. Franz. 2017. *The Indispensable Guide to Undergraduate Research: Success In and Beyond College.* New York: Teachers College Press.

Christiansen, Jonathan. 2009. "Four Stages of Social Movements." EBSCO Research Starters: Academic Topic Overviews, EBSCO Publishing.

"Clinic for Writing and the Public Good." n.d. University of Denver Writing Program https://pgwrit.wordpress.com/.

Coad, David T. 2017. "'That's My Face to the Whole Field!': Graduate Students' Professional Identity-Building through Twitter at a Writing Studies Conference." *Computers and Composition* 45: 51–66. https://doi.org/10.1016/j.compcom.2017.06.003.

Collins, Timothy W., Sara E. Grineski, Jessica Shenberger, Xiaodan Morales, Osvaldo F. Morera, and Lourdes E. Echegoyen. 2017. "Undergraduate Research Participation is Associated with Improved Student

Outcomes at a Hispanic-Serving Institution." *Journal of College Student Development* 58, no. 4: 583–600.
Conference on College Composition and Communication. 2018. "CCCC Position Statement on Scholarship in Rhetoric, Writing, and Composition: Guidelines for Faculty, Deans, and Chairs." http://cccc.ncte.org/cccc/resources/positions/scholarshipincomp.
—. 2017. "CCCC Position Statement on Undergraduate Research in Writing: Principles and Best Practices." http://www.cccc.ncte.org/cccc/resources/positions/undergraduate-research.
—. 2016. "CCCC Position Statement on Community-Engaged Projects in Rhetoric and Composition." https://cccc.ncte.org/cccc/resources/positions/community-engaged.
—. 2007. Committee on the Major in Rhetoric and Composition. "Writing Majors at a Glance." www.ncte.org/cccc/gov/committees/majorrhetcomp.
Cook-Sather, Alison, Catherine Bovill, and Peter Felten. 2014. *Engaging Students as Partners in Learning and Teaching: A Guide for Faculty.* San Francisco: Jossey-Bass.
Cook-Sather, Alison, and Crystal Des-Ogugua. 2018. "Lessons We Still Need to Learn on Creating More Inclusive and Responsive Classrooms: Recommendations from one Student–Faculty Partnership Programme." *International Journal of Inclusive Education* 23, no. 6: 594–608. DOI: 10.1080/13603116.2018.1441912.
Corroy, Jennifer. 2003. "Institutional Change and the University of Wisconsin-Madison Writing Fellows Program." *Young Scholars in Writing* 1: 20–34
Council of Writing Program Administrators (CWPA). 1998. "Evaluating the Intellectual Work of Writing Program Administration." http://wpacouncil.org/positions/intellectualwork.html.
Council of Writing Program Administrators, National Council of Teachers of English, and National Writing Project. 2011. *Framework for Success in Postsecondary Writing.* https://wpacouncil.org/files/framework-for-success-postsecondary-writing.pdf.
Council on Undergraduate Research (CUR). 2019. "Who We Are—Mission." https://www.cur.org/who/organization/mission/.
Council on Undergraduate Research and National Conferences on Undergraduate Research. 2005. "Joint Statement of Principles in Support of Undergraduate Research, Scholarship, and Creative Activities."

Craton, Lillian, Renée Love and Sean Barnette, eds. 2017. *Writing Pathways to Student Success*. Boulder: University Press of Colorado.

Crawford, Iain, Sara E. Orel, and Jenny Olin Shanahan, eds. 2014. *How to Get Started in Arts and Humanities Research with Undergraduates*. Washington, DC: Council on Undergraduate Research.

Cushman, Ellen. 2008. "Toward a Rhetoric of Self-Representation: Identity Politics in Indian Country and Rhetoric and Composition." *College Composition and Communication* 60, no. 1: 321–65.

— —. 1996. "The Rhetorician as an Agent of Social Change." *College Composition and Communication* 47: 7–28.

Daniels, Heather, Sara E. Grineski, Timothy W. Collins, Danielle X. Morales, Osvaldo Morera, and Lourdes Echegoyen. 2016. "Factors Influencing Student Gains from Undergraduate Research Experiences at a Hispanic-Serving Institution." *CBE—Life Sciences Education* 15, no. 3: 1–12.

Daniels, Sharifa, Rebecca Day Babcock, and Doria Daniels. 2017. "Writing Centers and Disability: Enabling Writers through an Inclusive Philosophy." *Praxis: A Writing Center Journal*, 13, no. 1.

Day, Michael, Susan H. Delagrange, Mike Palmquist, Michael A. Pemberton, and Janice R. Walker. 2013."What We Really Value: Redefining Scholarly Engagement in Tenure and Promotion Protocols." *College Composition and Communication* 65, no. 1: 185–208.

DeAngelo, Linda, Jessica Mason, and Dana Winters. 2016. "Faculty Engagement in Mentoring Undergraduate Students: How Institutional Environments Regulate and Promote Extra-Role Behavior." *Innovative Higher Education* 41, no. 4: 317–32. doi:10.1007/s10755-015-9350-7.

DelliCarpini, Dominic. 2007. "Re-writing the Humanities: The Writing Major's Effect upon Undergraduate Studies in English Departments." *Composition Studies* 35, no. 1: 15–36.

DelliCarpini, Dominic, and Cynthia Crimmins. 2010. "The Writing Center as a Space for Undergraduate Research." In *Undergraduate Research in English Studies*, edited by Laurie Grobman and Joyce Kinkead, 191–211. Urbana, Illinois: National Council of Teachers of English.

De Mueller, Genevieve Garcia, and Iris Ruiz. 2017 "Race, Silence, and Writing Program Administration: A Qualitative Study of US College Writing Programs." *WPA: Writing Program Administration* 40, no. 2: 19–39.

Denny, Harry, Robert Mundy, and Liliana M. Naydan. 2019. *Out in the Center: Public Controversies and Private Struggles*. Boulder: Utah State University Press.

Devitt, Amy, Mary Jo Reiff, and Anis Bawarshi. 2004. *Scenes of Writing: Strategies for Composing with Genres*. Toronto: Pearson/Longman.

Dickter, Cheryl L., Anne H. Charity Hudley, Hannah A. Franz, and Ebony A. Lambert. 2018. "Faculty Change from Within: The Creation of the WMSURE Program." *Scholarship and Practice of Undergraduate Research* 2, no. 1: 24–32.

Dolan, Erin L. 2016. "Course-based Undergraduate Research Experiences: Current Knowledge and Future Directions." National Research Council Commissioned Paper, Washington, DC, USA.

Dolan, Erin, and Deborah Johnson. 2009. "Toward a Holistic View of Undergraduate Research Experiences: An Exploratory Study of Impact on Graduate/Postdoctoral Mentors." *Journal of Science Education and Technology* 18: 487–500.

Downs, Doug. 2015. "Undergraduate Researchers and the Challenge of Finding the Conversation." Council of Writing Program Administrators Conference, Boise, ID.

Downs, Doug, and ZuZu Feder. 2010. "Undergraduate Research on Writing: Benefits to Faculty and Curriculum Development." *CUR Quarterly* 31, no. 1: 9–13.

Downs, Douglas, and Elizabeth Wardle. 2010. "What Can a Novice Contribute? Undergraduate Researchers in First-Year Composition." In *Undergraduate Research in English Studies*, edited by Laurie Grobman and Joyce Kinkead, 173–90. Urbana, Illinois: National Council of Teachers of English.

———. 2007. "Teaching About Writing, Righting Misconceptions: (Re)Envisioning 'First-Year Composition' as 'Introduction to Writing Studies.'" *College Composition and Communication* 58, no. 4: 552–84.

Downs, Doug, and Greg Young. 2012. "What Faculty Need and Want." In *Faculty Support and Undergraduate Research: Innovations in Faculty Role Definition, Workload, and Reward*, edited by Nancy H. Hensel and Elizabeth A. Paul, 26–34. Washington, DC: Council on Undergraduate Research.

Duersch, Morgan, et al. 2019. "The Rise and Fall of the Blue Book: An Examination of Essay Examination Books." *Young Scholars in Writing* 15: 102–13.

Durack, Katherine T. 2013. "Sweating Employment: Ethical and Legal Issues with Unpaid Student Internships." *College Composition and Communication* 65, no. 2: 245–72.

Eagan, Jr., M. Kevin, Jessica Sharkness, Sylvia Hurtado, Cynthia M. Mosqueda, and Mitchell J. Chang 2011. "Engaging Undergraduates in Science Research: Not Just about Faculty Willingness." *Research in Higher Education* 52, no. 2: 151–77.

Earley, Mark A. 2014. "A Synthesis of the Literature on Research Methods Education." *Teaching in Higher Education* 19, no. 3: 242–53. DOI: 10.1080/13562517.2013.860105.

Eiffert, Samantha, Yomi Noibi, Stephen Vesper, Jonathan Downs, Florence Fulk, Juanita Wallace, Melanie Pearson, and Andrea Winquist. 2016. "A Citizen-Science Study Documents Environmental Exposures and Asthma Prevalence in Two Communities." *Journal of Environmental and Public Health.* doi.org/10.1155/2016/1962901.

Elder, David, and Joona Smitherman Trapp. 2010. "Mentor as Method: Faculty Mentor Roles and Undergraduate Scholarship." In *Undergraduate Research in English Studies*, edited by Laurie Grobman and Joyce Kinkead, 3–12. Urbana, Illinois: National Council of Teachers of English.

Elliott, Richard. 1996. "Discourse Analysis: Exploring Action, Function and Conflict in Social Texts." *Marketing Intelligence and Planning* 14, no. 6: 65–68. https://doi.org/10.1108/02634509610131171.

ENGL3340 AdvComp 2017. 2017. *Great Explications: Some Related to Art, Some Related to Culture, and Some out of Left Field*. San Francisco: Blurb.

Enoch, Jessica, and Pamela VanHaitsma. 2015. "Archival Literacy: Reading the Rhetoric of Digital Archives in the Undergraduate Classroom." *College Composition and Communication* 67, no. 2: 216–42.

Eodice, Michele, Anne Ellen Geller, and Neal Lerner. 2017. *The Meaningful Writing Project: Learning, Teaching, and Writing in Higher Education*. Boulder: Utah State University Press.

Ervin, Christopher. 2016a "What Tutor Researchers and Their Mentors Tell Us About Undergraduate Research in the Writing Center: An Exploratory Study." *The Writing Center Journal* 35, no. 3: 39–75.

———. 2016b. "The Peer Perspective and Undergraduate Writing Tutor Research." *Praxis: A Writing Center Journal* 13, no. 2: 46–51.

Etmanski, Catherine, Budd L. Hall, and Teresa Dawson, eds. 2014. *Learning and Teaching Community-based Research: Linking Pedagogy to Practice.* Toronto: University of Toronto Press.

EvaluateUR. 2019. https://serc.carleton.edu/evaluateur/index.html.

Eyman, Douglas, Stephanie Sheffield, and Danielle Nicole DeVoss. 2009. "Developing Sustainable Research Networks in Graduate Education." *Computers and Composition* 26, no. 1: 49–57. https://doi.org/10.1016/j.compcom.2008.11.001.

Felten, Peter, John N. Gardner, Charles C. Schroeder, Leo M. Lambert, and Betsy O. Barefoot. 2016. *The Undergraduate Experience: Focusing Institutions on What Matters Most.* San Francisco: Jossey-Bass.

Feminist Digital Humanities Lab. Accessed January 10, 2019. University of South Florida, Department of English. https://www.usf.edu/arts-sciences/departments/english/opportunities/undergraduate-research.aspx.

Finley, Ashley, and Tia McNair. 2013. *Assessing Underserved Students' Engagement in High-Impact Practices.* Washington, DC: American Association of Colleges and Universities.

Fister, Barbara. 1993. "Teaching the Rhetorical Dimensions of Research." *Research Strategies* 11: 211–219.

Fitzgerald, Lauren. 2014a. "Undergraduate Research in Writing Studies." In *How to Get Started in Arts and Humanities Research with Undergraduates*, edited by Iain Crawford, Sara Orel, and Jenny Shanahan, 94–106. Washington, DC: Council on Undergraduate Research.

—. 2014b. "Undergraduate Writing Tutors as Researchers: Redrawing Boundaries." *The Writing Center Journal* 33, no. 2: 15–31.

Fitzgerald, Lauren, and Melissa Ianetta. 2015. *The Oxford Guide for Writing Tutors: Practice and Research.* Oxford University Press.

FitzGerald, Bill, and Brynn Kairis. 2019. "Year of Living DALNgerously: Breakthrough Encounters with Archival Pedagogy." *The Archive as Classroom: Pedagogical Approaches to the Digital Archive of Literacy Narratives*, edited by Kathryn Comer, Michael Harker, and Ben McCorkle. CCDigitalPress.Org. Boulder: Utah State University Press.

FitzGerald, William, and Natalie Midiri. 2013. "But Is It Really Research? Undergraduate Anxieties in the Humanities." *PURM: Perspectives on Undergraduate Research Mentoring* 2, no. 2: 1–13. blogs.elon.edu/purm/files/2013/04/PURM-2.2-Midiri-Fitz.pdf.

Flick, Uwe. 2015. *Introducing Research Methodology: A Beginner's Guide to Doing a Research Project.* 2nd ed. Thousand Oaks, California: SAGE Publications Ltd.

Free, Rhona, Suzanne Griffith, and Bill Spellman. 2015. "Faculty Workload Issues Connected to Undergraduate Research." *New Directions for Higher Education* 2015, no. 169 (March): 51–60. https://doi.org/10.1002/he.20122.

Fulkerson, Richardson. 2005. "Composition at the Turn of the Twenty-First Century." *College Composition, and Communication* 56, no. 4: 654–87.

Gaillet, Lynée Lewis. 2017. "Primary Research in the Vertical Writing Curriculum." In *Writing Pathways to Student Success*, edited by Lillian Craton, Renée Love, and Sean Barnette, 109-116. Boulder: University Press of Colorado/WAC Clearinghouse.

Gallup. 2014. "Life in College Matters for Life after College: New Gallup-Purdue Study Looks at Links among College, Work, and Well-Being." http://www.gallup.com/poll/168848/life-college-matters-life-college.aspx.

Garcia, Marissa. "Raab Writing Fellows Showcase Their Work." N.d. UC Santa Barbara Humanities and Fine Arts. Accessed June 13, 2019. https://www.hfa.ucsb.edu/news-entries/2019/6/2/raab-writing-fellows-showcase-their-work.

García, Romeo. 2017. "Unmaking Gringo-Centers." *The Writing Center Journal* 36, no. 1: 29–60. JSTOR, www.jstor.org/stable/44252637.

Gardner, Clint. 2017. "Our Students Can Do That: Peer Writers at the Two-Year College." *Praxis: A Writing Center Journal* 15, no. 1.

Giberson, Greg A., and Thomas A. Moriarty, eds. 2010. *What We Are Becoming: Developments in Undergraduate Writing Majors.* Logan: Utah State University Press.

Giberson, Greg, Jim Nugent, and Lori Ostergaard, eds. 2015. *Writing Majors: Eighteen Program Profiles.* Logan: Utah State University Press.

Giltrow, Janet, Richard Gooding, Daniel Burgoyne, and Marlene J. Sawatsky. 2014. *Academic Writing: An Introduction.* 3rd Edition. Peterborough, ON: Broadview Press.

Gladstein, Jill and Brandon Fralix. N.d. "Two-year Institution Survey." Accessed Dec. 24, 2018. *National Census of Writing.*

Godbee, Beth, et al. 2015. "Stretching beyond the Semester: Undergraduate Research, Ethnography of the University, and Proposals for

Local Change." *PURM: Perspectives on Undergraduate Research and Mentoring* 3 no. 2: 1–15.

Gofine, Miriam. 2012. "How Are We Doing? A Review of Assessments within Writing Centers." *Writing Center Journal* 32, no.1: 39–49

Graff, Gerald, Cathy Birkenstein, and Russel Durst. 2018. *They Say / I Say: The Moves That Matter in Academic Writing.* 4th ed. New York: Norton.

Green, Neisha-Anne. 2018. "Moving beyond Alright: And the Emotional Toll of This, My Life Matters Too, in the Writing Center Work." *The Writing Center Journal* 37, no. 1:–34. JSTOR, www.jstor.org/stable/26537361.

Greenfield, Laura, and Karen Rowan. 2011. *Writing Centers and the New Racism: A Call for Sustainable Dialogue and Change.* Logan: Utah State University Press.

Gries, Laurie E. 2018. "Introduction: Circulation as an Emerging Threshold Concept." In *Circulation, Writing, and Rhetoric*, edited by Laurie Gries and Collin Gifford Brooks, 3–24. Boulder: Utah State University Press.

Grobman, Laurie. 2017a. "Disturbing Public Memory in Community Writing Partnerships." *College Composition and Communication* 69, no. 1: 35–60.

—. 2017b. "'Engaging Race': Teaching Critical Race Inquiry and Community-Engaged Projects." *College English* 80, no. 2: 105–32.

—. 2011. "Expanding Honors Research Through Undergraduate Research: Another Look At Equity And Access." *CUR Quarterly*, 32, no. 1: 29–35.

—. 2009a. "The Student Scholar:(Re) Negotiating Authorship and Authority." *College Composition and Communication* 61, no.1: W175–W196.

—. 2009b. "'Speaking With One Another': Writing African American History in Berks County, Pennsylvania." *Reflections: Writing, Service-Learning, and Community Literacy* 9, no. 1: 129–61.

—. 2007. "Affirming the Independent Researcher Model: Undergraduate Research in the Humanities." *CUR Quarterly* 28, no. 1: 23–28.

Grobman, Laurie, Elizabeth Kemmerer, and Meghan Zebertavage. 2017. "Counternarratives: Community Writing and Anti-Racist Rhetoric." *Reflections: A Journal of Public Rhetoric, Civic Writing, and Service-Learning* 17, no. 2: 43–68.

Grobman, Laurie and Joyce Kinkead, eds. 2010. *Undergraduate Research in English Studies*. Urbana, Illinois: National Council of Teachers of English.

Grobman, Laurie and Candace Spigelman. 2003. "Editors' Introduction." *Young Scholars in Writing: Undergraduate Research in Writing and Rhetoric* 1: 1–5.

Guba, Egon. 1990. "The Alternative Paradigm Dialog." In *The Paradigm Dialog*, edited by Egon Guba, 17–27. Newberry Park, California: Sage, 1990.

Guzmán, Georgina. 2018-19. "Learning to Value Cultural Wealth Through Service Learning: Farmworker Families' and Latina/o University Students' Mutual Empowerment via Freirean and Feminist Chicana/o-Latina/o Literature Reading Circles." *Reflections: A Journal of Community-Engaged Writing and Rhetoric* 18, no. 2: 6–35.

Haas, Christina, and Abigail Bakke. 2013. "Editors' Introduction: Special Issue on New Methods for the Study of Written Communication." *Written Communication* 30, no. 3: 233–35.

Hadfield, Leslie, Joyce Kinkead, Tom Peterson, Stephanie H. Ray, and Sarah S. Preston. 2003. "An Ideal Writing Center: Re-Imagining Space and Design." In *The Center Will Hold: Critical Perspectives on Writing Center Scholarship*, edited by Michael A. Pemberton and Joyce Kinkead, 166–76. Logan: Utah State University Press, 2003.

Hackman, Heather W. 2008. "Broadening the Pathway to Academic Success: The Critical Intersections of Social Justice Education, Critical Multicultural Education, and Universal Instructional Design." In *Pedagogy and Student Services for Institutional Transformation: Implementing Universal Design in Higher Education*, edited by Jeanne L. Higby and Emily Goff, 25-48. Minneapolis: Center for Research on Developmental Education and Urban Literacy, University of Minnesota.

Hakim, Toufic. 1998. "Soft Assessment of Undergraduate Research: Reactions and Student Perspectives." *CUR Quarterly* 20, no. 2: 189–92.

Hall, Eric E., Helen Walkington, Jenny Olin Shanahan, Elizabeth Ackley, and Kearsley A. Stewart. 2018. "Mentor Perspectives on the Place of Undergraduate Research Mentoring in Academic Identity and Career Development: An Analysis of Award-Winning Mentors." *International Journal for Academic Development* 23, no. 1: 15–27. https://doi.org/10.1080/1360144X.2017.1412972.

Hairston, Maxine. 1985. "Breaking Our Bonds and Reaffirming Our Connections." *College Composition and Communication* 36, no. 3: 272–82.

Harris, Joseph. 2012. *A Teaching Subject: Composition Since 1966*. Logan: Utah State University Press. First published 1996 by Prentice Hall (Upper Saddle River, NJ).

Haswell, Richard. 2005. "NCTE/CCCC's Recent War on Scholarship." *Written Communication* 22, no. 2: 193–223.

Hayden, Wendy. 2017. "AND GLADLY TEACH: The Archival Turn's Pedagogical Turn." *College English* 80, no.2: 133–54.

—. 2015. "'Gifts'of the Archives: A Pedagogy for Undergraduate Research." *College Composition and Communication* 66, no. 2: 402–26.

Healey, Mick, Abbi Flint, and Kathy Harrington. 2014. *Engagement through Partnership: Students As Partners in Learning and Teaching in Higher Education*. York: Higher Education Academy.

Hensel, Nancy. 2018. *Course-Based Undergraduate Research: Educational Equity and High-Impact Practice*. Sterling, VA: Stylus.

Hensel, Nancy H., and Elizabeth L. Paul, eds. 2012. *Faculty Support and Undergraduate Research: Innovations in Faculty Role Definition, Workload, and Reward*. Washington, DC: Council on Undergraduate Research.

Hirschi, Charlene A. 1996. "The Re-Entry Student: On Both Sides of the Table." *Writing Lab Newsletter* 21, no. 2: 9–10.

Hocks, Mary E. 1999. "Feminist Interventions in Electronic Environments." *Computers and Composition* 16, no. 1: 107–19. https://doi.org/10.1016/S8755-4615(99)80008-5.

Hoffman, Rachel. 2019. "Getting Mouthy: The Displayed Authority of Dr. Katharine Berry Richardson." *Young Scholars in Writing* 15: 6–19.

Horner, Bruce. 2016. *Rewriting Composition: Terms of Exchange*. Carbondale: Southern Illinois University Press.

Horner, Bruce, and Min-Zhan Lu. 2010. "Working Rhetoric and Composition." *College English* 72, no. 5: 470–94.

Horowitz, Jessica and Kelly B. Christopher. 2013. "The Research Mentoring Program: Serving the Needs of Graduate and Undergraduate Researchers." *Innovative Higher Education* 38, no. 2: 105–16.

Hummel, Marc. 2012. "Community Writing Centers and Genre Literacy." *Young Scholars in Writing* 9: 58–63.

Hunter, Anne-Barrie, Sandra L. Laursen, and Elaine Seymour. 2007. "Becoming a Scientist: The Role of Undergraduate Research in Students' Cognitive, Personal, And Professional Development." *Science Education* 91, no. 1: 36–74.

Hurtado, Sylvia, Nolan L. Cabrera, Monica H. Lin, Lucy Arellano, and Lorelle L. Espinosa. 2009. "Diversifying Science: Underrepresented Student Experiences in Structured Research Programs." *Research in Higher Education* 50, no. 2: 189–214.

Hutchinson, Terry C. 2010. *Researching and Writing in Law*. 3rd ed. Pyrmont, NSW, Australia: Thomson Reuters.

Inoue, Asao. 2012. "Racial Methodologies for Composition Studies: Reflecting on Theories of Race in Writing Assessment Research." In *Writing Studies Research in Practice: Methods and Methodologies*, edited by Lee Nickoson, Mary P. Sheridan, and Gesa E. Kirsch, 125–39. Carbondale: Southern Illinois University Press.

Ishiyama, John. 2001. "Undergraduate Research and the Success of First Generation, Low Income College Students." *CUR Quarterly* 22, no. 1: 36–41.

—. 2002. "Does Early Participation in Undergraduate Research Benefit Social Science and Humanities Students?" *College Student Journal* 36, no. 3: 381–87.

Jackson, Judy, and Bessie M. Guerrant. 2012. "Exposing Hidden Barriers for Faculty of Color." In *Faculty Support and Undergraduate Research: Innovations in Faculty Role Definition, Workload, and Reward*, edited by Nancy H. Hensel and Elizabeth L. Paul, 57–67. Washington, DC: Council on Undergraduate Research.

Jackson, Karen Keaton. 2013. "Don't Knock the Hustle: HBCU Writing Center Life." *Academic Exchange Quarterly* 17: 135–41.

Johnson, Donna M., and Judith A. Fox. 2003 "Creating Curb Cuts in the Classroom: Adapting Universal Design Principles to Education." In *Curriculum Transformation and Disability: Implementing Universal Design in Higher Education*, edited by Jeanne L. Higbee, 7–21. Minneapolis: Center for Research on Developmental Education and Urban Literacy, University of Minnesota.

Johnson, Lindy L., Jacqueline Chisam, Peter Smagorinsky, and Katalin Wargo. 2018. "Beyond Publication: Social Action as the Ultimate Stage of a Writing Process." *L1-Educational Studies in Language and Literature* 18: 1–21.

Johnson, Steven. 2009. *The Invention of Air: A Story of Science, Faith, Revolution, and the Birth of America*. New York: Riverhead.

Johnson, W. Brad. 2016. *On Being a Mentor*. 2nd ed. New York: Routledge.
—. 2002. "The Intentional Mentor: Strategies and Guidelines for the Practice of Mentoring." *Professional Psychology: Research and Practice* 33, no. 1: 88–96.
Johnson, W. Brad, Laura L. Behling, Paul Miller, and Maureen Vandermaas-Peeler. 2015. "Undergraduate Research Mentoring: Obstacles and Opportunities." *Mentoring & Tutoring: Partnership in Learning* 23: 441–53.
Juzwik Mary M., Svjetlana Curcic, Kimberly Wolbers, Kathleen D. Moxley, Lisa M. Dimling, Rebecca K. Shankland. 2006. "Writing into the 21st Century: An Overview of Research on Writing, 1999 to 2004." *Written Communication* 23, no. 4: 451–76.
Ketcham, Caroline J., Eric E. Hall, Heather Fitz Gibbon, and Helen Walkington. 2018. "Co-Mentoring in Undergraduate Research: A Faculty Development Perspective." In *Excellence in Mentoring Undergraduate Research*, edited by Maureen Vandermaas-Peeler, Paul Miller, and Jessie L. Moore, 155–79. Washington, DC: Council on Undergraduate Research.
Kim, Christopher S., Anna Leahy, and Lisa Kendrick. 2017. "Credit Where Credit Is Due: A Course-Load Banking System to Support Faculty-Mentored Student Research." *Scholarship and Practice of Undergraduate Research* 1, no. 1: 55–62. DOI:10.18833/spur/1/1/8.
King, Patricia, and Karen Strohm Kitchener. 1994. *Developing Reflective Judgment: Understanding and Promoting Intellectual Growth and Critical Thinking in Adolescents and Adults*. San Francisco: Jossey-Bass.
Kinkead, Joyce. 2019. "An Empirical Research Project in English and Writing Studies." *Prompt* 3, no. 2: 39–69. http://thepromptjournal.com/index.php/prompt.
—. 2018. "Engaging Undergraduate Researchers in the Assessment of Communication across the Curriculum Courses. *Across the Disciplines* 15, no. 2: 15–30. https://wac.colostate.edu/docs/atd/articles/kinkead2018.pdf.
—. 2016. "Transcending Institutional Boundaries and Types: Undergraduate Research." In *A Critical Look at Institutional Mission: A Guide for Writing Program Administrators*, edited by Joseph Janangelo, 24–39. Anderson, SC: Parlor Press.
—. 2015. *Researching Writing: An Introduction to Research Methods*. Logan: Utah State University Press.

—. 2012. "What's in a Name? A Brief History of Undergraduate Research." *CUR Quarterly* 32, no. 5: 20–29.

—. 2011a. *Advancing Undergraduate Research: Marketing, Communications, and Fundraising*. Washington, DC: Council on Undergraduate Research.

—. 2011b. "Undergraduate Researchers as Makers of Knowledge in Composition in the Writing Studies Major." In *The Changing of Knowledge in Composition: Contemporary Perspectives*, edited by Lance Massey & Richard C. Gebhardt, 137–60. Logan: Utah State University Press.

—. 2007. "How Writing Programs Support Undergraduate Research." In *Developing and Sustaining a Research-Supportive Curriculum: A Compendium of Successful Practices*, edited by Kerry K. Karukstis and Timothy E. Elgren, 195–208. Washington, DC: Council on Undergraduate Research.

—. 2003. "Learning Through Inquiry: An Overview of Undergraduate Research." In *Valuing and Supporting Undergraduate Research*, edited by Joyce Kinkead, 5–17. San Francisco: Jossey-Bass.

Kinkead, Joyce, and Laurie Grobman. 2011. "Expanding Opportunities for Undergraduate Research in English Studies." *Profession*: 218–30.

Kinkead, Joyce, and Jessie L. Moore. 2017. "The Naylor Workshop in Undergraduate Research in Writing Studies," September 18, 2017. *Literacy & NCTE* (blog). http://www2.ncte.org/blog/2017/09/naylor-workshop-undergraduate-research-writing-studies/.

Kinzie, Jillian, Robert Gonyea, Rick Shoup, and George D. Kuh. 2008. "Promoting Persistence and Success of Underrepresented Students: Lessons for Teaching and Learning." *New Directions for Teaching and Learning* 115: 21–38.

Kleinfeld, Elizabeth. 2018. "Increasing Access to Undergraduate Research through Writing Centers." Unpublished Manuscript.

Koch, Sara Stein, Betsy Q. Griffin, and Betsey O. Barefoot. 2014. *National Student Success Initiatives at Two-Year Colleges*. Brevard, North Carolina: John Gardner Institute.

Kuh, George D. 2008. *High-Impact Educational Practices: What They Are, Who Has Access to Them, and Why They Matter*. Washington, DC: Association of American Colleges and Universities.

Kuh, George D., and Ken O'Donnell. 2013. *Ensuring Quality and Taking High-Impact Practices to Scale*. Washington, DC: Association of American Colleges and Universities.

Lancaster, Zak. 2016. "Do Academics Really Write This Way? A Corpus Investigation of Moves and Templates in 'They Say / I Say.'" *College Composition and Communication* 67, no. 3: 437–64.

Langley-Turnbaugh, Samantha, Jean Whitney, Lynn Lovewell, and Babette Moeller. 2014. "Benefits of Research Fellowships for Undergraduates with Disabilities." *CUR Quarterly* 35, no. 2: 39–45.

Lewis, Lynn. November 7, 2018. Re: Listserv to Listserv: A Response from nextGEN [Electronic mailing list message].

Lindemann, Heather, and Justin Lohr. 2018. "What Changes When We 'Write for Change?': Considering the Consequences of a High School-University Writing Partnership."
Reflections: A Journal of Public Rhetoric, Civic Writing, and Service Learning 18, no. 1: 8–38.

Lockett, Alexandria. 2019. "Why I Call it the Academic Ghetto: A Critical Examination of Race, Place, and Writing Centers." *Praxis: A Writing Center Journal*.

—. 2017. "The Traditional Research Paper is Best." In *Bad Ideas about Writing*, edited by Cheryl Ball and Drew M. Loewe, 236–41. Morgantown: West Virginia University Libraries, Digital Publishing Institute.

—. 2015. "Multimedia Academic Literacy." https://www.slideshare.net/anova8/multimedia-literacy-researchlockett.

Lockett, Alexandria, and Sarah Rude Walker. 2016. "Creative Disruption and the Potential of Writing at HBCUs." *Composition Studies* 44, no. 2: 172–78.

Longmire-Avital, Buffie. 2019. "Recognizing Student Capitol in Mentored Undergraduate Research" (blog). March 4, 2019. Center for Engaged Learning, Elon University. https://www.centerforengagedlearning.org/recognizing-student-capitol-in-mentored-undergraduate-research/.

—. 2018. "Seven Potential Barriers to Engaging in Undergraduate Research for HURMS" (blog). September 18, 2018. Center for Engaged Learning, Elon University. https://www.centerforengagedlearning.org/seven-potential-barriers-to-engaging-in-undergraduate-research-for-hurms/.

Lopatto, David. 2010a. *Science in Solution: The Impact of Undergraduate Research on Student Learning.* Washington, DC: Council on Undergraduate Research. Tucson, AZ: Research Corporation for Science Advancement.

—. 2010b. "Undergraduate Research as a High-Impact Student Experience." *Peer Review* 12, no. 2: 27–30.

—. 2004. "Survey of Undergraduate Research Experiences (SURE): First Findings." *Cell Biology Education* 3, no. 4: 270–77.

—. 2003. "The Essential Features of Undergraduate Research." *CUR Quarterly* 23, no. 3: 139–42.

Lueck, Amy J., Beverlyn Law, and Isabella Zhang. 2019. "Inclusivity in the Archives: Expanding Undergraduate Pedagogies for Diversity and Inclusion." In *Diversity, Equity, and Inclusivity in Contemporary Higher Education*, edited by Rhonda Jeffries, 1–12. Hershey, Pennsylvania: IGI Global, 2019.

Lyons, Scott Richard. 2000. "Rhetorical Sovereignty: What do American Indians Want from Writing?" *College Composition and Communication* 51, no. 3: 447–68.

MacNealy, Sue. 1999. *Strategies for Empirical Research in Writing*. New York: Allyn & Bacon.

Malachowski, Mitchell. 2012. "Living Parallel Universes: The Great Faculty Divide Between Product-Oriented and Process-Oriented Scholarship." In *Faculty Support and Undergraduate Research: Innovations in Faculty Role Definition, Workload, and Reward*, edited by Nancy H. Hensel and Elizabeth L. Paul, 7–8. Washington, DC: Council on Undergraduate Research.

Malenczyk, Rita, Susan Miller-Cochran, Elizabeth Wardle, and Kathleen Blake Yancey, eds. 2018. *Composition, Rhetoric, & Disciplinarity*. Logan: Utah State University Press.

Margolin, Stephanie, and Wendy Hayden. 2015. "Beyond Mechanics: Reframing the Pedagogy and Development of Information Literacy Teaching Tools." *The Journal of Academic Librarianship* 41, no. 5: 602–12.

McDorman, Todd. 2004. "Promoting Undergraduate Research in the Humanities: Three Collaborative Approaches." *CUR Quarterly* 25, no. 1: 39–42.

McIsaac, Claudia Monpere. 2015. "'Beneath Thatched Shelters, We Paint Wide-brimmed Straw Hats': Creative Writing and Social Justice." In *Service Learning and Literary Studies in English*, edited by Laurie Grobman and Roberta Rosenberg, 188–200. New York: Modern Language Association.

McMillan, Laurie. 2019. *Focus on Writing: What College Students Want to Know*. Peterborough, ON: Broadview.

McNair, Tina Brown, Susan Albertine, Michelle Asha Cooper, Nicole McDonald, and Thomas Major Jr. 2016. *Becoming a Student-Ready College: A New Culture of Leadership for Student Success.* San Francisco: Jossey-Bass.

Mendoza, Susan G., and Dave A. Louis. 2018. "Unspoken Criticality: Developing Scholarly Voices for Minoritized Students Through UREs." *Scholarship and Practice of Undergraduate Research* 1, no. 4 (Summer): 18–23.

Micciche, Laura R. 2018. "Writers Have Always Loved Mobile Devices." *The Atlantic*, August 18. https://www.theatlantic.com/technology/archive/2018/08/writers-have-always-loved-mobile-devices/567637/.

Moore, Jessie L. 2016. "Undergraduate Research in SoTL as a High-Impact Practice." August 6, 2018. (blog) Center for Engaged Learning, Elon University. https://www.centerforengagedlearning.org/undergraduate-research-in-sotl-as-a-high-impact-practice/.

Moore, Sean E., Glen T. Hvenegaard, and Janet C. Wesselius. 2018. "The Efficacy of Directed Studies Courses as a Form of Undergraduate Research Experience: A Comparison of Instructor and Student Perspectives on Course Dynamics." *Higher Education* 76, no. 5: 771–88.

Morrison, Charles D. 2012. "'Boyer Reconsidered': Fostering Students' Scholarly Habits of Mind and Models of Practice." *International Journal for the Scholarship of Teaching and Learning* 6, no. 1, Article 16. https://doi.org/10.20429/ijsotl.2012.060116.

Mueller, Derek N. 2017. *Network Sense: Methods for Visualizing a Discipline*. Fort Collins, CO: WAC Clearinghouse and University Press of Colorado. https://wac.colostate.edu/books/writing/network/.

Mutnick, Deborah. 2007. "Inscribing the World: An Oral History Project in Brooklyn." *College Composition and Communication* 58, no. 4: 626–47.

National Census of Writing. 2013. https://writingcensus.swarthmore.edu/.

National Survey of Student Engagement (NSSE). 2018. "Annual Results 2018: Engagement Insights: Survey Findings on the Quality of Undergraduate Education." http://nsse.indiana.edu/html/annual_results.cfm.

Naylor Workshop for Undergraduate Research in Writing Studies. Accessed June 18, 2019. mschoett.wixsite.com/naylorconference.

Nelson Laird, Thomas F., Brian K. Bridges, Carla L. Morelon-Quainoo, Julie M. Williams, and Michelle Salinas Holmes. 2007. "African American and Hispanic Student Engagement at Minority Serving and Predominantly White Institutions." *Journal of College Student Development* 48, no. 1: 39–56.

New Faculty Majority. 2018. http://www.newfacultymajority.info/.

North, Stephen. 1987. *The Making of Knowledge in Composition: Portrait of an Emerging Field*. Upper Montclair, New Jersey: Heinemann.

Osborn, Jeffry M., and Kerry K. Karukstis. 2009. "The Benefits of Undergraduate Research, Scholarship, and Creative Activity." In *Broadening Participation in Undergraduate Research: Fostering Excellence and Enhancing the Impact*, edited by M. K. Boyd & J. L. Wesemann, 41–53. Washington, DC: Council on Undergraduate Research.

Ostergaard, Lori, Greg Giberson, and Jim Nugent. 2015. "Oakland University's Major in Writing and Rhetoric." In *Writing Majors: Eighteen Program Profiles*, edited by Greg Giberson, Jim Nugent, and Lori Ostergaard, 73–84. Logan: Utah State University Press.

Palmer, Ruth J., Andrea N. Hunt, Michael R. Neal, and Brad Wuetherick. 2018. "Mentored Undergraduate Research: An Investigation of Students' Perceptions of its Impact on Identity Development." In *Excellence in Mentoring Undergraduate Research*, edited by Maureen Vandermaas-Peeler, Paul Miller, and Jessie L. Moore, 19–42. Washington, DC: Council on Undergraduate Research.

—. 2015. "Mentoring, Undergraduate Research, and Identity Development: A Conceptual Review and Research Agenda." *Mentoring & Tutoring: Partnership in Learning* 23 no. 5: 411–26.

Paul, Elizabeth L. 2012. "New Directions for Faculty Workload Models: Focusing on High-Impact Learning Practices." In *Faculty Support and Undergraduate Research: Innovations in Faculty Role Definition, Workload, and Reward*, edited by Nancy H. Hensel and Elizabeth L. Paul, 133–46. Washington, DC: Council on Undergraduate Research.

Pennebaker, James W. 2011. *The Secret Life of Pronouns: What Our Words Say About Us*. New York: Bloomsbury.

Perdue, Sherry Wynn, et al. 2014. "Negotiating the Sponsorship Continuum: Preparing Humanities Undergraduates to Conduct RAD Research." *Perspectives on Undergraduate Research and Mentoring* 3, no. 2: 1-19.

Perryman-Clark, Staci M. 2014. "Writing, Rhetoric, and American cultures (WRA) 125—Writing the Ethnic and Racial Experience." In

Students' Right to Their Own Language: A Critical Sourcebook, edited by Staci Perryman-Clark, David. E. Kirkland, and Austin Jackson, 258-275. Boston: Bedford St. Martin's.

—. 2013. "African American Language, Rhetoric, and Students' Writing: New Directions for SRTOL." *College Composition and Communication* 64, no. 3: 469–95.

Perryman-Clark, Staci M., and Collin Lamont Craig, eds. 2019. *Black Perspectives in Writing Program Administration: From the Margins to the Center*. Urbana, IL: National Council of Teachers of English.

Phelps, Louise Wetherbee. 1991. *Composition as a Human Science: Contributions to the Self-Understanding of a Discipline*. New York: Oxford University Press.

Poe, Mya, Asao B. Inoue, and Norbert Elliot, eds. 2018. *Writing Assessment, Social Justice, and the Advancement of Opportunity*. Fort Collins, CO: WAC Clearinghouse.

Renee Posselt, Julie, and Kim R. Black. 2012. "Developing the Research Identities and Aspirations of First-generation College Students: Evidence from the McNair Scholars Program." *International Journal for Researcher Development* 3, no. 1: 26–48.

Robertson, Liane, and Kara Taczak. 2017. "Teaching for Transfer." In *Understanding Writing Transfer: Implications for Transformative Student Learning in Higher Education*, edited by Jessie L. Moore and Randall Bass, 93–102. Sterling, VA: Stylus.

Robillard, Amy E. 2006. "'Young Scholars': Affecting Composition: A Challenge to Disciplinary Citation Practices." *College English* 68, no. 3: 253–70.

Royster, Jacqueline Jones, and Gesa E. Kirsch. 2012. *Feminist Rhetorical Practice: New Horizons for Rhetoric, Composition, and Literacy Studies*. Carbondale: Southern Illinois University Press.

Ruiz, Iris D. 2016. *Reclaiming Composition for Chicano/as and Other Ethnic Minorities: A Critical History and Pedagogy*. New York: Palgrave Macmillan.

Scott, J. Blake, and Elizabeth Wardle. 2015. "Using Threshold Concepts to Inform Writing and Rhetoric Undergraduate Majors: The UCF Experiment." In *Naming What We Know: Threshold Concepts of Writing Studies*, edited by Linda Adler-Kassner and Elizabeth Wardle, 122–39. Boulder: University Press of Colorado.

Seymour, Elaine, Anne-Barrie Hunter, Sandra L. Laursen, and Tracee Deantoni. 2004. "Establishing the Benefits of Research Experiences for Undergraduates in the Sciences: First Findings from a Three-Year Study." *Science Education* 88: 493–534.

Shanahan, Jenny Olin. 2012. "Curricular Support for Faculty Who Engage in Undergraduate Research." In *Faculty Support and Undergraduate Research: Innovations in Faculty Role Definition, Workload, and Reward*, edited by Nancy H. Hensel and Elizabeth L. Paul, 68–76. Washington, DC: Council on Undergraduate Research.

Shanahan, Jenny Olin, Elizabeth Ackley-Holbrook, Eric Hall, Kearsley Stewart, and Helen Walkington. 2015. "Ten Salient Practices of Undergraduate Research Mentors: A Review of the Literature." *Mentoring & Tutoring: Partnership in Learning* 23: 359–76. DOI: 10.1080/13611267.2015.1126162

Shanahan, Jenny Olin, Helen Walkington, Elizabeth Ackley, Eric E. Hall, and Kearsley A. Stewart. 2017. "Award-Winning Mentors See Democratization as the Future of Undergraduate Research." *CUR Quarterly* 37, no. 4: 4–11. https://doi.org/doi: 10.18833/curq/37/4/14.

Shuy Roger. 2001. "Forensic Linguistics." In *The Handbook of Linguistics*, edited by Mark Aronoff and Janie Rees-Miller, 683–91. Oxford: Blackwell.

Simmons, Michele. 2018. "Engaging Circulation in Urban Renewal." In *Circulation, Writing, and Rhetoric*, edited by Laurie Gries and Collin Gifford Brooke, 43-60. Logan: Utah State University Press.

—. 1992. "Studying Risk at the Oak Ridge National Laboratory." (with C. C. Travis) *Federal Facilities Journal* 3, no. 3: 295–300.

Simmons, Michele, and Tim Amidon. 2016. "Negotiating 'Messy' Research Context and Design Through Adaptive Research Stances: Experience Report." Proceedings of the 34th Annual ACM International Conference on the Design of Communication. Silver Springs, MD.

Small, Meg L., and Emily A. Waterman. 2017. "Time Use During First Year of College Predicts Participation in High-Impact Activities During Later Years." *Journal of College Student Development* 58, no. 6: 954–60. doi:10.1353/csd.2017.0075.

Smith, Kevin G. 2017. "A (New)ish Approach to Markup in the Undergraduate Classroom." Women Writers Project Blog https://wwp.northeastern.edu/blog/classroom-markup.

Sorcinelli, Mary Dean, and Jung Yun. 2007. "From Mentor to Mentoring Networks: Mentoring in the New Academy." *Change* 39, no. 6: 58–61.

Stenberg, Shari J. 2015. *Repurposing Composition: Feminist Interventions for a Neoliberal Age*. Logan: Utah State University Press.

Strada Education Network and Gallup, Inc. 2018. *2018 Strada-Gallup Alumni Survey: Mentoring College Students to Success*. https://news.gallup.com/reports/244058/2018-strada-gallup-alumni-survey.aspx.

Stuart, Kate. 2013. "Flinging Myself into the Broader World." *Young Scholars in Writing* 10: 5–10.

SURE III (Survey of Undergraduate Research Experiences). 2017–18. https://www.grinnell.edu/academics/resources/ctla/assessment/sure-iii.

Swales, Jonathan. 1990. *Genre Analysis: English in Academic and Research Settings*. Cambridge: Cambridge University Press.

Sweat, Jeffrey, Glenda Jones, Suejung Han, and Susan M. Wolfgram, 2013. "How Does High Impact Practice Predict Student Engagement? A Comparison of White and Minority Students." *International Journal for the Scholarship of Teaching and Learning* 7, no. 2. https://doi.org/10.20429/ijsotl.2013.070217

"The Challenge of the Count" 2012. Special Issue, *CUR Quarterly* 32, no. 3. https://www.cur.org/assets/1/7/323TOC.pdf.

Thieme, Katja, e-mail message, February 11, 2019.

Thieme, Katja, and Shurli Makmillen. 2017. "A Principled Uncertainty: Writing Studies Methods in Contexts of Indigeneity." *College Composition and Communication* 68, no. 3: 466–93.

Toth, Christie, Mitchell Reber, and Aaron Clark. 2015. "Major Affordances: Collaborative Scholarship in a Department of Writing and Rhetoric Studies." *Composition Studies* 43, no. 2: 197–200.

Traywick, Deaver. 2010. "Preaching What We Practice: RCR Instruction for Undergraduate Researchers in Writing Studies." In *Undergraduate Research in English Studies*, edited by Laurie Grobman and Joyce Kinkead, 51–73. Urbana, Illinois: National Council of Teachers of English.

Tuhiwai Smith, Linda. 2012. *Decolonizing Methodologies: Research and Indigenous Peoples*. London: Zed Books.

University of British Columbia Vancouver Campus. "WRDS 350 Course Descriptions." Accessed March 21, 2017. https://asrw.arts.ubc.ca/WRDS-350-course-descriptions/.

University of California Santa Barbara. n.d. *Raab Writing Fellows Program*. Accessed June 13, 2019. http://raabwritingfellows.com/.

University of California Santa Barbara Library. n.d. *UCSB Library Award for Undergraduate Research*. Accessed June 1, 2019. https://www.library.ucsb.edu/library-award-undergraduate-research.

University of California Santa Barbara McNair Scholars Program. n.d. Accessed June 9, 2019. https://mcnair.ucsb.edu/.

University of California Santa Barbara Undergraduate Education. n.d. *Undergraduate Research and Creative Activities (URCA) Grant*. Accessed June 14, 2019. https://www.duels.ucsb.edu/research/urca.

University of Massachusetts Amherst Institute for Teaching Excellence & Faculty Development. N.d. Mutual Mentoring Model. Accessed November 2, 2018. https://www.umass.edu/tefd/mutual-mentoring-model.

University of Utah, Department of Writing and Rhetoric Studies. 2019. "WRTG 3030: Writing Across Locations." https://writing.utah.edu/_resources/documents/classes/2019-classes/summer/WRTG-3030.pdf.

Valles, Sarah Banschbach, Rebecca Day Babcock, and Karen Keaton Jackson. 2017. "Writing Center Directors and Diversity: A Survey." *The Peer Review* 1, no. 1.

Villanueva, Victor. 2011. "The Rhetorics Of Racism: A Historical Sketch." In *Writing Centers and the New Racism: A Call for Sustainable Dialogue and Change*, edited by Laura Greenfield and Karen Rowa, 17–32. Boulder: University Press of Colorado. DOI:10.2307/j.ctt4cgk6s.

Waitoller, Federico R., and Kathleen A. King Thorius. 2016. "Cross-pollinating Culturally Sustaining Pedagogy and Universal Design for Learning: Toward an Inclusive Pedagogy that Accounts for Dis/ability." *Harvard Educational Review* 86, no. 3: 366–89.

Walkington, Helen, Eric Hall, Jenny Olin Shanahan, Elizabeth Ackley, and Kearsley Stewart. 2018. "Striving for Excellence in Mentoring Undergraduate Research: The Challenges and Approaches to 10 Salient Practices." In *Excellence in Mentoring Undergraduate Research*, edited by Maureen Vandermaas-Peeler, Paul Miller, and Jessie L. Moore, 105–29. Washington, DC: Council on Undergraduate Research.

Wardle, Elizabeth. 2013. "Intractable Writing Program Problems, Kairos, and Writing about Writing: A Profile of the University of Central Florida's First-Year Composition Program." *Composition Forum* 27.

—. 2012. "Creative Repurposing for Expansive Learning: Considering 'Problem-Exploring' and 'Answer-Getting' Dispositions in Individuals and Fields." *Composition Forum* 26, no. 1.

Wardle, Elizabeth, and Doug Downs. 2019. *Writing about Writing: A College Reader*. 4th ed. Boston: Bedford/St.Martin's.

—. 2017. *Writing about Writing: A College Reader*. 3rd ed. Boston: Bedford/St. Martins.

Wayment, Heidi A., and K. Laurie Dickson. 2008. "Increasing Student Participation in Undergraduate Research Benefits Students, Faculty, and Department." *Teaching of Psychology* 35, no. 3: 194–97.

Welch, Nancy and Tony Scott, eds. 2016. *Composition in the Age of Austerity*. Boulder: University Press of Colorado, 2016.

Wenger, Etienne. 1998. *Communities of Practice: Learning, Meaning, and Identity*. Cambridge, UK: Cambridge University Press.

Werder, Carmen, and Megan M. Otis, eds. 2010. *Engaging Student Voices in the Study of Teaching and Learning*. Sterling, VA: Stylus.

Wetherbee, Ben. 2012. "Toward a Polyphonic Model of Student Coauthorship: A Response to Joseph Harris and Julie Lindquist." *JAC* 32, no. 3-4: 743–51.

White, Allison. 2018. "Understanding the University and Faculty Investment in Implementing High-Impact Educational Practices." *Journal of the Scholarship of Teaching and Learning* 18, no. 2 (June): 118–35. DOI:10.14434/josotl.v18i2.23143.

White, Kate, Suzanne Kesler Rumsey and Stevens Amidon. 2016. "Are We 'There' Yet? The Treatment of Gender and Feminism in Technical, Business and Workplace Writing Studies." *Journal of Technical Writing and Communication* 46, no. 1: 27–58.

Wierszewski, Emily. 2012. Celebration of Writing at SHU. www.youtube.com/watch?v=BCFo4fqQIsw.

Wuetherick, Brad, John Willison, and Jenny Olin Shanahan. 2018. "Mentored Undergraduate Research at Scale: Undergraduate Research in the Curriculum as Pedagogy." In *Excellence in Mentoring Undergraduate Research*, edited by Maureen Vandermaas-Peeler, Paul C. Miller, and Jessie L. Moore, 181–202. Washington, D.C.: Council on Undergraduate Research.

Yancey, Kathleen Blake. 2018."Mapping the Turn to Disciplinarity: A Historical Analysis of Composition's Trajectory and Its Current Moment." In *Composition, Rhetoric, and Disciplinarity*, edited by Rita

Malenczyk, Susan Miller-Cochran, Elizabeth Wardle, and Kathleen Blake Yancey, 15–35. Logan: Utah State University Press.

Yancey, Kathleen, Liane Robertson, and Kara Taczak. 2014. *Writing Across Contexts: Transfer, Composition, and Sites of Writing.* Logan: Utah State University Press.

YMV. 2012. "Summer Institute for Literary and Cultural Studies." Preparing for Graduate School. Accessed Dec. 28, 2018. mmufgradprep.wordpress.com/2012/12/19/summer-institute-for-literary-and-cultural-studies/.

Young Scholars in Writing. N.d. Journal Mission. Accessed July 18, 2019. arc.lib.montana.edu/ojs/index.php/Young-Scholars-In-Writing/about/editorialPolicies#focusAndScope.

Contributors

Sophia Abbot is a Graduate Apprentice in the Center for Engaged Learning and a graduate student in Elon University's Masters of Higher Education program. Since her undergraduate participation in Students as Learners and Teachers at Bryn Mawr College, she has been active in student-faculty partnerships and partnership research. Prior to graduate school, she spent three years as an academic developer and launched and led a student-faculty pedagogic partnership initiative during that time. She serves on the International Advisory Board for the International Journal for Students as Partners and is a member of the International Society for the Scholarship of Teaching and Learning (ISSOTL) Board of Directors. In her recent work, Sophia has been looking at mentorship as a form of partnership.

Heather Brook Adams is Assistant Professor of English at the University of North Carolina at Greensboro. Her research investigates discourses of gender, reproduction, and shame as well as decolonial/intersectional methodologies. Adams's work has appeared in journals such as *Rhetoric Review*, *Women's Studies in Communication*, *Peitho*, and *Composition Forum* as well as in various edited collections. Adams has been granted funds for implementing undergraduate research while teaching at the University of Alaska Anchorage as well as at UNC-Greensboro. In her current position, she teaches courses on contemporary rhetoric, rhetorics of health and medicine, and advocacy and argumentation.

Rebecca Day Babcock is the William and Ordelle Watts Professor at University of Texas, Permian Basin, where she teaches courses in writing and linguistics. She also serves as the Freshman English Coordinator and Director of Undergraduate Research. She has authored, co-authored, or edited several books on tutoring, writing centers, disability, and meta-research, including *Researching the Writing Center*, the revised edition written with Terese Thonus, and *Theories and Methods of Writing Center Research*, edited with Jo Mackiewicz. She has also published research in *Writing Lab Newsletter*, *Linguistics and Education*, *Composition Forum*, *Praxis*, *The Peer Review*, and others. She won the IWCA best article award in 2011 for her article on interpreted writing tutorials with a deaf writer, and in 2019, she received the Council of Writing Program

Administrators (CWPA) Outstanding Scholarship Award for "Writing Center Directors and Diversity: A Survey," co-authored with Sarah Banschbach Valles and Karen Keaton and published in *The Peer Review*.

Hannah Bellwoar is Associate Professor of English and Director of Writing at Juniata College, where she teaches professional and digital writing. Her research interests include digital literacies, undergraduate research in writing studies, professional writing and usability studies, and the rhetoric of health and medicine. Her work has been published in *Kairos: A Journal of Rhetoric, Technology and Pedagogy*, *Harlot Journal*, *OneShot: A Journal of Critical Games and Play*, and *Technical Communication Quarterly*.

Ljiljana Coklin is a lecturer in the Writing Program at the University of California, Santa Barbara. She is a co-director of the Civic Engagement track of the Professional Writing Minor and a coordinator of the Raab Writing Fellows Program, for which she is also a seminar leader and a mentor.

Emily Murphy Cope is Assistant Professor of Rhetoric and Writing Studies at York College of Pennsylvania, where she directs the integrated written, oral, and visual communication program and teaches courses focused on the history of rhetoric and research methods. Her scholarship has appeared in *Rhetoric Society Quarterly* and several edited collections. Beginning in 2020, Emily is a co-editor of *Young Scholars in Writing*.

Cynthia Crimmins, Director of the Center for Academic Innovation at York College of Pennsylvania, leads initiatives to advance high impact practices such as undergraduate research and project-based learning. From 1997–2015, she directed the Writing Center and in 2011 founded the Center for Teaching and Learning at York College. As a Teagle Assessment Scholar, she consults with colleges and universities around the country to improve student learning. At York College of Pennsylvania, Crimmins teaches first-year seminars and communication courses and mentors undergraduate researchers.

Gabriel Cutrufello is Chair of the Department of Communication and Writing and Associate Professor of Rhetoric and Composition in the Professional Writing program at York College of Pennsylvania, where he teaches courses in first-year composition, technical writing, document design, and research methods. His scholarship on the rhetoric of science has been published in *Rhetoric Review*, and his work on technical writing and writing-about-writing pedagogy has been published in *Next Steps: New Directions for/in Writing about Writing*, edited by Barbara Bird, Doug Downs, Moriah McCracken, and Jan Rieman (2019).

Dominic DelliCarpini is the Naylor Endowed Professor of Writing Studies and Dean of the Center for Community Engagement at York College of Pennsylvania. He also served as WPA for thirteen years and Chief Academic Officer for five years. His areas of research, publication, and presentation include writing and civic engagement, writing program administration, first-year writing, and writing centers as sites for undergraduate research. He is author/editor of four textbooks: *The Prentice-Hall Guide for College Writers* (with Stephen Reid); *Composing a Life's Work: Writing, Citizenship, and your Occupation*; *Issues: Readings in Academic Disciplines*; and *Conversations: Readings for Writing* (with Jack Selzer).

Doug Downs is Associate Professor of Writing and Rhetoric at Montana State University, founder of its writing major, and Director of its Core Writing Program, 2013–18. He served as editor of *Young Scholars in Writing*, the national journal of undergraduate research in rhetoric and writing studies, from 2015–2019. Downs researches conceptions of writing, student reading, and writing pedagogy. With Elizabeth Wardle, he is coauthor of the textbook *Writing about Writing* and a foundational 2007 *College Composition and Communication* article on writing about writing. He is a co-editor of *Next Steps: New Directions for / in Writing about Writing* (2019) and has published numerous chapters and articles on first-year composition, writing pedagogy, student reading practices, and the disciplinarity of Writing Studies.

Andrea Rosso Efthymiou is Assistant Professor of Writing Studies and Rhetoric and Writing Center Director at Hofstra University. Andrea's work on institutional mission in writing program administration and tutors' discursive practices has appeared in various edited collections. Andrea's research interests include sustainable mentorship of undergraduate research through tutor education and facilitating undergraduate students' civic engagement. She is currently developing a longitudinal assessment plan to measure the impact of writing center tutors' extended work beyond sessions, looking specifically at tutors' writing center research, conference presentations, and publications as artifacts of undergraduate research.

Heather Falconer is Assistant Professor of Writing at Curry College and Coordinator of the Reading/Writing Enrichment program. She serves as an editor with the Perspectives on Writing book series (The WAC Clearinghouse), as well as Chair of the Research and Publications Committee for the Association for Writing Across the Curriculum. Dr. Falconer's research has appeared in *Written Communication, The WAC Journal,* the *Journal for Research in Science Teaching,* and the *Journal of Hispanic Higher Education,* as well as numerous edited collections.

Jenn Fishman is Associate Professor of rhetoric and composition/writing studies and a writing administrator at Marquette University. The author of more than a dozen articles and book chapters, she has edited the Research Exchange Index and issues *of CCC Online, Peitho,* and *Community Literacy Journal.* Her grant- and award-winning research centers on longitudinal projects from the Stanford Study of Writing to Kenyon Writes. Past President of the Coalition of Feminist Scholars in the History of Rhetoric and Composition, her national professional leadership includes stewardship of undergraduate research on behalf of the Conference on College Composition and Communication and the Rhetoric Society of America.

William FitzGerald is Associate Professor of English at Rutgers University-Camden, where he directs the Writing Program and the Teaching Matters and Assessment Center. He is the author, among other publications, of *Spiritual Modalities: Prayer as Rhetoric and Performance* (Penn State Press) and co-author/co-editor with Joseph Bizup of reference guides for the University of Chicago Press, including *The Craft of Research,* 4e; *A Manual for Writers of Research Papers, Theses, and Dissertations,* 7e; and *The Student's Guide to Writing College Papers,* 5e.

Jane Greer, University of Missouri Curators' Distinguished Teaching Professor, is the editor of *Girls and Literacy in America: Historical Perspectives to the Present* (ABC-Clio, 2003) and, with Laurie Grobman, coeditor of *Pedagogies of Public Memory: Teaching Writing and Rhetoric at Museums, Archives, and Memorials* (Routledge 2015). From 2010 to 2015, she served as editor of *Young Scholars in Writing,* and her scholarship has appeared in *College English, College Composition and Communication, Peitho, WPA Journal,* and numerous edited collections. A professor of

English and Women's, Gender, and Sexuality Studies at the University of Missouri, Kansas City (UMKC), she teaches composition courses as well as classes on the rhetorical practices of girls and women. She also serves as UMKC's Director of Undergraduate Research.

Dr. Laurie Grobman, Professor of English and women's studies at Penn State Berks, has published two single-authored books and four coedited collections, including *Pedagogies of Public Memory: Teaching Writing and Rhetoric at Museums, Archives, and Memorials* (Routledge, 2015, with Jane Greer) and *Undergraduate Research in English Studies* (NCTE, 2010, with Joyce Kinkead). Grobman's article, "'Engaging Race': Critical Race Inquiry and Community-Engaged Scholarship," received the 2018 NCTE Richard C. Ohmann Outstanding Article in *College English* Award. She was the 2014 Carnegie Foundation for the Advancement of Teaching Outstanding Baccalaureate Colleges Professor of the Year. Grobman's most recent book, coauthored with Dr. E. Michele Ramsey, is *Major Decisions: College, Career, and the Case for the Humanities*, and is forthcoming from the University of Pennsylvania Press. With her late colleague and friend, Candace Spigelman, Grobman co-founded *Young Scholars in Writing: Undergraduate Research in Writing and Rhetoric* in 2003. She edited the journal through 2009.

Michelle Grue's interdisciplinary research in education and writing draws on Black feminism to investigate diversity issues in academia. Her forthcoming article in the *Journal of Multimodal Rhetoric* explores rhetorical performances in the dress practices of Black women professors. Her current project focuses on the official and unofficial ways graduate students learn how to research race and gender in writing and rhetoric doctoral programs. She earned her MA at the Gevirtz Graduate School of Education at the University of California, Santa Barbara and is at the time of publishing a doctoral candidate in the same program.

Eric Hall is Professor of exercise science at Elon University. His disciplinary research interests include the importance of physical activity on mental health and exploring the short and longer-term impacts of concussions on student-athletes. Additionally, he is interested in the influence of high-impact practices on student development, as well as, the importance of high-quality mentorship in undergraduate research and other high impact practices. He has co-authored eighty research articles and six book chapters, and he is co-editor of a book on concussions in athletics. At Elon University, he has received multiple awards for his mentorship of undergraduate students and his scholarship.

D. Alexis Hart, Director of Writing at Allegheny College, is the editor of *How to Start an Undergraduate Research Journal* (CUR, 2012), and her published work has also appeared in *CUR Quarterly*, *College Composition and Communication*, *Pedagogy*, *Writing on the Edge*, *Composition Forum*, and several edited collections. She serves on the editorial boards of *Kairos*, *The Peer Review*, the *Journal of Veteran Studies*, and the *International Journal for ePortfolio*, among others. As Director of Writing, she is responsible for training and supervising the peer writing consultants in Allegheny's Learning Commons and for leading faculty development related to the teaching of writing across the curriculum.

Kristine Johnson is Associate Professor of English at Calvin College, where she directs the written rhetoric program and teaches courses in composition pedagogy, linguistics, and first-year writing. Her work has appeared in *College Composition and Communication*, *WPA: Writing Program Administration*, *Pedagogy*, *Composition Studies*, and various edited collections. At Xavier University, she co-founded the *Xavier Journal of Undergraduate Research*, and at Calvin College, she regularly collaborates with undergraduate researchers through the McGregor Undergraduate Research Program for summer research in the arts and humanities.

Dr. Joyce Kinkead is Distinguished Professor of English at Utah State University. In 2012, she was named a Fellow of the Council on Undergraduate Research, an award that recognizes her national reputation for promoting undergraduate research, the first and only humanist to be so honored. The US Professors of the Year Program designated her the Carnegie Professor for the State of Utah in 2013. She is the 2018 D. Wynne Thorne Career Researcher, the highest honor awarded to a faculty researcher at USU. As Associate Vice President for Research overseeing undergraduate research, she instituted a number of programs: University Undergraduate Research Fellows; the Utah Conference on Undergraduate Research; and Research on Capitol Hill. She has authored or edited a number of books that focus on undergraduate research, including the following: *Researching Writing: An Introduction to Research Methods* (2016); *Undergraduate Research Offices & Programs* (2012); *Advancing Undergraduate Research: Marketing, Communications, and Fund-raising*

(2011); *Undergraduate Research in English Studies* with Laurie Grobman (2010); *Valuing and Supporting Undergraduate Research* (2003).

Elizabeth Kleinfeld is Professor of English and Writing Center Director at Metropolitan State University of Denver. She teaches courses on rhetoric and composition theory and practice, including authorship studies and digital rhetoric. She researches student source use, academic integrity, and ways of teaching and assessing writing that promote inclusivity and social justice. Her pedagogy and research are informed by disability studies, feminism, and social justice theory. She has co-authored a textbook on multimodal and multi-genre composition and has published articles on writing center work, digital rhetoric, and student source citation practices.

Dr. Alexandria Lockett is Assistant Professor of English at Spelman College. She publishes about the technological politics of race, surveillance, and access. Her work has appeared in *Composition Studies, Enculturation,* and *Praxis* as well as *Black Perspectives on Writing Program Administration: From the Margins to the Center* (SWR Press), *Out in the Center* (Utah State University Press), and *Bad Ideas about Writing* (West Virginia University Digital Publishing Institute). An extended biography, which contains more information about her grants, service, works-in-progress, and consulting experience is available via her portfolio at: www.alexandrialockett.com, ORCID link: https://orcid.org/0000-0002-6267-8875.

Shurli Makmillen is Assistant Professor at Claflin University in South Carolina. Her research draws from rhetorical theories of language and genre to understand a variety of literary and non-literary texts. This includes work on the ways Indigenous methodologies and knowledges are finding form in academic and legal genres. Publications along these lines have appeared in *Linguistics in the Human Sciences* and *College Composition and Communication*.

In a former life, **Mike Mattison** sold vacuum cleaners, fixed sump pumps, and worked on Park Avenue. For the past twenty years, though, he has been involved with writing centers, where he has been fortunate to collaborate with undergraduate advisors on a variety of research projects. He is the Director of the Writing Center, Associate Provost of Academic Support Services, and Associate Professor of English at Wittenberg University, where he teaches courses in writing center theory, composition theory, and rhetoric/grammar. He co-chaired the 2019 IWCA-NCPTW conference, and is the 2020 president of NCPTW. Two of his recent articles, in *WLN: A Writing Center Journal* and *Praxis,* were co-written with undergraduates.

Laurie McMillan is Assistant Dean in the College of Arts, Humanities, and Social Sciences at Millersville University. Her research focuses on feminist writing and rhetoric as well as composition studies. She published a composition textbook, *Focus on Writing* (Broadview Press, 2019), and is working on a book manuscript titled *Slut Rhetoric: Social Media, Pop Culture, and Politics.* She has published articles in journals such as *Peitho, Feminist Media Studies,* and *Radical Pedagogy* as well as in a number of edited collections. She is teaching less frequently now, but she has a record of supporting undergraduate research in writing studies, with mentorship occurring both inside and outside the classroom.

Jessie L. Moore is Director of the Center for Engaged Learning and Professor of English: Professional Writing and Rhetoric at Elon University. Jessie coordinates the Center's research seminars, which support international, multi-institutional inquiry on engaged learning topics. She is the co-editor of *Critical Transitions: Writing and the Question of Transfer* (with Chris Anson, The WAC Clearinghouse and University Press of Colorado, 2016), *Understanding Writing Transfer: Implications for Transformative Student Learning in Higher Education* (with Randy Bass, Stylus, 2017), and *Excellence in Mentoring Undergraduate Research* (with Maureen Vandermaas-Peeler and Paul Miller, CUR, 2018).

Kim Fahle Peck is the Writing Center Director at York College of Pennsylvania, where she leads the writing tutoring and writing fellows programs and teaches courses on writing and writing center pedagogy. She currently serves as the Membership and Communication Chair of the Global Society of Online Literacy Educators (GSOLE) and the Web Coordinator for the Mid-Atlantic Writing Center Association (MAWCA), and she will serve as a co-editor of *Young Scholars in Writing* starting in 2020.

Patricia Roberts-Miller, Professor of Rhetoric and Writing and Director of the University of Texas at Austin University Writing Center, is the author of *Rhetoric and Demagoguery* (SIUP 2019), *Demagoguery and Democracy* (The Experiment 2017), *Fanatical Schemes: Proslavery Rhetoric and the Tragedy of Consensus* (U of Alabama P 2009), *Deliberate Conflict:*

Argument, Political Theory, and Composition Classes (SIUP 2007), and *Voices in the Wilderness: The Paradox of the Puritan Public Sphere* (U of Alabama P 1999).

Megan Schoettler is a PhD candidate in Composition and Rhetoric and a Graduate Assistant Director of Composition at Miami University. Her research centers on feminist pedagogy and rhetorics as well as writers' learning dispositions. At York College of Pennsylvania, Megan was an undergraduate researcher and co-facilitator of the first annual Naylor Workshop for Undergraduate Research in Writing Studies. At Miami, Megan teaches composition theory and research to college and secondary-level writing teachers and has been recognized by the English department with an Outstanding Teacher Award. Megan also serves as an Editorial Assistant for the journal *Women & Language*.

Jenny Olin Shanahan, PhD, is Assistant Provost for High-Impact Practices at Bridgewater State University—Massachusetts, where she supports Undergraduate Research, the Honors Program, National Fellowships, and a Research Internship program for students from underserved groups. Dr. Shanahan has co-edited five books and authored thirteen articles on undergraduate research. Her research focuses on inclusion and equity in high-impact practices for all students, excellence in mentoring undergraduate research and creative scholarship, and scaffolding research and inquiry across curricula.

Field Watts is a graduate student in chemistry at the University of Michigan, conducting discipline-based education research in collaboration with the Sweetland Center for Writing. His work is focused on the implementation and assessment of writing-to-learn pedagogies in large-enrollment STEM courses. A National Science Foundation Graduate Research Fellow, he works as a graduate student instructor within the chemistry department and as a graduate student instructional consultant within the Center for Research on Learning and Teaching.

Index

academic writing, 56, 78, 109, 191
academy, the, xv, 3, 7, 61–63, 74, 113, 116, 125, 167
access, xii, xvi, 4, 8, 10–12, 16, 23, 30, 32, 34–35, 37, 46, 48, 62, 72, 81, 89, 94–96, 104, 111, 113–134, 135–137, 141, 144–145, 147, 150, 155, 159–161, 163, 165, 176–177, 182, 185, 204, 207, 209, 211
adaptability, 58
adjunct instructors, 4, 136–137, 139, 150, 206, 221
admissions, 114, 116, 120, 197
Advanced Placement Research, 84
Advancement Offices, 169, 170, 174, 201, 208–209
advising, 31, 44, 78, 114, 164, 167
affordances, 5, 34, 51, 96
African-American rhetorics, 18, 55, 77, 92
anti-racist writing instruction, 92, 93
archival research, 7, 9, 49, 53–55, 57, 60, 75, 80, 85, 101, 130, 145, 146–147, 149, 152, 216–217
assessment, 13, 54, 58, 73, 78, 86, 88, 131, 144, 151, 162, 166–169, 171, 199, 208
assignments, xiii, xiv, 39, 40, 42, 54, 59, 75, 102, 115, 122, 163, 204

audience, xv, 39, 40, 42–43, 82, 85, 87, 95, 99, 119, 130, 193, 197
austerity, 81, 180, 182, 211
authority, 56, 93, 182, 193
authorship, 43, 80, 92–93, 193; faculty/student, 43, 168, 209

barriers to participation, xi, xvi, 50, 114, 116–118, 120–121
Bazerman, Charles, 56, 146, 191
Belmont Report, The, 53
benefits of undergraduate research, xii, 29, 46, 48, 51, 54, 62–63, 76, 89, 111, 114, 129, 136, 140, 151, 205
best practices, 5, 216
Boyer, Ernest L., xii, 3, 7, 10, 13, 17, 23, 27, 29, 59, 77, 82, 94, 138, 158, 165, 180, 194–196
budgeting decisions, 202
budgets, 81, 166, 172, 204, 210–211
Burke, Kenneth, 55, 106, 153–154

capacity (for undergraduate research), 5, 8–9, 35, 46, 186–188, 195, 212, 220
capstone courses and projects, 37, 41, 54, 60, 84, 116, 144, 196
career placement, 202
careers, 9, 47, 58, 81–82, 83–84, 120, 123, 150, 202, 208, 219

CCCC Position Statement on Undergraduate Research, 13, 49, 50, 71, 72, 73, 74, 76, 77, 159, 193, 215

circulation of knowledge, xvi, 4, 12, 27, 41, 72, 85, 94–110, 115, 120, 131, 149, 161, 153, 176, 178, 182, 185, 187, 196, 208

civic engagement, 84

Civil Rights Movement, 92–93

Coalition for Community Writing, 179, 212

coauthoring, 47, 91–93

collaboration, xi, 31, 33, 35, 37, 42, 45, 46, 49, 52, 54, 63, 68, 73, 77, 87, 91–92, 103–104, 108, 119, 129, 133, 144, 145, 149, 152, 163, 184, 188, 194–195, 213, 216, 219

College Board, 84

community writing, xv, 5–7, 9, 11, 17, 18, 20, 32, 37, 40, 42, 46, 55–56, 60, 64, 69, 71, 73–74, 76–77, 79, 80, 83, 86–87, 89, 92, 96–97, 101, 104, 107, 115–116, 121–122, 131, 145, 152, 155–156, 161, 162, 163, 172–173, 176–179, 184–185, 187–188, 193, 208, 210, 212, 217–220, 223

community-based research, xv, 64, 71, 74, 101, 156, 179, 193, 217–218

community-engaged projects, 7, 9, 73, 74, 76–77, 92, 104, 115, 155

compensation, 137, 172, 182

composition: first-year, 9, 11, 60, 78, 181, 198; see also first-year composition and first-year writing

Conference on College Composition and Communication (CCCC), 10, 13, 49–50, 62, 71–72, 74, 76–77, 86, 101, 103, 118, 128, 159, 187–188, 192–193, 212, 216, 221, 223

Council of Writing Program Administrators (CWPA), 58, 78, 83, 121, 144, 150, 166, 179, 182, 213

Council on Undergraduate Research (CUR), xiii–xiv, xv, 4, 71, 94, 192, 195, 222

course-based undergraduate research experiences, 12, 37, 40–42, 50, 53, 61, 134, 148, 151, 198, 210

coursework, xvi, 44, 58, 81, 93, 120, 138, 141, 151, 157, 160

creative writing, 76, 82, 174

creativity, xiii, 8, 58, 84, 130,

critical thinking, xiv, 78, 82

culture: academic, 5, 124, 125, 129, 140, 162

cultures, 5, 81, 165–166

curation, 97–98, 104, 149,

curiosity, xiv, 57–58, 61, 99, 119, 150, 195

curriculum, xvi, 4–5, 8,–12, 23, 30–31, 39, 44, 48, 51, 53–54, 56–63, 65–66, 68–69, 76, 78–79, 82, 84–85, 89, 92, 105, 111, 115–117, 131, 133, 138–157, 162–163, 165–167, 175–176, 179, 185, 192, 196, 198–199, 203, 206–207, 215–217, 220;

Cushman, Ellen, 55, 94

data, xi, xii, 9, 35, 37, 50, 52–54, 57, 59, 60, 63, 70, 78, 80, 84, 104, 117–118, 131, 143, 145, 146, 181, 188, 192, 195, 197, 199, 213, 218, 221,

declarative knowledge, 65, 67

demographics, xi, 114–115, 125, 131, 210

development: of curriculum, 79, 156, 167, 220; of faculty, 33, 193, 206; professional, 33, 35, 44, 46, 73, 84, 114, 120, 137, 166, 204, 216, 219–220; of research, 35, 39, 97, 103, 116, 135, 174; student, 8, 32, 34–35, 43–44, 47, 60, 133, 139, 161, 167, 174, 184–186, 188, 194; of networks, 31, 45

developmental writing, 9, 51,

Digital Archive of Literacy Narratives (DALN), 104, 123

digital humanities, xiii, xv, 80, 142, 149,

digital literacies, 9, 80, 97, 101, 146, 162, 217

dis/abilities, 117, 125–126

disciplinary knowledge, 8, 65, 71, 78, 81, 91, 105, 109, 166, 208, 218–219

disciplinary research methods, xiii, xv, 8, 49–70, , 85–86, 89, 91, 95, 96–99, 109–110, 113, 115–116, 122, 124, 128, 143, 146, 150, 154, 156, 161, 163, 166, 185, 188, 192, 196, 199, 203–204, 208, 210, 213, 214, 218–220

disciplines, xi–xvi, 3–4, 7, 9, 12, 23, 32, 33–35, 36, 39, 46, 48–51, 53, 59, 62–63, 64,71–72, 81–82, 84–85, 86, 88, 90, 95–99, 102, 109, 115–118, 121, 127, 136–138, 141–144, 146, 157–158, 160, 162, 164–165, 175, 178, 186, 193–194, 199, 203–204, 208, 210–211, 212, 215–217

discourse analysis, 37, 52, 64

discourse community, 69, 98, 143, 162

dissemination, xv–xvi, 23, 32, 37, 95, 98, 106–107, 196, 216, 218, 221

diversity, xii, xiii, xiv, 7, 9, 30, 76, 99, 111, 113, 117, 121–122, 124, 146, 188, 204, 209; see also access

education: general, 3, 7, 66, 83–84, 130, 138, 142, 161–162, 192, 198; higher, xi–xii, 9, 33, 43, 81, 82, 113, 115, 121, 125, 131–133, 162, 188, 192

Elon University, 52, 169, 178, 193, 213

engagement, xii, 3, 29, 58, 66, 69–70, 79, 84, 97, 117, 121, 124–125, 129, 147, 176, 182, 184, 202, 208, 210

enrollment, 116, 172, 201, 207, 209

equity, xii, xvi, 13, 23, 48, 56, 111, 113, 116, 120, 130, 132–133, 136, 145, 147, 160, 163, 164, 168, 177, 201, 213; see also access

ethical standards, 217–218

ethics, 8, 50, 53–55, 66, 70, 94, 155, 166, 185, 188, 197, 217–219

ethnographic research, 55, 78, 119, 146

ethos, 33, 139

evidence, use of, xi–xii, 3, 32, 86, 156, 185, 197–198

experiential learning, 66, 139–140, 142, 146, 147

expertise, xv, 11, 21, 23, 36, 43, 50–51, 57, 69–70, 78, 84, 103, 104, 146, 150, 158, 192, 196–197, 203, 219

extracurricular opportunities, 139–140, 144, 151, 160, 215–217

Index

feedback, xiii, 21, 23, 30, 33, 39–40, 41, 42, 54, 62, 73, 75, 116, 128, 147, 216, 218, 223
feminist methods, xvi, 55, 56, 212
first-generation students, xii, 82, 134, 147, 161, 167, 181, 185
first-year composition, *see* first-year writing
first-year writing, 6, 9, 11, 30, 53, 57, 60, 66, 78, 79, 83–85, 88–89, 98, 100, 101, 115–116, 120, 123, 130, 135, 136, 143, 160–162, 166, 181–182, 193, 196, 198, 203–204, 207, 208
flexibility, 58
Framework for Success in Postsecondary Writing, The, 58
funding, xii, 52, 97, 102, 105, 121, 129, 159, 161, 162, 163, 168, 172, 175, 181, 198, 206–208, 211, 218
fundraising, 42, 82, 169, 170, 195

general education, 7, 66, 83–84, 130, 161–162, 198, 207
genre, 12, 50, 52, 62, 64, 69, 80, 113, 115, 117, 123, 125, 133, 140, 143
goals, 30, 33, 39, 47–48, 82, 94, 114, 122, 123, 133, 138, 140, 144, 151, 154, 159, 160, 163, 202, 207–209, 217–219
graduation, xi, 82, 114, 122,131, 223
grammar, 73
Guerrant, Bessie M., 165, 168

habits of mind, xiv, 58–59, 144, 150
handbooks, 53, 166
Harris, Joseph, 6, 138
Harris, Muriel, 86

Haswell, Richard, 102, 104
HBCUs (Historically Black Colleges and Universities), 4, 129
heuristics, 44, 201
higher education, xi–xii, 9, 33, 43, 81–82, 113, 115, 121, 125, 131–133, 162, 188, 192
high-impact practices, 4, 7, 10, 17, 29–30, 33–34, 37, 43–44, 71, 81–82, 90, 113, 127, 140, 142, 146, 155, 158, 166, 176, 180, 194, 196, 202, 206–207, 215–216, 223
high-transfer/declarative knowledge pedagogies, 65–67
Hofstra University, 167
honors programs, 35, 81, 85, 120, 207
Human-Centered Design, 21
humanities, xv, 32, 34–35, 50, 67, 98, 120, 122, 141, 196, 220
hyper-professionalization, 72, 81

identities, 111, 113–114, 137, 147, 185
impact, 4–5, 7, 11, 23, 29–31, 33, 61, 72, 74, 76–77, 84, 88, 93, 95–96, 102, 105, 111, 114, 116, 129, 131–132, 134, 137, 149, 150–151, 153, 155–156, 176–178, 184–189, 191–192, 198–199, 209, 220, 223
inclusion, 9, 111, 117, 163, 172, 197

inequity, 13, 116, 126, 147, 164
information literacy, 58
innovation, 21, 194, 207, 216
inquiry, xi–xiv, 7, 21, 33, 35, 43, 50, 63, 66–67, 72–73, 80, 89, 99, 103, 133, 139, 141–143, 147, 149, 151, 153, 155–156, 192,

194–196, 198, 201, 207–208, 212–213, 215, 217
inquiry-based learning, xii, xiv, 98, 133
institutional mission, 5, 43, 139, 142, 146, 150–151, 158, 160–161, 172–173, 202, 209,
institutional support, xvi, 43, 47, 102, 113, 148, 150, 158–180, 181–183, 184–186, 187–189, 201–211, 217–218, 220
institutions, xi–xiii, xvi, 4–6, 16, 39, 43–44, 46–48, 51, 54, 59, 62, 77, 81–82, 84, 85, 94, 96, 113, 115–116, 120–121, 126–129, 131–132, 134, 142, 144, 151, 156, 158–162, 169–170, 172, 176, 178, 180, 187–188, 211, 215–216, 220
interdisciplinarity, xii, 63, 72, 131, 202–203
internships, 54, 60, 61, 63, 81, 114, 36, 141, 144, 146, 151, 172
intersectional identities, 113, 138, 150, 154, 165, 203
interviews, 52, 61, 156, 195
IRB (Institutional Review Board), 37, 53, 54, 66, 68, 70, 185, 195,

journals, 10, 43, 50–51, 56, 72, 74, 86, 99–101, 103–104, 109, 124, 139–140, 179, 185, 187, 193–194
JUMP+, The, 10, 74, 100–101, 103, 193, 221

Kairos (journal), 86, 100, 193–194, 221
Kemmerer, Elizabeth, 92
Ketcham, Caroline J., 31, 32, 46
Kinkead, Joyce, 8, 14, 50, 53, 66, 71, 120, 139, 146, 156, 160–161, 164, 192, 193, 194, 195, 215

knowledge, xi–xii, xiv, xvi, 4, 8, 11, 12, 17, 23, 27, 31, 35, 43, 57–58, 60, 62–63, 65–67, 69, 71–87, 88–90, 91–94, 95–99, 105, 106–107, 109, 113, 115, 117–118, 124, 126, 135, 137, 139, 141, 143–144, 147, 154, 156–157, 161–163, 165, 166, 184, 188, 194–196, 198, 208, 216, 218–219, 223
Kuh, George D., xii, 3, 10, 29–30, 71, 82, 86, 114, 140, 146, 176, 194, 196, 207, 223

labor practices, 5, 23, 81, 85, 97, 133, 135–137, 142, 151, 155, 159, 164, 165, 167–168, 181, 182, 204–206, 213
leadership teams, 202
learning objectives, 59, 161
liberal arts, 4, 9, 35, 88, 115
literacies: digital, 27, 54, 61, 72, 80, 146–147, 160. 162, 196, 197, 216, 217
literacy, 6, 9, 54–55, 65–66, 76, 84, 89, 96, 122, 123, 139–140, 143, 176, 210
literature, 72, 76, 118
Lockett, Alexandria, 8, 115, 117, 124–125
low-income students, xii, 76, 120

majors, xi, 109, 163, 217;
majors, writing, 7, 9, 30, 32–34, 45, 139, 155, 166, 172, 196, 203
marketing (of programs), 142, 170–171, 173, 209
McNair Scholars Program, 120, 124, 185
mentees, 32, 46, 48, 219, 221
mentoring, xi, xiii–xiv, xvi, 8, 12, 14, 16, 27, 29–44, 45–48, –49, 62, 70–73, 81, 84–86, 95–96,

105, 111, 113–114, 116, 118, 120–124, 126–129, 136–137, 138, 141–142, 144, 148, 150–151, 155, 159,163–165, 168, 172, 177, 179, 181, 182, 184–185, 192–194, 197,204–206, 209, 212, 216, 217, 218–220; co-mentoring, xiii, 31–32, 34, 46; mutual-mentoring, xiii, 16, 29–44, 45–48, 163

methodology, xiv, 4, 39, 46, 49–64, 65–67, 68–70, 72, 73, 79–80, 103, 118, 122, 143–144, 156, 163, 216, 218, 220

methods instruction, 49–64, 65–67, 68–70

methods, research, xiv, 4, 8–10, 12, 17, 27, 35, 49–64, 65–67, 68–70,78, 80, 116–118, 122, 128, 150, 163, 185, 187, 191, 194–195, 196, 203, 214, 218

methods-based research, 53, 56, 58, 62

models of undergraduate research, xvi, 27, 34, 41, 44, 46, 50, 76, 84, 95, 102, 113, 116, 122, 128, 139, 142, 165, 188

modes of circulation, 100, 105, 108–110, 113, 149

Moore, Jessie, 14, 33, 116, 193, 215

Morrison, Charles D., 150

multilingual students, 117, 161

multimodal texts, 76, 103

narrative, of Naylor Symposium, 14–24,

narrative inquiry, 55

narratives, literacy, 37, 85, 123, 151,

narrative, research as 67

narratives of research, 95, 100–101, 103–104, 141, 196–197

National Census of Writing, 6, 115, 131, 192

National Conference on Undergraduate Research (NCUR), 174–175, 192

National Science Foundation (NSF), 175, 259

National Survey of Student Engagement (NSSE), 129, 202, 207, 223

Naylor Symposium, 3, 14–24 25, 45, 47, 106, 180, 182, 18199

near-peers, 31–32, 34–35, 37, 44

new media projects, 84, 185

oral history, 76, 77, 80, 92–93, 124, 131

outcomes, xiii, 39, 43, 61, 72, 87, 94, 114, 153, 208; outcomes, learning, 8, 31, 59, 89, 161–162, 166, 213, 217–218

Palmer, Ruth, 34, 127

pathways, 114–115, 122, 125, 139, 141, 144, 147, 153, 156, 159

pedagogy, 33, 41, 44, 55, 65–67, 70, 84, 85, 93, 113, 125–126, 133, 140, 150, 160, 161, 188

peer review, 93, 216

peers (working with), xii, 30, 32, 34, 37, 41, 44, 46, 48, 54, 62, 86, 116, 128, 144, 163, 223

Perryman-Clark, Staci, 55, 163, 181

persistence, xi, 8, 58, 88, 114, 150

portfolios, 78, 144,185

posters, 62, 94, 96, 99, 101, 109, 140, 144, 149, 214, 221

post-graduation goals, xi, 122

power, xi–xii, xv, 14, 31, 46, 76–77 91–92, 194, 197

praxis, 154, 156, presentations, 62, 73, 74, 79, 96, 103, 105, 109,

116,126, 174, 204, 207, 209, 210, 214. 216, 219
priorities, xiii, 21, 31, 39, 69, 108, 109, 141–142, 159, 160–161, 168, 170, 172, 177, 188, 207, 210
professions, 84, 87
project management, 146
promotion and tenure criteria, 43, 94, 105, 166, 168, 207
proposals, 17, 54, 103, 121, 149, 175
protocols, 55, 178, 179, 188, 219
publications, xv, 11, 52, 74, 79, 89, 90 91, 94–105, 106–107, 108–110, 116, 118, 124, 165, 171, 177–178, 193, 209–210, 219–220
publicness, 94–105

qualitative research, 9, 49, 51, 53, 61, 69, 80, 96, 122, 143, 146, 185, 217
quantitative research, 49, 51, 53, 61, 69, 96, 122, 143, 185, 195, 197, 217

Raab Writing Fellows Program (RWF), 184–186
racism, 13, 93; see also access; anti-racist writing instruction; barriers to participation; inclusion; inequity; intersectional identities; and under-represented groups
reciprocity, 33, 45–48, 74, 92
recruitment of undergraduate researchers, 117,
recruitment and retention, 202, 208–210
Reinventing Undergraduate Education (Boyer Commission Report), 3, 17, 29, 94, 194

research design, 50, 53, 54–55, 59–60, 70, 80, 120, 178
research methods, xiv, 4, 8–10, 12, 17, 27, 35, 41, 42, 49–70, 78, 80, 116, 117, 118, 122, 128, 145, 150, 152, 163, 185, 187, 191, 194–196, 203, 214, 218
research skills, 46, 58, 84, 186
research-based learning, 3, 5, 10, 104, 133, 143, 185
retention, 3, 82, 88, 114, 166, 167, 184, 202, 207–208, 223
rhetoric, 51, 56, 65, 84, 86, 96, 143, 149, 175, 192, 193–194, 208, 212, 213, 215, 219
rhetoric and composition, 71, 139, 192, 219
rhetorical situation, xiii, xv, 42, 56, 201
Robertson, Liane, 65–66
Ronald E. McNair Post-Baccalaureate Program, 120, 124, 175, 185

scaffolding, 60, 66, 114–115, 159, 217, 220
scholarly research, xi, xiii–xiv, xvi–xvii, 11, 16, 18, 67, 71–72, 78, 86, 88, 94, 96, 98–99, 107, 115, 141, 163, 178, 193–194, 203, 213, 219
self-studies, 13, 160, 166, 178, 179, 184, 187, 207, 210, 211
showcases, 37, 43, 85, 171, 174, 184, 187, 210
silos, 150, 203
skills: literacy, 6; management, 62; practical, 147, 150; research, 46, 58, 84, 186; technical, 32, 37
social media, 11, 61, 76, 96, 171, 198
social sciences, xv, 51, 122, 220

sponsors, of research, 8, 31, 53, 77, 101, 117, 121, 125, 128, 130, 169, 174, 177, 179, 187, 207, 213
stakeholders, 5, 64, 76, 78, 79, 81, 95, 97, 151, 159, 179, 206
STEM fields, xii, 38, 88, 142, 148, 175
stories of discovery, xi, xiv, 95, 96, 100, 102, 105, 141, 149, 152, 153, 194, 196
student-centered learning, xii, 7, 8, 109, 117, 216
students-as-partners (SaP), 33, 35, 39, 43, 45, 46, 48
sustainability, 12, 46, 76, 111, 140, 142, 151–152, 154, 160, 164, 168, 181

teachers, 3–7, 13, 31, 72–73, 81–82, 84–85, 95, 102, 135–136, 138–140, 147, 150, 151, 153, 182, 191, 193, 197, 212
teacher-scholars, xiii, 34
teaching for transfer, 65–66
teams, 32–35, 37, 38–39, 41, 42, 44, 46, 60, 66, 104, 172, 174, 178, 195, 201, 209, 213, 219
technical communication, 56, 82, 139, 149, 162, 175, 193
technology, xiii, 46, 48, 73, 79, 80, 84, 94, 98, 124,
tenure, 4, 31, 43, 47, 72, 94, 105, 159, 165–166, 167, 168, 204–207, 220–221
textbooks, 11, 53, 65–66, 69, 72, 137, 194
theses, 9, 85, 116–117, 130, 1
Thieme, Katja, 55–56, 64
time management, 127, 185
transfer, 41, 63, 65–67, 81, 148, 186, 196, 219, 223
tutor training and development, 9, 41, 73, 118, 145, 203

tutoring, 11, 61, 63, 73–74, 77–78, 79, 85, 103, 116–118, 119, 131, 163, 164, 194–195, 203–204, 207, 214, 217

undergraduate research: benefits for students, xii, 29, 51, 54, 56, 62, 63, 76–77, 81–82, 87, 89, 111, 114, 136, 149, 151; benefits for mentors, 46, 48, 151
Undergraduate Research Network in Writing Studies, 102–104, 129, 131, 176–179, 182–183, 187–188, 197, 211–213
underrepresented groups, 12, 34, 48, 82, 113–131, 141, 167, 181; see also Robert E. McNair Baccalaureate Program; racism; low-income students; intersectional identities; barriers to participation; anti-racist writing instruction
Universal Design for Learning (UDL), 113, 126

values, discipline of writing studies, xii, 5, 8, 44, 86voice, student, xii–xiii, 33, 72, 86, 90, 91, 93, 96, 109, 110, 124, 184

Wardle, Elizabeth, 6, 53, 62, 65, 100, 133, 135, 137, 139, 143, 146, 156, 194
Wetherbee, Ben, 91–93
White privilege, 56, 166
workshops, professional and research, xv, 6, 16, 17, 52, 62, 114, 122, 124–125, 178–179, 193, 213; for tutor training, 203; Naylor Workshop, 16–17
writing across the curriculum (WAC), 30, , 77, 89, 116, 121, 203–204, 217

writing centers, 5, 7, 9, 11, 30, 32, 34, 44, 54, 60–63, 73, 77, 78, 85, 86, 105, 116–118, 131, 139, 146, 150, 154, 155, 163, 170, 181, 192, 194–195, 203–205, 207
writing fellows, 9, 32, 53, 63, 170, 184–185, 194–195
writing in the disciplines, 9, 53, 116, 217; see also writing across the curriculum (WAC)
writing processes, 60, 69, 80, 82, 104, 108, 122, 124, 218
writing program administrators (WPAs), 55–56, 77, 85, 131, 137, 160, 166, 168, 170, 181–182, 205
writing programs, 5, 30, 33–34, 45, 60, 62, 158, 182, 187, 203

writing-about-writing curriculum, 65–67, 122–123, 137, 155, 160, 204
writing-intensive courses, xii, 7, 62, 121, 124, 149

Xchanges (journal), 10, 74, 100, 193, 221
Yancey, Kathleen Blake, 6, 65–66, 96, 109
York College of Pennsylvania, 3, 4, 16–20, 68
Young Scholars in Writing (journal), 10, 35, 50, 74, 82, 86, 100, 140, 163, 192–193, 196, 221

Zebertavage, Meghan, 92

www.ingramcontent.com/pod-product-compliance
Lightning Source LLC
Chambersburg PA
CBHW030119240426
43673CB00041B/1335